The Power of Positive Fishing

The Power of Positive Fishing

A STORY of FRIENDSHIP and the QUEST FOR HAPPINESS

MICHAEL J. TOUGIAS
and ADAM GAMBLE

Essex, Connecticut

An imprint of Globe Pequot, the trade division of
The Rowman & Littlefield Publishing Group, Inc.
4501 Forbes Blvd., Ste. 200
Lanham, MD 20706
www.rowman.com

Distributed by NATIONAL BOOK NETWORK

Front cover art by Katherine Blackmore.

British Library Cataloguing in Publication Information available

Library of Congress Cataloging-in-Publication Data
Names: Tougias, Michael J., 1955- author. | Gamble, Adam, author.
Title: The power of positive fishing : a story of friendship and the quest for happiness / Michael J. Tougias and Adam Gamble.
Description: Essex, Connecticut : Lyons Press, an imprint of Globe Pequot, the trade division of The Rowman & Littlefield Publishing Group, Inc., [2023]
Identifiers: LCCN 2023004824 (print) | LCCN 2023004825 (ebook) | ISBN 9781493075416 (hardcover ; acid free paper) | ISBN 9781493075423 (epub)
Subjects: LCSH: Fishing--Anecdotes. | Friendship
Classification: LCC SH441 .T665 2023 (print) | LCC SH441 (ebook) | DDC 799.1–dc23/eng/20230405
LC record available at https://lccn.loc.gov/2023004824
LC ebook record available at https://lccn.loc.gov/2023004825

♾️™ The paper used in this publication meets the minimum requirements of American National Standard for Information Sciences—Permanence of Paper for Printed Library Materials, ANSI/NISO Z39.48-1992.

Contents

Contents

To Robin and Nate

New Waters, New Friend

MT

I have this crazy belief that I can turn any—well almost any—bad event or disappointment into something much better. But when I first met Adam several years ago, I wasn't practicing this technique, and my life was in the dumps. In early 2001, I was desperately trying to escape the corporate world, and thought I was well on my way to doing so through a career as an author.

I had begun to write books, but something happened to my original publisher, and the simple solution was for me to buy the stock of books they had produced. I sent them a check, and a week later an enormous truck pulled up to my house, and two men off-loaded pallets of book boxes. I was now the proud owner of a couple thousand books that filled my garage, with more still back at the warehouse. And if my checking account had a fuel gage, it would have been on empty.

I needed a publisher to distribute and sell the books fast. Another writer mentioned a Cape Cod publisher named Adam Gamble to me, explaining that he published the types of books I wrote, which at the time were mostly local history and travel guides. Adam and I met at my house, and quickly came to an agreement whereby he would publish and distribute my previously written books as well as a new one. We then had a cup of coffee and talked of writing and ideas for future projects. As we talked I felt like I found a great business partner, but nothing more. He struck me as a serious, well-organized young man who gave careful consideration to his words and actions. I thought of myself as the opposite. There was an age difference as well; I was forty-six and Adam was thirty-four. My wife and I had two teenage children while Adam and his wife were raising a one-year-old. His second child wasn't even born yet. We even dressed differently: Adam in a blazer, gray slacks, and shined shoes, and me in a pair of fifteen-year-old jeans and frayed flannel shirt. I had also learned he was devoted Buddhist, while I had traded my Catholic religious upbringing for my own concoction of Christianity and a reverence for nature as a way to nurture my soul. But I didn't belong to any organized spiritual groups, and my thoughts on the spiritual changed with each month.

After we talked I walked Adam out to his car, exiting the house through the garage. He noticed all my fishing rods, stacked in a tangled heap.

"What kind of fishing do you do?" he asked.

"Mostly trout in rivers in Vermont where I have a little cabin."

"Have you fished for striped bass?"

"Well, about the only ocean fish I've caught are bluefish."

Hearing that, Adam invited me down to Cape Cod where he lived and explained we could fish for stripers using his kayaks. I was game, and we set up a time to meet the following week, which was early October.

The bad event with the former publisher had led to something better, but I just felt relieved. I should have felt a profound sense of gratitude and excited for new opportunities.

I wasn't perceptive enough to analyze the power of manifestation—transforming ideas into reality—and how to bring it to the next level. That would come later when I opened my mind to the full power of possibilities.

***

We launched our kayaks in a large bay, and I followed Adam as he paddled out to a sandbar where the outgoing tide swept around its edges. It would be twilight soon, but now the sun was low in the sky, creating pink and gold hues near the horizon. In the distance I could see what looked to be an island with a small lighthouse on it, and I thought how beautiful Cape Cod was when seen from the water.

As we paddled, Adam seemed like a very different person than the one I met at my house. He started talking fast, giving me tips about where to cast, what speed to work my lure, and to be cognizant of the strength of the tide. I asked if he thought our odds were good to catch stripers.

"Mike," he said laughing, "there are stripers right beneath you. I've already seen some race pass us and two have broken the surface. If you can't catch a fish today, I'll double your royalties!"

Gone was the serious and thoughtful young man I first met. Fishing can do that.

Adam paddled off to the far side of the sandbar, leaving me to work my side. My kayak was in about three feet of water and I saw a dark object pass beneath me. My heart skipped a beat. It had to have been a striper, and it looked to be three feet long. I cast and cast but nothing hit my lure, so I began paddling in a circle around the sandbar, intending to eventually intersect with Adam. I could see him in the distance and soon heard him shout something. He held up a fish of about twenty inches long and then dropped it back in the sea. While I paddled toward him, I trolled my lure behind my kayak and when I was within shouting distance my rod jerked and almost popped out of the rod holder. The fish stripped line from the reel, and I hoped it was a striped bass. I'd caught big bluefish from a boat, but in a kayak, with the ocean just inches away, I felt I was more in the fish's element and it controlled the fight. I was more directly connected to the fish; I could feel when it thrashed its head, used its tail for power, or bull-dogged down. This was a more intimate kind of ocean fishing than I was familiar with. It reminded me a bit of trout fishing in the river where the fish telegraphs its movements right through the line to my hands.

In the shallow water the fish came to the surface in a swirl, and the quick glimpse I got convinced me that this was indeed a striper. The fish submerged again and made another run. It was a good-sized fish, because when I managed to take some line in, the striper soon responded by taking more out. I worried the drag on my reel was set too tight and the fish would bust my line, but I didn't dare make any corrections. What saved me was the kayak itself. The vessel acted like a second drag, and the fish pulled the kayak in a semi-circle. Finally I gained more line and the tired fish was next to the kayak. I shouted for Adam. Slowly I reached over with my left hand and pulled on the leader until the fish's head was near the surface. The silver body with the dark stripes confirmed it was a bass.

At the time it looked enormous next to the kayak. My heart pounded from the ordeal. Adam told me earlier that stripers, unlike bluefish, do not have sharp teeth, so I felt safe grabbing it by the lower jaw and swinging it into the cockpit. I was lucky it slid down by my feet and didn't thrash around too much, or I could have got a hook in the crotch—not the best way to start a new sport!

I managed to get the hook out of its mouth, lifted it up and let out a whoop of joy. It was about twenty-five inches long, and was one of the biggest fish I ever caught. It was not, however, large enough to keep, as the legal size is twenty-eight inches, so I reluctantly started lowering it toward the water.

"Hold on a minute," said Adam, who had paddled his kayak next to mine. "Let me take a look." He glanced at the striper, gave me a high five, and I let the fish go.

In that moment two things happened. I became an avid striper fisherman and a friendship was born. Little did we know that the friendship would be a much-needed anchor when life threw storms our way and crucial decisions had to be made.

***

Without a mutual passion for fishing two people as different as Adam and I might not have become friends at all. Many men seem to need a shared activity to bring them together. While women, in my humble observation, are perfectly comfortable getting to know one another while meeting over a cup of coffee, men have to be actively engaged in the same hobby, business interest, or sporting event. That's one of the reasons so many men golf. It's a chance to enjoy and even compete at a game, while at the same time offering an opportunity to talk and share ideas. For Adam and me, fishing was the activity and the ocean the setting which afforded us the opportunity to exchange ideas, to brainstorm, and get to know the true measure of the other person.

We did, however, view our "coffee shop" with a slightly different perspective. Adam seemed to appreciate the beauty of nature more than me, though he was an intense fisherman, for sure. I, on the other hand, was focused on the fish first and then the setting, sometimes not even fully appreciating where we were until I had landed a fish. Even my conversation was governed by the hunt for fish. Until we caught a couple of stripers or bluefish I'd only want to talk about *how* we were going to catch them and where we should fish. It was a bad habit to be so locked into catching fish—I'd measure if the day was good or bad by the number and size of fish we caught.

***

We were back at the bay a week later, and this time we were ready to fish into the evening and maybe an hour or two past dark. Each of us wore a headlamp, and we both had a spare flashlight onboard.

While we unloaded the kayaks from the top of the car Adam confided that he was considering buying a boat. Being ever practical, I cautioned that he might not have enough time to justify its cost, and that boats were expensive to maintain. Adam said he knew all that, but a boat meant greater freedom, new waters, and bigger fish. I couldn't argue with that part, but being twelve years older than he I felt it was my job to bring up opposing views and advised him to take his time, and maybe buy the boat when his kids were older.

It was a mild evening with no wind and after we launched the kayaks we trolled for a short distance, fishing rods held in special kayak rod-holders. I hooked into a fish that was quite large, and while I hoped it would race out in the front of my vessel and pull my kayak, it instead decided to dive straight down, wrapping my rod around the outside of the little vessel. Adam shouted, "Tip up!" but I couldn't move the rod, let alone get its tip up. I was sure the rod would break as I hung on for dear life, but the line parted first and came back with a snap. I cursed, loosened my drag, and vowed I'd never lose another fish because of line tension.

Later, Adam hooked into a striper and it was pure pleasure to watch him play the fish with the sun setting behind him. The light from the sun illuminated the horizon with the most beautiful orange and red hues.

We saw a few birds working and headed that way. The stripers we paddled to were small schoolies but it was fun to catch a couple. We continued to chase pods of fish, but the light waned, and we had to follow the schools more by the sounds of their splashing and slapping than by sight. We turned our headlamps on so we could see our gear, and so other boaters would see us. A boat or two did go by, and in the dark we had to swing around and get our bows pointed at them, preparing to ride over the unseen wake that was sure to follow.

When the fish stopped biting, it really hit me that we were out on the ocean in tiny kayaks—in the pitch black. A few thoughts crossed my mind—well actually it was one thought but it came over and over. The thought was this: I was not at the top of the food chain out here. Sharks do cruise New England's coast, and after visualizing what I would do if I saw a fin I felt more and more uncomfortable. I mentioned this to Adam, and he replied, "Nothing to worry about. I do this all the time. Never had a problem."

It wasn't until a couple hours later when we were back on land in the safety of his car, that Adam clarified his statement about never having a problem. "While it's true I've never had a problem, my cousin Donny did tell me something that gave me pause."

Adam hesitated, and of course I said, "Well, what happened, was it a shark?"

"No, but you're close. A whale surfaced next to his kayak."

"You're joking." I said, but Adam only smiled and nodded. "Was it at night?" I asked.

"Yup. Donny said it was just a wee bit spooky."

"And where did this happen?"

"Not far from where we were fishing a couple hours ago."

This was when I encouraged Adam to buy that boat he was thinking about, pointing out he deserved one and you can't always be thinking about the cost.

***

We fished a few more times by kayak and talked a bit more about Adam buying a boat (even as a rookie fisherman I knew a friend with a boat was better than me owning one!). About a year later, Adam took the plunge and bought a small boat, making us both quite happy. It was a used Scout, eighteen feet long with a center console that he could trailer to different boat ramps on Cape Cod. Rather than give the boat a name, Adam simply called it the *Scout*, and that's what we planned to do with it—scout out every bit of water we could. I fell in love with that boat on the first trip because it only drafted a couple of feet of water, and Adam could maneuver it right next to shore to some of the productive spots he had discovered during his years of fishing from a kayak.

We quickly developed our respective roles on the boat. Adam would be at the wheel guiding us through the maze of rocks and shoals, while I would stand on a cooler in the bow directly in front of the center console where I could grip a steel bar that came over the top of the windshield to help steady me and keep me from falling out. My duties were to spot fish in the shallows and warn Adam if I saw a big rock ahead. By standing on the cooler, I obstructed some of Adam's view, so he often stood off center so he could see around me.

Perhaps because of that first trip in the kayaks to the sandbar, I was fixated on fishing in shallow water, using light tackle, and "hunting" fish where I could see them. Adam preferred the exact same type of fishing, so consequently we only ventured far offshore when we were getting skunked (fishless) at our inshore haunts.

As I got to know Adam better over that first year of fishing I realized that while our outward personalities were different we shared many of the same inner traits that dictated the direction we wanted our lives to follow. We each had an entrepreneurial streak that made us fiercely independent and brimming with ideas, but we lacked the know-how to turn those ideas into money-making ventures. One thing we had going for us was unflagging energy. Heck, I knew Adam had uncommon energy because there are not many people who fish the way I do—hunting and casting continuously from dawn to dusk. There were even a few days where we'd find ourselves out on the water in the pitch dark, going beyond twelve hours of fishing.

Adam once said, "I'm unemployable," meaning he simply had to be running his own business, had to be in control. And I was beginning to think the same about myself, even though I still clung to a corporate job three days a week while moonlighting as a writer. I felt fortunate to have part-time job with benefits, but the reason I chose the position was anything but pleasant. In fact, it's a perfect example of how poorly some corporations treat loyal and productive employees.

I had been the manager of a department at one of the country's major insurance companies. My department was making money hand over fist but we were woefully understaffed and our customer service was abysmal. Three coworkers and I made a presentation to the company's new president highlighting our profitability, growth, and staffing needs. We hoped it would lead to proper staffing but the presentation had unintended consequences: the upper management decided my qualifications were inadequate to lead such a successful division. They decided a manager with an MBA from an Ivy League college should be running the department and within a few months I was pushed out and replaced. After years of running a short-staffed department and still managing to be quite profitable, my "thanks" was being "re-engineered" out of a job. The whole experience left me bitter and depressed, to the point that getting out of bed in the morning became a battle.

With the help of another "old-timer" I was able to find another position in the same company, but that position was highly technical, and that was never my strong suit. Gone were the days of managing a team of employees for whom I had the utmost respect. My new position basically kept me glued to a computer screen every hour of the day. After a short time in this position I ignored the advice of most friends and family and made another change, this time to the part-time position at a lower grade level. While my peers were climbing the corporate ladder, I found myself descending it. At least the move preserved my sanity. It also allowed me to build my writing and speaking career in a slow but steady way, and be creative in a manner that large corporations stifle.

Nonconformists like Adam and I have a hard time fitting ourselves into structured jobs where protocols and procedures trump the ability to make changes in strategy and capitalize on opportunities. So on the boat we'd toss out any and all ideas regarding our publishing and writing businesses, knowing the other person would give a frank opinion that was not born of conformity. We used those fishing trips to not only catch striped bass but also try to catch business ideas that would bring us financial freedom. We wanted to create joy for ourselves and those around us. In that first year, most of our ideas were like the bass we caught: good, but not good enough to keep. With our rods and reels we mostly caught "schoolies," fish below the legal size limit that tended to travel in schools. And with our brains—or lack thereof—we hatched business ideas that just weren't strong enough for us to take to the next level. Still, we had fun in the process of trying to get "keeper" fish and "keeper" business ideas.

Adam was the deeper thinker of the two of us, and in our brainstorming he'd push the conversation beyond our entrepreneurial goals, into what we wanted to accomplish here on earth—how could we improve not just our businesses, not just ourselves, but also improve the world around us.

Before we could make an impact on the lives of others, we first needed to get our own lives in order. We knew we could help each other make the adjustments needed. However, we had no idea of the changes that were going to be both forced upon us. I simply could not have imagined what was coming our way, nor could I imagine our responses. It wasn't just storm clouds heading into our lives, there were some unbelievable blessings as well. As with our fishing, we had a lot to learn.

CHAPTER 2

Casting Buffalo

AG

"Slow it up, I just saw one," Mike called to me from his perch atop the boat cooler on the deck of the *Scout*.

I promptly throttled down and killed the engine. Our momentum carried us a little. Mike hopped up onto the small casting deck at the peak of the bow, his lightweight six-foot rod in hand. As I grabbed my own, he made a cast straight off our nose.

"There's a lot here," he declared.

An offshore breeze blew opposite an incoming tide. It was May, about an hour before sunset. I had on a heavy, zip-up sweatshirt with the hood pulled up over my baseball cap. We were in about three and a half feet of water on sand flats in Cape Cod Bay, perhaps a mile offshore. Before casting, I quickly scanned the water. I imagined I spotted a shadow under the surface, perhaps thirty yards away.

Hurling my lure high, it tumbled in an arc against a sky dappled with clouds before splashing down a short distance beyond the shadow.

"Fish on! Yeah, baby," Mike called out.

At that moment, my shadow, obviously a fish, shot quickly away. I turned and saw Mike's rod arch out in front of him, line zipping out through the guides. It held all the tension of a hunter's bow just prior to the release of an arrow. His face was all delight.

We had been out on the water four hours with only three small schoolies between us. We were finally into fish. This one took yards of Mike's line before finally slowing up and changing direction, parallel to the boat rather than away from it. Mike was forced to follow it counter-clockwise around the center console of the *Scout*. He made his way first along the port to the stern next to me, so I had to duck under his line. Then the fish brought him back up the starboard side and off the bow again. After a couple of minutes, he cranked back a bit of his line, forcing the fish toward us. But then it shot out again.

"You got it, Mike," I encouraged him, even though I was thinking the opposite. The way it pulled him around, it looked like the fish had caught Mike.

"You should keep casting. This might take a while," he told me after another minute of what appeared to be a stalemate. "There's more fish out there."

Mike didn't dare put another ounce of pressure on his line for fear of snapping it. So I scrambled up onto one of the platforms in the stern and took another cast.

"Let's get a double hookup," my friend hooted. "You gotta get some of this action."

I was retrieving my topwater lure and thinking that there was little chance of that, given the skittishness of the first fish I had cast at when a swirl emerged behind my retrieve. I stopped and let the lure sit a second. A wide fish mouth suddenly opened from below it and my lure was gone. I yanked back to set the hook, and then line started streaming out with a high-pitched whine from my reel.

"Fish on!" I bellowed.

An extraordinarily fun ten minutes later or so, Mike and I exchanged high fives and draped our measuring tape across the two big fish bodies on the deck. Then we snapped photos with Mike's film camera. (It was that long ago.) Our broad smiles were strained by the effort of holding up yard-long striped bass at the ends of our arms, both more than twenty-five pounds.

It was one of many bright highlights of our now twenty-five-year fishing friendship. But however exciting the fishing has been—like glittering waves on a choppy summer sea—it really does pale in comparison to the warm sunshine of our friendship. Fishing may be the glue that has bound us, but our friendship has transcended it. In fact, our relationship didn't even start with fishing, but with the book business. Mike does not remember the incident, but he and I met four years prior to my visiting his house and our subsequent kayak trips.

***

"I'm giving my two-week notice," I told my editor at the small-town weekly newspaper I worked for in 1996. I was twenty-nine years old, and those few syllables were among the most terrifying I had ever uttered. I had meager savings, and my only plan was to focus full-time on writing a book that didn't have a publisher. Still, there I was—finally—with the guts to pursue my dream of being a full-time author.

The book didn't come out until more than a year later, and only then as a self-published work. *In the Footsteps of Thoreau: 25 Historic & Nature Walks on Cape Cod* is a hiking guide with literature and history mixed in. It sold relatively well for a local book of its type. My timing was fortuitous. It was probably a high-water mark for regional book publishing in the United States. Amazon.com was only starting to nibble at market share, and even the advent of bookstore chains hadn't driven many local shops out of business just yet, at least not in New England. Virtually every town on Cape Cod had a bookshop or even two. As had been the case for millennia, ink on paper was still the primary medium for storing and sharing knowledge and wisdom. In short, the internet hadn't transformed the world yet, and people still relied on the printed word.

My problem was that I didn't know how good I had it. No sooner had my dream come true then I started letting it slip out of my grasp. Because I had paid for the printing, design, and editing from credit cards, I felt obliged to earn that high-interest debt back as quickly as I could. In fact, I was filled with financial fears and worries. I immediately began selling copies to stores throughout the region directly out of the trunk of my beat-up little Dodge K-car. This income was supplemented by my giving paid slideshows about Henry David Thoreau to local civic groups, and by leading Cape Cod "Thoreau nature walks."

My dream was to be a full-time author. I hadn't realized it, but I had been living it, albeit impecuniously, for more than a year. Now I was embracing the life of a book salesman and publisher who often did not "have the time to write."

Then one day a customer grabbed my shoulder. "Adam, I heard a guy give a lecture the other night. You've got to meet him. He's so much like you!"

"Who?" I asked.

Next thing I knew I was sitting on the edge of a metal folding chair at the Middleboro, Massachusetts, public library watching Michael Tougias project a slideshow onto a screen. He told story after story of one of America's bloodiest, least-known conflicts, King Philip's War, 1675 to 1676. Mike spoke with an enthusiasm grounded in practical realities. I recall him talking about both authoring and coauthoring books.

After turning off his projector, Mike made his way to the back of the room where not just one but two tables were covered by stacks of different books, each with Mike's name somewhere on the cover. He proceeded to sell dozens and dozens of autographed copies to the crowd of about seventy-five people. I had given presentations to only a few groups that even compared in size to this one of Mike's, and I only had one book to sell at my events. I was even more impressed when I saw all the greenbacks happily handed over to him by his fans.

This is why, when I eventually got a call from Mike four years later, asking if my business, On Cape Publications, would be interested in working with him, I immediately drove more than an hour to his house to close the deal.

In retrospect, it seems obvious our paths would cross. The books business in New England isn't all that big, and there are only so many authors writing about local history, the outdoors, and who give slide presentations. Still, as Mike has acknowledged, if it wasn't for fishing, we probably would have remained colleagues and may never have become friends.

***

One of the earliest memories I can clearly place is from the age of four. It is of my father taking me fishing in a pond in Delaware Park near our home in Buffalo, New York. We encountered a few bicyclists and walkers on our way from the car to the pond. It was a relatively early weekend morning, and the sun glistened off the glassy water. A grass lawn ran down a small hill to the edge of the pond where we stood with my father's fishing rod and tackle box. The water bugs intrigued me.

"How do they walk on the water, Dad?"

It seemed like magic. My younger brother, Matt, was a babe-in-arms still, at home with our mother. My father was spending the whole morning, just with me. I remember his warm masculine presence.

I thought of my father very differently than my mother. There was some resistance in me to his roughness, his dark voice, and his thick scratchy beard and moustache. I didn't know him anywhere nearly as well as my mother, or even as well as his parents, my grandparents. My mother stayed at home and took care of Matt and me full-time, while my father seemed to mainly be at work. I remember returning home with him later that morning and his telling my mother multiple times what a good fisherman I was.

"That Adam is a good fisherman. He's a good fisherman."

I recall my four-year-old brain thinking that he was not quite telling the truth, because I didn't actually catch any fish by myself. He had done the catching. I just reeled in some that my father had hooked. I was already starting to learn about fishermen and exaggeration.

That was one of the only father-and-son activities we had together. From all accounts, he was a compassionate young man, twenty-seven years old at the time. He was passionate about the civil rights movement that remained so active back in 1971. A teacher by training, he purposely chose to work in the poorer parts of Buffalo with underprivileged kids. He later worked in drug and alcohol counselling, a fact that makes me wonder today what struggles he himself may have had with those substances. I've never been involved with drugs myself, but I've suffered from alcohol problems, and we all know what they say about apples and trees.

At one point around then my father received a psychiatric diagnosis of bipolar. Tragically, he died the year after our lone fishing trip together by suicide. His bouts with depressions had become so intense that he was checked into hospitals for short periods a few times that year. The final time, he apparently grew terrified of what people would think of him when he was to be discharged. There were even greater social stigmas attached to mental illness back in the early seventies than there are now. Unable to cope with it all, the night before he was to be released he wrapped the belt from his robe around his neck and hanged himself in the closet.

It was a violent act, abruptly ending his young life and deeply wounding our surviving family. When five-year-old me was informed by my mother and grandmother that my father "would not come back" as they put it, I burst into a tantrum. "He didn't even say goodbye!" was my inconsolable lament. I don't recall much of the event, but I recall picking up on the intense grief that permeated the house. Children are like emotional tuning forks. I'm told my grandmother eventually called our family doctor who came to the house and administered a sedative to me. (Yes, you read right; our doctor made a house call. It was a long time ago.)

My mother, brother, and I felt abandoned by my father. Fortunately, I've come to feel differently about it. When someone has a heart attack and dies, we usually don't conceive of them as abandoning anyone. I now believe it's very similar in the case of mental illness leading to suicide. Instead of having a heart attack, people like my dad have what I think of as a "brain attack." Their brains fail in a way that results in death, not unlike any diseased major organ. That's how I've come to think about my father's case. He had a brain attack.

Working on *The Power of Positive Fishing* with Michael, I have come to wonder how much my fishing has been concerned with seeking the sense of connection I felt during that trip to the park. I also wonder how much of my enthusiasm for fishing was inherited from my dad. His obituary doesn't include a lot of biographical details, but one sentence notes his having been a fisherman:

"Mr. Gamble was a member of the Buffalo Casting Club."

Who knew they built fishing rods strong enough to cast buffalo?

CHAPTER 3

Icarus and the Kayak Incident

MT

Even though Adam now had a boat, every now and then I'd insist we take the kayaks out instead. Maybe I was trying to recapture that magical first kayak outing that got me hooked on striper fishing. I also liked the stealth a kayak provided for approaching fish, the exercise from paddling, and the lack of engine noise. But there was one outing where I wished we'd taken the boat.

We used Adam's kayaks. He gave me the bigger one that was more suitable for the ocean, and he used a smaller one more suitable for a bathtub. No matter; he was the more experienced ocean kayaker, and seemed to handle the shorty just fine. When we first launched we were in the marginally protected confines of a harbor, and the brisk wind did little to deter us from paddling out toward the same sandbar we fished on our very first trip together. But this time the fish did not cooperate, and not wanting to go home empty-handed we ventured toward the distant mouth of the harbor. That's when Adam spotted the terns hovering above the water far out in the distance. He pointed them out to me and hollered, "What do you say?"

I replied, "Let's do it!"

"Ok, but let's stick together. It's going to be choppy. And let's turn back if those birds are too far out."

And so off we went, paddling full steam, plowing our way through one-foot seas. The ocean looked different than that first trip, gone was the touch of light blue, replaced by a steely gray, as if the sea's mood had changed. But the sight of birds working over fish does something to me, something that happens to impulsive anglers, something that causes what little common sense we possess to go out the window and be replaced by a single thought—*there are probably big fish under those birds, and I gotta get there quick.* I was a modern-day Icarus, drawn to the birds like he was to the sun, oblivious to the risk that should have been obvious.

I went racing ahead of Adam, and was surprised by the speed with which I reached the wheeling terns and gulls. Tiny bait fish leapt from the water and the little patch of ocean boiled with big fish breaking the surface. Here was predator and prey in action, and I felt an intimate connection to nature, awed by the deadly dance of birds and what I hoped were keeper stripers intent on capturing every little fish they had corralled and trapped near the surface. Being in a kayak smack in the middle of the feeding frenzy is about as close as you can get to this violent side of the natural world—without actually being a fish. I cast a top water plug into the fray thinking I'd be into a fish within seconds. Three times I cast through the churning water without so much as a fish taking a swipe at it. Maybe it's too big I thought, and replaced the plug with a small, gray, soft plastic lure about six inches long that looks like a worm, eel, or snake.

The fish, which I now knew were stripers, were likely feasting on sand eels and the small lure did the trick. I was soon hooked up with a striped bass, similar to the size I caught with Adam on our very first trip.

It took a while to work the striper to the kayak and release it. I had drifted far from the birds, and when I tried to paddle back toward them I realized the combination of the wind and outgoing tide was formidable. Now it would be a long slog back into the harbor, but maybe I could squeeze in one more cast.

I could see Adam in his "toy" kayak still coming out of the harbor, and after a few minutes we were side by side.

"I lost sight of you for a few seconds," Adam shouted. "The wind is picking up and I don't like the look of these clouds, so let's head in."

He didn't need to tell me twice. I felt badly that I had bolted ahead of him and caught a fish, simply because he had given me the faster vessel. But my kayak didn't feel so fast now, fighting the wind and current.

I really had to dig the paddle in deep to make headway. The rain that Adam feared soon materialized. It decreased visibility, making it look more like twilight than 10 a.m.

Adam was quite a ways behind me and I shouted, "Let's head to the nearest land!"

He hollered back in agreement, "Straight ahead!"

I fought the chop toward shore, thankful for my life jacket, but wished I had some drinking water to sustain my energy. The waves were not even big enough for a small craft advisory, but a two-foot wave looks plenty large from a kayak, and occasionally one slapped the side of my vessel hard enough to send water into the cockpit. Thank God the coast was still discernible, and I simply focused on paddling as hard as I could, worried that conditions would deteriorate. When I was almost at the welcoming sand of the shoreline I twisted in my seat to see how Adam was progressing in his little toy. He was nowhere in sight. The gloom from the rain seemed to have swallowed him up.

Do I go back and look for him? Could he be ahead of me?

My arms felt as heavy as cement, and I decided to first get myself off the water, and catch my breath. The beach I pulled out at was bordered by a salt marsh behind it, and I had no idea where I was. Even worse, there wasn't a house in sight. I thought perhaps Adam had landed on the same beach either to my right or left, and first I jogged one way and then the other. He was nowhere in sight, and I could feel the panic rising, and fought it back by considering my next move. If I could find a house, I'd be able to use their phone and dial 911. Then I'd relaunch my kayak and do my best to look for him.

Crazy thoughts go through your mind when you're scared, and I was already having the conversation with Adam's wife that he was missing. Then I'd have to explain why I didn't stay with him.

I forced that imaginary conversation from my head and turned toward the marsh, running along its edge behind the beach, hoping for a path through it. That marsh seemed to stretch out endlessly, and I gave up the idea and instead retraced my steps back to my kayak. *I've got to get back out there, and start shouting for him.*

Chapter 3

Something on the ocean caught my eye, but I couldn't make out what it was. I took my rain and salt splattered glasses off and wiped them off, and looked again.

It might be Adam, but something is wrong.

Either his kayak got a lot smaller or I was looking at a little log bobbing on the waves. Whatever it was, it was coming my way.

Then it all made sense. It was Adam alright, but he was facing away from me, paddling in backwards.

When he was in shallow water I waded out to him, and of course my first question was not about his welfare but instead wanting to know what the hell he was doing paddling backward.

"I was taking on water," he said, shaking his head. "This piece of crap isn't made for the ocean. The waves were rising up under me so the kayak was kind of surfing them. But with the smooth surface and no keel, I was going to tip over. Facing the waves and letting them push me backward allowed me to have some control. I figured it out on the fly. It was either that or swim."

I think I was more relieved than he was to have him safely onshore.

"Geez, we did everything wrong," I said. "We should have never gone racing after those birds. We should have a compass, flares, the works."

"I know," Adam said. "We'll make some changes before our next trip."

"So where are we?"

Adam explained that we were north of where we parked the car, but not more than a mile and half. We dragged the kayaks through the shallows for the first part of our journey to the car, and then in more protected water were able to paddle them. Once at his butt-ugly yellow Dodge K-car we were cold, wet to the bone, and thirsty as hell. We each drank two bottles of water, then loaded the kayaks onto the roof.

"Don't tell my wife about what happened," Adam said.

Then we decided that since we aborted the trip ahead of schedule we had time to go get coffee and a midday breakfast at a restaurant near his house.

Over coffee, I told him this wasn't the first time a kayak got me in trouble. I explained that the incident in question happened on the

Connecticut River, about thirty miles from its source on the Canadian border. My friends, Boomer and Cogs—whom I have fished with since elementary school—had joined me in a combo kayak/fly-fishing trip. There was plenty of white water, with large boulders scattered across the river, and the occasional sharp bend where the current flowed under fallen trees on the outside edge of the curve. Cogs and I were ahead of Boomer, and we had gotten out of our kayaks to cast into a fishy-looking pool. I had just mentioned to Cogs that Boomer must have stopped upriver to fish, when his wooden paddle came floating by us. Not a good sign.

We expected him to come drifting down the river paddle-less in his kayak like a fallen leaf, so we continued casting. But when he didn't appear after a few minutes, we decided we'd better go looking for him, so we jogged upstream along the riverbank. We found him all right. His kayak had him pinned against a fallen tree which crossed part of the river just above the water's surface. Some people call them "strainers" because the tree separates you from your canoe or kayak, but in Boomer's case he was still in the kayak, holding himself upright with the tree across his lap as the current held the vessel in this perfect trap.

We helped extricate him, and he told us that he thought he would surely have drowned if we hadn't come, as he couldn't hold on much longer. He may have been right, because his kayak was half filled with water, and behind the fallen tree were more branches and logs submerged in the river. Boomer asked us what took us so long, and before I could answer, Cogs did:

"We saw your paddle, but Toug wanted to take a few more casts. He was convinced a lunker brown trout was in that pool."

Adam interrupted my story. "And you probably wouldn't have helped me today if you found fish along the shore. Well, at least you have your priorities straight."

We had a good laugh, discussed how we would be more safety conscious, and counted our blessings that in the case of Adam's kayak misadventure there was a safe outcome.

I said, "That close call we just had is making me really think about the fear that crews must experience in boats during truly big storms. While

I was writing the *Blizzard of '78* book you are going to publish, I came across an incredible story of bravery and sacrifice."

I then explained that the incident occurred during the blizzard when a Coast Guard forty-four-foot motor lifeboat went to the aid of a foundering oil tanker off Salem, Massachusetts, and the Coast Guard vessel's radar went out, making them unsure of their position. A private boat, a pilot boat named the *Can Do* with five men on board, went out to try and assist both the motor lifeboat and possibly offer help to the men on the tanker. But they left just as the storm was really exploding and the seas were an enormous forty feet.

I told Adam I had already started the research for this new story, and that's how I was learning about seamanship, storms, and even superstitions. He could see my excitement and told me this potential book had a chance to really put me on the map because it had national appeal, and that I should get an agent and go for a big New York publisher. "I'd be happy to publish it, but I don't have the distribution outside of New England; at least not yet."

I liked his optimism. Little did either of us know that one day he'd have worldwide distribution.

We talked about the project, and he gave invaluable feedback and advice.

"Think big," Adam said. "It's a great story, so shoot for the stars."

"Exactly—I'm manifesting a blockbuster."

He asked me how I manifest, and I explained how I first state aloud exactly what I want to happen, then I try to imagine the good feelings that will come my way when it happens, and finally try to believe the wheels of the universe or God or whatever is out there are setting this dream in motion.

"Well, it's not a dream," Adam remarked. "You have already started the research, you're a damn good writer, and you've found the story you've been looking for. It's going to happen."

That was exactly the encouragement I needed to hear. Other people I told about this potential project said kind things, like "sounds good," but then moved on to another subject. Adam wanted to hear the details, offered specific advice, and more importantly he intuitively understood that through manifesting—and hard work—it was going to work. He explained the manifesting was not unlike his Buddhism, and that he had big thoughts for his business but wasn't quite sure about the next steps to take.

It was around then that Adam first told me that he had attended one of my presentations on King Philip's War, and I told him I'd seen his *In the Footsteps of Thoreau* book.

"When I first saw your book," I told Adam, "I thought that it was just the kind of thing I would write."

"I guess we're kindred spirits," Adam replied.

"Let's keep brainstorming every time we go fishing," I said. "That way we have something more than a fish or a near drowning to show for our day."

CHAPTER 4

The Seal

AG

"Manifesting" was a new term to me before Mike articulated his practice of it back around the year 2000.

"I'm aiming to manifest a national bestseller," he told me.

"What do you mean manifest?" I asked.

I don't remember exactly what Mike said. But I do remember that I didn't believe he would write a blockbuster book. It wasn't that I doubted his ability as a writer. I wholeheartedly cheered him on as a friend and colleague. I just couldn't conceive of someone so close to me having that kind of success.

What he told me about manifesting also reminded me of a book someone else had recommended to me back then, *The Power of Positive Thinking* by Norman Vincent Peale. Having flipped through it at a bookstore, I had dismissed it and even derided it a little, not only because it focuses so intensely on a deep Christian faith I wasn't used to, but also because it seemed very much a book of its time, the early 1950s. Since then, having finally actually read it cover to cover, I've come to appreciate it and to truly enjoy the author's unbridled optimism, passion, and faith. It's a great book.

Fortunately, I wasn't as closed off to Mike's ideas, which struck me as more organic than that of the *Power of Positive Thinking*. I had myself converted to Buddhism several years before I met Mike, and I had also been a longtime listener to audio self-improvement programs. As a result,

I appreciated the importance of focusing one's mind, the idea that if we focus consistently on a particular outcome that our actions naturally begin to align with those thoughts, yielding positive results. This seemed sensible. Yet Mike was also talking about something more than that. He seemed to allude to something transcendental, something spiritual. This also resonated with Buddhism and its emphasis on the interconnectedness of individuals and their environments—essentially that one's outer world is inextricably intertwined with one's inner world. Mike's explanation also dovetailed with the Buddhist belief in the boundless potential of each living being. To be one with the universe is to be one with the infinite. Difficult for me to swallow was that I personally could have such potential too. The truth was that I often felt crippled inside, perhaps by my family history and probably also by at least two ongoing problems. One, my alcohol abuse. Two, my compulsively overeating. I was carrying a lot of extra fat and wasting a lot of evenings imbibing booze, as well as a lot of mornings being hungover. I realize now that I was using both to distract me from my inner feelings of inadequacy. This all fed into a downward spiral of self-recrimination and negativity.

There was a civil war waging in me, between my lesser impulses and my greater aspirations. I desperately desired to be a better person while simultaneously slipping further into negative behaviors. Frankly, that was a big part of Mike's attraction as a friend. He's so darn positive. To fish with Mike while he talked about manifesting a hit book was inspiring.

Around that time, I started visualizing stacks of books piled up around me, each written by me. My imagination brought forth different colored covers, various sizes, thicknesses, papers, bindings. In my mind's eye, they steadily piled high. I only half believed this vision. But half believing was incalculably more than not believing.

And as my dreams grew, fishing seemed to beckon me more and more too. Both were leading me into new challenges, as dramatized by the close-call kayak trip Mike wrote about in the last chapter. By then I had a few seasons of kayak fishing experience, not only with Michael, but also with others, particularly my brother-in-law, Richard. Our favorite method was to trail sand eels behind us. Richard was born and bred in Hertfordshire, England, where he was instilled with a wry sense of humor. We'd launch evenings after work with lunchbox coolers between our legs, just big enough to hold six-packs of beer next to bait bags of sand eels. As darkness crept in, we'd don headlamps and paddle and fish under the stars until around midnight.

Once, under a nearly full moon, we were out on the water talking to each other. Richard bemoaned the fact that we'd been catching nothing but small schoolie stripers for weeks. As the summer had progressed, the waters had warmed and the inlets got less comfortable for big fish.

"Catching a keeper is like hitting the lottery," he complained loudly as he tossed his hook and sand eel in behind him. And then almost instantly he yelled, "Bloody hell, I've got a fish!"

Sure enough, Richard hooked into a hog. It was large and strong enough to give him a nice little "Nantucket Sleighride." The expression is derived from the whaling days of old, when Nantucket was the center of the industry. Back then large whaleships, upon encountering whale pods, launched smaller boats, each rowed by crews with a harpooner in the bow. The long, narrow-shafted weapons were attached to the boats by rope so that when whales were successfully harpooned, they would literally drag the boat behind them, not unlike the way Richard's massive striper pulled him and his little kayak in circles that night. He laughed and yelled with joy.

"This beast better not drag me out to sea, mate. Whoa!"

After a protracted fight, Richard worked it alongside him. His challenge was to get hold of it and lift it into his little kayak without capsizing or dropping his fishing rod. He was, in fact, in the same small, tippy kayak that I had been in with Mike when we had our trouble. Fortunately, we both also carried a "lip grip" tool in our kayaks, as well as a small club to kill them with. Richard always referred to his club as a priest. When he used his to knock his fish out, we measured it at a whopping 44 inches, and it probably weighed nearly as many pounds. Once he finally slid it into the space behind his seat, he found it didn't quite fit. Its thick tail poked up into the night air behind him until we returned to shore.

The rest of that summer, and even into the autumn, Richard superstitiously called out before all his casts, "Catching a keeper is like hitting the lottery! Catching a keeper is like hitting the lottery! Catching a keeper . . ."

Alas, Richard's new mantra didn't lead to many more big fish that summer. But it made me wonder: does an angler who thinks positively about fishing, who makes every cast with anticipation, get better results than one whose thoughts and feelings are all over the place? Of course the answer is yes. All the best fishermen I've known exude strong feelings of anticipation. Nearly every cast, every retrieve, every flick of the rod tip, is endowed with positive anticipation for a big fish.

This anticipation of good results seems to be a key component of manifesting. It seems to be about aligning one's inner life with a positive external outcome.

One of my first experiences of manifesting came the very next spring after our incident. After visualizing a fishing boat for many wintry months and after working my tail off on a publishing project, I received a windfall profit of about $8,000 above and beyond what was planned. This was just enough to buy the *Scout*, the slightly used eighteen-foot center-console that would serve as the primary setting for about a decade of Michael's and my friendship.

Frankly, to call the *Scout* a boat feels like an injustice to her. True, she was not a car, or a truck, or even an aircraft, and she certainly operated well on the water, just like a "boat." But to me at least, the *Scout* was far more than a boat. She was as much a mystic portal as a watercraft. The *Scout* facilitated direct passage out of everyday realities into radically different realms where vast skies, endless horizons, unfathomable depths, and untamed nature flourished all around. She transported Mike and me to places where we could explore our own true natures in ways we didn't expect. Truly, the broad, bright, spacious environment out on the water served as a balm for our souls.

One trip our first season with the *Scout* seems especially emblematic. We arrived at the boat ramp about 6 a.m., towing the boat with my ugly, used little Dodge K-car. I had purchased three different K-cars over the years, all four-door sedans. All had belonged to elderly women and had low miles. I had learned that ugly cars were significantly cheaper than handsome ones. Problem was that the weight of the trailer and the

Scout were on the outer edge of the manufacturer's guidelines for towing. Anything but annoyingly gradual acceleration on the road was impossible, and I had to allow for about twice the normal distance for braking. Moreover, we were always the only non-truck at the boat ramp, drawing plenty of bemused looks from other fishermen, most of whom sported full-size pickups with plenty of torque and power.

Mike turned to me at the parking lot that morning beaming with his usual excitement. "Hey, you've got to teach me how to tow the boat. I want to learn how to back up with a trailer."

Mike still repeats the same sentiment all these years later, to which I continue to smile quietly without comment, because he has yet to learn how to trailer anything. When Mike gets close to the water, he becomes way too fixated on the prospect of fishing to do anything else. Why learn how to tow a boat on land when you could be out on the water fishing?

Mike still worked at a national insurance company in the underwriting department back then. He often told me how much he disliked it, so much so that he was spending every lunchtime and every train commute scribbling away on whatever book he was working on, or on his latest proposal letters for prospective publishers, or on his latest press release for whatever book had just come out. It was amazing to watch him build his career, not one book at a time, not one page at a time, but one word at a time.

After tying up to the public dock, I was priming the *Scout*'s ninety horsepower engine by squeezing the bulb on the fuel line between the tank and the engine when Mike stepped aboard and declared, "We are so lucky. How many poor people are going to be stuck in windowless cubicles all day?"

I was myself working sixty or more hours a week on what quickly developed into my local publishing business, On Cape Publications. I ran it from my home office and rarely took time off, except to fish or to fulfill family obligations. Despite my dream of being a full-time author, I split my time between my own writing and publishing books by other authors, including by Mike. On Cape Publications released titles on subjects like Cape Cod lighthouses, Cape Cod windmills, Cape Cod geology, even Cape Cod ghosts. The business handled a few titles about New England

and Boston, but it was very Cape-focused. And how was it all financed? From the same credit cards that were used to publish my first book. Then I'd scramble like a madman to sell enough books to pay the debt down and hopefully make a living.

I held tight to the belief that I'd one day write or publish a book that would yield enough money to allow me to focus full-time on my own writing again. But with two young children at home, I was on a treadmill of my own making. Yes, I was self-employed in a business I seemed to have a predilection for, but like Henry David Thoreau's "mass of men" I too was starting to live a life of "quiet desperation."

When we finally left the harbor and felt the sea breeze on our faces from the open water, I let out my tongue-in-cheek boating battle cry, "Yippee kai-yay!" to signal we were leaving dry land behind. I stole the salute from Bruce Willis' character in the over-the-top eighties action movie *Die Hard*. Mike gave me the tolerant grin he typically reserves for small dogs and young children.

That first year we mainly cruised around arbitrarily in search of obvious fish signs.

"Birds!" Mike eventually called out. "Looks like they're on fish."

A cloud of gulls circled chaotically above the water in the distance. We raced toward them at thirty miles an hour. As we neared, we saw striper heads and tails splash up through the surface. About them tiny baitfish burst like hot kernels of popcorn. Countless seagulls squawked in competition with one another, plunging down after the bait. We slowed and cut the engine before we got too close. Mike hurled a shiny metal lure into the mix.

"Got one!"

His rod bent fiercely.

"Oh my God. This thing is huge. Whoa!"

I could hear the line coming off his reel.

"I've never felt a fish like this."

Mike's line was flying out.

After another five seconds, he announced, "I think it's going to spool me," meaning the fish was going to take all his line.

Fortunately, someone had once warned me of what to do in such a situation. I hopped to the helm, restarted the engine, and steered the *Scout* in the direction of his line.

"See if you can reel it in."

Sure enough, Mike was able to recall line as we gained on his catch.

"Must be a monster."

As we continued to pursue, we spotted something splashing ahead.

"What the hell?"

"Slow up! Slow up!"

There was a harbor seal in the water.

"Did you hook a seal?"

It dove and fled further away to our right. It looked about five feet long and more than a hundred pounds.

We followed and pulled up near it. Then it turned to face us, displaying a shiny two-foot striped bass in its mouth.

We could clearly see Mike's metal lure dangling from the fish's lips.

The seal looked at us over its whiskers with large, watery eyes and an unmistakably accusatory expression.

"Why are you chasing me? Leave me and my fish alone!" the seal clearly seemed to say.

Then it dove and swam again.

Not knowing what else to do, we pursued.

This pattern continued a while, during which time one of us recalled laws against harassing marine mammals by boating too close to them. Then again, this seal had stolen a fish that was already hooked onto Mike's line. Who was harassing who?

"Damn, I don't want that seal to get hooked with my lure,"

"It's pretty adorable," I responded.

"Should I cut the line? I don't think it's going to let that fish go."

"I don't know."

"I just bought that lure."

The seal submerged and swam again.

"Hey, get my camera out of my bag," Mike said.

I rummaged in his bag with one hand while trying to steer with the other. I found it and handed Mike the camera. Then all of a sudden the lure came free and popped into the air.

"Darn it, we didn't even get a photo. Oh well, at least the seal won't get hurt," Mike said. "That was cool, actually."

"Wow," I concurred.

We learned later that it's not uncommon for seals to steal fish off lines. It often happens while they are hunting a school. When an unlucky fish gets snagged by an angler, the fish loses the ability to swim freely and becomes easy prey for the seal.

Neither of us knew it, but we had experienced a harbinger of the future. In the early 2000s, seals were still fairly inconsequential within Cape Cod Bay. They mainly stayed around Monomoy Island on the Atlantic side of the Cape. But even then, the population was estimated at forty thousand. That's a larger number than the human population of most Cape Cod towns. As I write this chapter in the 2020s, there are seals living year-round on Cape beaches on all sides, including Cape Cod Bay. No wonder shallow-water fishing has dropped so precipitously.

In point of fact, Cape Codders have long competed with seals for fish. Back before they were protected by federal law, towns tried to get rid of them by paying locals to kill them off. One anecdote tells of two neighboring Cape townships in the early twentieth century. One offered a bounty for every seal's nose turned in as proof it had been killed. Typical of the "incompetence of governments," the adjacent town offered a similar bounty for every seal's tail turned in. Fishermen loved that deal, and the seal population dwindled quickly.

Of course, today's seals have brought with them an even bigger problem than the odd striper theft. And I do mean bigger, as in "we're going to need a bigger boat" bigger. But sharks are a topic we will pick up later.

The rest of the trip was fishless. We trolled, we jigged, we cast, we searched for birds, but it was all to no avail. We remained hapless rookies that maiden boating year. I won't say we didn't land some nice fish. We put in long hours out on the *Scout* and tried many methods during different weather, tides, times of day and night. The vessel was only eighteen-foot long, but she provided ample room for both our fishing and our friendship to develop, as well as for our minds and our lives to expand. We relished each adventure out into this realm known as "on the water," where unexpected, amazing things happen all the time.

CHAPTER 5

Jon Hyde the Fishing Guide

MT

One of the more frustrating fishing problems—really a good problem, if we could solve it—was seeing schools of keeper bass on the tidal flats but only getting a hit on maybe one out of a hundred casts. True tidal flats are those mostly sandy areas that are void of water at low tide but then fill with the incoming tide. At high tide there may be only four feet of water a full mile out from shore. The more gradual the bottom drops off, the longer the flats extend out toward a depth where ocean water is found even at low tide. Cape Cod Bay has scores of tidal flats, from small ones to the large expanses, and I've had some success fishing flats on the Merrimack River and some no-name flats in Buzzards Bay. They are especially attractive to striped bass in the spring because these flats often have the warmest water—at low tide the sand can bake in the sun, and even at high tide the shallow water retains its warmth.

On our first forays onto the flats we were cautious about having the boat's propeller hit the sand and the concern over getting stranded on an outgoing tide. We soon developed our roles to mitigate the problem: Adam would stay at the helm, keeping us under five knots, and I'd stand on a cooler in the bow, which gave me some elevation to spot any rocks or sand bars ahead. Standing on the cooler was also useful in spotting schools of fish, and polarized sunglasses were essential. I began to notice that my assumption that the bottom was relatively uniform was all wrong: there were channels, weed beds, and even the occasional rock—some as big as a car. Scouting, along with utilizing Adam's depth finder, were essential for not running aground or damaging the propeller and hull.

There were some sections of flats that Adam knew like the back of his hand from years of kayaking, and he could maneuver his boat through a myriad of channels right up to the grass beds along the shore. Still, I'd stand on the cooler just in case.

The first time we took the eighteen-foot Scout into just two feet of water I wondered why. But from my perch on the cooler the answer became clear: giant stripers were there, sometimes entire schools, other times loners.

The "cooler scouting" did more for my understanding of the habits of striped bass than any other form of education. Reading fishing magazines or studying the bottom of the flats from a kayak, could not compare to the knowledge gained from having my eyes approximately seven or eight feet above the water. I could only imagine the detail that an osprey sees when looking down during flight. But the cooler was the best I could do, and I loved the view, even though I'm sure the constant staring into the glare of the water was not helping the long-term health of my eyes.

Shrimp, crabs, and sand eels are at home in the flats and that brings in the predatory fish. On some of our earlier forays I mistook tight-knit schools of stripers for weed beds, but after hours on the cooler perch, my eyes were sensitive to movement. Fish would hear or see the boat coming, and they would cruise out of the way, often making their escape at the ten o'clock or two o'clock hand of the clock (with the bow pointing at twelve o'clock). The best way to describe seeing the bass on the sand while in a moving boat is like looking out your car window at the pavement as you slowly roll down a beat-up back road. Fresh tar has been put over cracks on the road, and those dark spots remind me of the bass. (More than once after a day of scouting on the boat, I've tried to fall asleep in bed, and all I see are black "tar" marks going by.)

We never tried poling the boat with the motor off, in part because the *Scout* didn't have a poling stand and because we needed the engine to find the fish over a large expanse of water, often spending more than an hour looking for fish. Once we found them, we'd cut the motor and drift. We figured if we saw even just a couple fish there might be more in the area, and we'd let the wind and current carry the boat and hopefully intersect with stripers. That often happened. Wind could be our enemy or friend depending on how much it was blowing. I found that five to ten knot winds moved us along quite nicely and sometimes we'd cast for half an hour and never start the engine. Too much wind would bring us quickly to the fish and our casting time was cut short before they spooked. Dead calm was what I dreaded most, because we barely moved and I can be an impatient fisherman. Sometimes, however, I'd be surprised on a windless day and see fish coming toward the boat, not veering off until just ten feet away. But perfectly calm seas seems to make the fish especially wary about taking a fly or lure. Some wind is better, and wind along with low light is best. The fish are more aggressive.

I began to notice that a school of stripers was usually uniform in size. "Rats," the smallest ones of about a foot long, tended to swim with other rats. Schoolies, those fish I classify in the 20 to 27 inch range, stayed with fish their own size. And "nice fish," those between 28 to 39 inches all seemed to stay together. Even the hogs—those 40 inches or greater—stuck together. I can understand this behavior with bluefish, where the big will cannibalize the little ones, but I wasn't aware that stripers did the same. Yet I've learned big stripers—being opportunistic—won't turn down a very small relative. I'll bet that innate fear of bigger fish keeps the fish schooling with similar sizes. (Anglers have reported small striped bass fry in the stomach of big ones!)

While this rule of thumb of fish keeping within their own class size is what I observed most of the time, every now and then we'd spot a keeper bass hanging on the fringe of a school of smaller size fish. That exception is why I always take a few casts even when the fish I can see are mere toddlers.

Adding to the challenge of flats fishing is that fish in shallow water spook easily. And who can blame them—they can't dive and hide, and their backs often stand out from a light sandy bottom. Incredibly, however, striped bass can gradually adjust their skin pigmentation to more closely match their surroundings. A bass that stays on the flats will lighten their color significantly. Still, they are in shallow water, and I'm sure instinctively, small striped bass know they take a risk from being plucked from the sea by a bird of prey such as an osprey, and that wariness stays with them as they grow. Their caution tends to increase as spring turns to summer. Perhaps this is because of the rise in fishing pressure or the influx of more predators such as seals and sharks. Poor casts can scare the fish as well. It's best to have your lure land in front of the fish at least six feet away and then retrieve it away from the fish. If you put the cast right on their heads, most fish will scatter, although every now and then I've seen a big hog inhale the offering immediately—maybe they think a bird dropped if from the sky. But generally speaking, you don't want to do anything to put the fish on edge. Avoid casting over the pod of stripers because then your lure will be coming at them, which doesn't happen very often in the natural world. Bait flees big fish, it doesn't come toward them, and it's better to let stripers believe they've discovered your lure as an escaping fish.

Later in my angling days I fished a little bit with a fly rod, and there were many advantages to its "soft" presentation, and of course even the smallest striper feels bigger on a fly rod. Fly fisherman also have the advantage of working smaller offerings, and often that is key. So many times while standing on the cooler I'd see stripers focused only on one kind of bait at a certain size, and watch them ignore casts that Adam and I make with anything that wasn't a perfect match. Seeing stripers locked in to a certain bait, sometimes incredibly small, and ignore every lure in your tackle box is frustrating indeed. Yet it is still a thing of beauty—feeding fish can fuel winter dreams.

***

Our knowledge of striped bass increased every trip, and Adam and I were smitten with shallow water fishing. We liked catching bass on the surface so we could get the visual thrill of seeing the bass the second it hit or swiped at and missed our lure. Our most exciting catches were those in shallow water where we could see fish both before and after the strikes. In depths of four feet or less the bass couldn't bulldog downward once on the hook so instead they would take off to the races, peeling line against our drag as they ran. Occasionally the bass would even jump or do a head shake above the surface of the ocean. Our only problem with this kind of fishing was that if the bass were not feeding or aggressively checking out our lures we couldn't entice them to strike. We might spot hundreds fish in a day of scouting and only catch one after what seemed like a thousand casts trying all different surface lures and plugs. Subsurface lures did little better.

Salvation came in the form of a very unique fishing guide named Jon Hyde who specialized in light tackle, shallow water, surface action. Adam had heard some good things about Jon's skill at coaxing big fish to strike in as little as two feet of water. This was music to my ears, because prior guides I'd used were quite different. While they always managed get me into fish, most did so by trolling deep-diving lures or jerking heavy jigs along the bottom of the ocean in depths between twenty and forty feet. The fish struck hard, but much of the battle was unseen as the bass fought to stay deep. And there was little skill required of the angler because instead of trying to make pinpoint casts, I found myself sitting at the back of the boat holding onto the rod as the captain slowly motored at trolling speed while using his electronic fish-finder to locate the bass.

Jon would be different. He'd use his knowledge of the flats to determine where the productive spots would be at different tides, and then his superior eyesight—and knowing the signs—to locate fish. And so we hired Jon one spring afternoon, and it was the best money Adam and I ever invested.

Most of the guides I'd met grew up on Cape Cod and had done some commercial fishing or lobstering cobbled with off-season work to help pay the bills. Not Jon; he was a New Jersey boy who had made a small fortune on Wall Street in the 1980s as a bond salesman. He told me that the lifestyle he fell into, coupled with the grueling hours at the trading desk and on the phone, made him fear for his health. To regain his sanity, he left Wall Street and moved to the Cape where he had spent many summer vacations fishing with his dad. They had perfected techniques that caught fish in skinny water. One of his favorites involved lures that stayed on the ocean's surface. Jon wasn't sure if he could make it as a guide, but he borrowed a friend's boat and took a few customers out where he would patiently show them his techniques. While I won't give away the details of how he turned non-feeding fish into attacking missiles, anyone with enough patience and willingness to use good old trial and error can become proficient at working top-water lures at varying rates of retrieves and motions.

Jon's true skill is reading the water. He spots fish long before others can, and seems to know when and where they are likely to turn up. Stealth is key. That one outing with Jon improved the fishing Adam and I preferred by leaps and bounds. Often we'd be fishing, and if things were going poorly, one of us would say, "What would Jon do?"

Jon and I have become good friends, and in the years that followed we often fished together just for the fun of it, where he didn't have to worry about guiding and he could fish as much as he liked. Some trips produced big fish; some only a couple little ones; and once, when he took my family out for a day of fishing, we got skunked. I mention that to remind readers that even the top-notch fishermen, who know their local water like the back of their hand, cannot pull a rabbit out of their hat if there are no rabbits around.

My most memorable day with Jon occurred recently, during a year that the fishing had been below average most of the summer. My girlfriend at the time had helped Jon with his website, so he took her and me, along with a friend of my girlfriend, out for a late afternoon of fishing. We didn't have much luck with our top-water lures, so Jon had us jig up a few mackerel. The ladies live lined the mackerel but I stuck with a top-water lure Jon had originally taught Adam and me how to use. The mackerel were the ticket, and they each caught a keeper, while I flailed away with nothing to show.

Usually as the sun goes down the wind dies with it, but on this evening the breeze kept us in a perfect drift in about seven feet of water. The waves were about a foot in size, and every now and then I'd see a flash of a striper's side as it struck some unlucky bait fish. I stood on the bow, and I did see a couple good-sized fish dash up from the bottom and inspect my offering, only to turn away when they were within a couple inches of the lure. Suddenly my girlfriend's line started screaming out against the drag, and she was into a big fish. It was quite a battle, and from my perch on the bow I got glimpses of the fish. It seemed every time she reeled it in to within ten feet of the boat, the fish found the energy to make another dash. But with Jon's guidance, she played the fish to the boat, and soon Jon hauled it onboard and measured it.

"Michael Tougias," he said, "I have an announcement. Her fish is forty-four inches!"

"Way to go!" I shouted, but never stopped casting.

Now because Jon and I have fished together many times he knew my biggest fish to date was forty-three inches. "You are never going to live this down, my man!"

I continued my casts. The breeze was certainly helping, and it seemed my lure flew a mile from the boat on each toss.

The sun was down but we had some ambient light and the sky had tinges of pink and orange.

"We're going to have to head in soon," said Jon.

And like the four-year-old that I am, I said, "Just a few more casts."

I thought I saw a big striper in the curl of a wave, and I cast at it. For once, the fishing gods weren't playing a cruel joke on me. I watched that fish rocket about ten feet and slam the lure, but not get hooked. I was shaking with excitement, but managed to keep my head and remembered a trick Jon had taught Adam and me years earlier. I stopped my retrieve and just gave the lure a slight twitch.

That big bass inhaled it. The fight was incredible and we all got glimpses of the fish and knew it was a big one. When I look back on that battle, I recall the one thing going through my mind was don't horse it in—my braided line was about three years old and only twenty pound test. (I didn't tell Jon that.) It took about ten minutes to tire that fish out, and I certainly didn't have the strength to reach down and grab its lip and haul it in. Nor would it have fit in the net Jon carried on the boat. But luckily Jon was able to grab it by the lower lip, and with two hands haul it in.

I collapsed on the deck I was so tired. That must have been my thousandth cast, followed by fighting the fish. Those efforts, combined with being dehydrated, made me feel spent.

"Stand up, Mr. T!" Jon bellowed. "Your fish is forty-six inches."

"Wow," I managed to say as I sat up on the deck. "We gotta let that big guy go. But first let's get a picture of the two of us and the fish."

After the picture, Jon carefully revived the fish while the rest of us looked on. Then in a flash it flipped its tail and was gone.

CHAPTER 6

Sight Fishing

AG

There is an old theory that if you set a monkey at a typewriter and let him bang away long enough, given enough time, eventually he'll produce *Hamlet* word for word. Well, the two monkeys named Mike and Adam could have spent eons banging away with our fishing rods out on the flats and never produced the kind of Shakespearean fishing Jon Hyde showed us. Angling is a skill. As such, it is acquired most readily through an in-person teacher, coach, or mentor.

It was sometime in the spring of the second year with the *Scout* that I found myself wandering around a tackle shop in bewilderment at all the choices. There were umbrella rigs that trailed five to nine imitation fish behind them, designed to look like a school swimming in unison. There were a hundred different top-water plugs meant to be splashed along the surface. Many cost upward of twenty bucks apiece back then, a fair amount, I thought, for something that I was literally going to chuck into the ocean in hopes that it be mauled by a predator. I looked over swimming lures that were every bit as expensive as the top-water plugs, each designed to appear like a fish at various depths. There were also hook-and-weight and float systems, each created to bring frozen or live bait to different parts of the water table.

There was also a particularly preposterous rig called a tube and worm that both Mike and I still find fascinating. The tube looks much less like a fish than like what really it is—a piece of cheap plastic tubing. Its effectiveness seems primarily to be as a means of moving a live seaworm through the water at a given depth. Striped bass have amazing senses of smell, which might also be described as their ability to taste the water. They greatly prefer fresh over frozen or old bait, so a living seaworm twirling through the water can apparently be close to irresistible to them, even when attached to a brightly colored plastic tube. I believe part of its effectiveness comes from the fact that once the seaworm gets old it tends to fall off, so anglers are forced to keep fresh ones on the hook.

The tackle shop also offered an endless array of metal lures: Hopkins, Deadly Dicks, Cast Masters, and more, most made to be flung shockingly long distances. I also examined both vertical and lead-headed jigs meant to be "bounced" off the bottom.

I won't even try to get into all the fly-fishing equipment for sale, or the pricey tuna gear, mostly because a lot of it is beyond me. Mike and I still mainly use light spinning gear.

Eventually I was distracted from my shopping by a forceful voice at the front of the store near the register.

"What a day. We caught eight keepers this morning, all between thirty and forty inches, all in less than two and a half feet of water."

The speaker was a middle-aged guy with prep-school good looks made swarthy from daily exposure to the sun and wind. He had a brash sparkle in his eye when he turned and looked at me.

"Hey," he said. "Didn't you come to my house last year to look at a boat I was selling?"

"Yeah. I remember you," I replied. "I wound up buying a smaller boat, an eighteen-foot Scout."

"Those are nice," he said. "I'm Jon Hyde the fishing guide."

Jon offered me his hand. After an engaging chat with him, I left the shop with my wallet a lot lighter, thanks to all the tackle I bought. But it was also just the tiniest bit heavier due to Jon's business card now tucked inside. Little did I know I had been hooked by Jon myself. His stories of behemoth fish caught in skinny waters attracted me like a striper to a seaworm. His business card acted like a barbed hook in me. Not three weeks later, after confirming through the grapevine he had a great reputation, Mike and I chipped in $200 a piece for his services.

Neither of us wasted a penny. As Mike has said, it turned out to be one of our wisest investments. In half a day we learned more than from countless books and magazines. If there's a single piece of advice any non-expert angler takes away from this book it should be to find and hire the right guide for the type of fishing you want to learn.

We quickly picked up many basic techniques for sight fishing the flats around the Cape. But perhaps most important was that Jon gave us confidence. By getting us into big fish in shallow waters, he quickly converted us into believers. As any angler (or positive thinker) will readily admit, confidence is everything.

One courtesy we extended to Jon afterward was to make sure never to crowd his boat out on the water but to give him plenty of space with his other clients. We fish recreationally. He fishes professionally. To this day when we encounter Jon with a client, we try to tip our hats to his kindness with greetings like, "How's the best fishing guide on Cape Cod?"

Sight fishing required more work and skill from us than the other types we attempted, but Mike and I found ourselves loving it. We started scouring great swaths of shallows—often for long hours—our eyes peeled for telltale ripples, silvery glints, subtle shadows. And only after finding fish does the real challenge begin. Knowing is one thing, execution another.

Sight fishing adds a simple but incomparable component to fishing, that of witnessing all the action. In deep water fishing you never know what exactly is happening at the other end of the line, until and unless a fish strikes and you feel it, or see the rod respond. Unless you have high-quality sonar, or see other boats pulling up fish nearby, you often don't even know if there are fish around. You might well pull a lure through a massive school below you (that isn't interested in your offering) and never know it. Or you might have many fish follow your lure and inspect it closely but still not strike it. You don't know that, either.

With sight fishing, when one attacks your lure, you see the action whether they get hooked or not. A fishing friend once commented that deepwater fishing compared to sight fishing was like the difference between sex at night under the covers and sex during the day outdoors.

"What do you prefer?" he asked. His question immediately called to mind a spring day back in high school when a girlfriend and I skipped and hung out together in the dunes. I knew my answer.

One of my favorite moments fishing came just a couple of weeks after Jon first taught us some of his techniques. I spotted a fish a long distance from the *Scout* in the general direction of our slow drift. I estimated it to be just beyond the outer edge of my range. But with a cool breeze behind me, I gave it a shot. I double-hand casted with my six-foot rod, throwing the lure higher than usual in an attempt to catch the wind. After lifting my right index finger from the fifteen-pound braided line, I followed the lure with my rod tip in order to minimize the friction on the line as it passed through the guides. Splash, it landed, and only a moment later a second splash erupted in the same spot. A flash of a silver head and curving back, and then a fishtail passed just above the surface. I flipped my bailer. The rod bent abruptly, my arm was yanked hard, and the small reel started giving up line. The fish took nearly half the spool before it slowed. Then I began working it back toward the *Scout*. The tension was intense, but after a protracted give and take, it finally appeared alongside the *Scout*. Hauling it aboard, I could see and feel it was a true "hog linesides," as old-time Cape fishing writer Phil Schwind calls them.

I was hooked on sight fishing.

As time passed, Mike and I began experimenting with our retrieves, trying various paces and rhythms. These subtleties are often inconsequential, as aggressive stripers can be known to attack just about anything, and bluefish can be even less discerning. But sometimes the devil is in the details. We slowly learned how to work varying waves, light, current, and fish behaviors.

One of the most enticing things is that there is no waiting around in sight fishing. You are either hunting or casting. Of course, not every cast is made to a fish you spot in advance. Mike and I often set up a drift and cast blindly into waters where we suspect they may lurk but really don't know until we either get a hit, spot an actual fish, or see signs of follows in the forms of ripples and swirls.

Sight fishing also forces us to face our many mistakes, such as getting overexcited and trying to set the hook prematurely.

"Nicely done, Adam. I love how you yanked your lure out of that fish's open mouth!"

Sight fishing paralleled our professional lives in the book business, as Mike has pointed out, because it requires countless hours of work for unpredictable payoffs. Back then neither of us were full-time writers. Even today, I rely as much on my publishing work as my writing for my income, and Mike sometimes brings in as much from his speaking as from royalties. But especially in the early days of our friendship, we were what might be described as sight-fishers of the book businesses, constantly casting for the next hit, day after day, season after season. We had no choice except to painstakingly promote each book we were involved in. Mike has always been especially diligent about reaching out to magazines, newspapers, radio, and television, never completely relying on a publisher, an agent, a publicist, or salespeople to do it for him. I've watched him do an incredible job of updating his social media and corresponding with his fans. He seems to always be out there, engaged. I know that some years he has spoken at as many as a hundred venues.

My work as a publisher of authors other than myself has been similar. I have personally made many hundreds of in-person sales calls to book and gift stores. Each relationship is critical. I've learned it's like building a brick house. Every brick matters. My Uncle Billy, who was an insurance rep for years, shared the saying with me, "Belly-to-belly twenty-five." The expression, taken from sales trainer Tom Hopkins, emphasizes the import of in-person connections, getting "belly-to-belly" with at least twenty-five buyers per week.

As the fishing adage goes, "You can't catch anything if your line isn't in the water."

The more you cast. The more you catch.

We both also rapidly discovered sight fishing is best done in tandem, with one person at the helm and the other on a lookout perch. It's perfectly possible solo or with a bigger crew, but two seems ideal. Neither of us has ever been comfortable maneuvering within large organizations, but we aren't strictly lone-wolf types either. Working with one partner at a time fits our personalities.

Chapter 6

Our first joint project was on a book Mike wrote titled *Quabbin: A History and Explorer's Guide*, about a former valley that was flooded to create what is today a great water reservoir serving about a million people in Massachusetts. When I proposed an unexpected cover and book design, Mike countered with several reasonable objections. We both had to do a lot of listening to create a final product we remain proud of. It was not unlike the negotiations we go through all the time fishing.

"Do you want to keep fishing here, or try the channel?"

"You want to do what?!"

Our second book was *The Blizzard of '78*. Mike worked intensely to research and write this retrospective of one of New England's worst storms, just as I strove to publish it in time for the twenty-fifth anniversary in 2003. Mike landed many notable TV and radio interviews, and I made some strong sales. In the long run it proved profitable, but in the short term we learned an expensive lesson. A national chain store I approached and pitched agreed to take seven thousand copies in advance. The only stipulation was that they would only buy through a wholesale company from which they exclusively purchased all their books. This meant my company had to sell to the wholesaler at a deeper discount than usual, not directly to the chain. Still, I jumped at the opportunity (this time like a striper on the flats after a topwater lure.) I even ordered an additional ten thousand books from my printer to handle all the additional demand I thought the big order foreshadowed.

Sure enough, when payment came due, the wholesaler not only failed to pay what they owed, but they also presented me with a declaration of bankruptcy which shielded them from legal action. (Like a fish after a lure, I too had been fooled.) I'm convinced the managers of the wholesaler had been well into the process of declaring bankruptcy when they ordered our books, and they knew all along they'd never pay my company. Yet they were sheltered by laws that left me with little recourse. In short, I had been swindled. My business not only failed to receive the tens of thousands of dollars owed but also had to pay our printer for all the extra books printed, a supply that would last many years. Worst of all, the loss cut into Mike's expected profits, as he would not receive royalties on the copies sold through the chain store. Such is the publisher-author partnership. We gain and lose together. This situation could have ruined our friendship, but instead it strengthened it. Though it no doubt hurt him, Mike proved sympathetic and understanding, something I'll never forget. We both kept plugging away together on the *Scout* and in the book world.

A few years later, Mike came up with a new way we could both earn extra cash by teaching amateur authors how to get published, both through traditional means and through the growing self-publishing trend. We co-taught a daylong seminar in the function room of a local restaurant, filling it mainly with Mike's public-speaking fans. He shared the many lessons he learned as an author, while I offered my perspective as a working publisher. As with any form of teaching, such as when we taught our kids how to fish, we had to hone our own skills in order to pass them on.

At some point during each seminar Mike would turn to me and ask, "Adam, can you please tell everyone how to make a million dollars in the book business?"

I always answered confidently. "Sure, it's easy. All you have to do is to start with two million dollars."

We'd usually get a laugh, because people sensed the truth in it. There are more than a quarter million new books published every year in the United States alone, and more than two million worldwide. This doesn't count the countless millions of books published in previous years. There truly is a vast ocean of books in print at any moment.

"There's a lot of water out there . . ."

My move into publishing edged me toward my dreams, but it was only partially. The truth is that I was afraid. Just as I struggled with my unhealthy eating and drinking, I struggled to muster the courage to fully pursue my dreams. Sight fishing based on Jon's techniques, writing, publishing, even teaching alongside Mike were all helping, but in many ways I remained adrift, still casting blindly into unknown and sometimes even perilous waters. I had a lot to learn.

CHAPTER 7

Catching More Than Fish

MT

I believe the words I say to myself are a self-fulfilling prophecy. We become what we think about and say, and I was telling myself good things are coming because of my dedication to research and writing. The positive results, however, don't come as fast as I would like, but I knew if I just kept on plugging a little longer, my goal of being a full-time author with meaningful work would eventually come to me. I'd been honing my craft with several regional books including those with Adam's company and articles in the *New York Times*, *Boston Globe*, *Yankee*, *Fine Gardening*, and just about every outdoor and fishing magazine under the sun. I supplemented those with a weekly outdoor column that ran in several newspapers, and I wrote freelance business articles for large companies.

My big break finally came when my book *Ten Hours Until Dawn* was released by St. Martins Press in 2005. I was fifty years old, and felt blessed that some of the inspirational talks, dreams, and attempts at manifesting while on Adam's boat were yielding results. It was my first national book, and both sales and reviews were strong. It provided me some vindication that I could make it as a full-time writer someday soon . . . but not just yet. My daughter Kristin was heading off to college, and my son Brian would be doing the same in a couple years.

My dad, whom I've written about in my book *The Waters Between Us*, worked his ass off to put me through any college of my choosing, and I was determined to give my kids that same option. It might seem odd that at age fifty I still wanted to provide in the same way as my father, but he was such a remarkable, larger-than-life figure, I couldn't help but try to emulate him. I'm convinced he shortened his own life by taking care of my sister for forty-three years after she was severely disabled in a car accident. My level of responsibility paled in comparison to his devotion. He was a living symbol of determination, and through osmosis I absorbed his drive. I like to think that my father provided me with an example, while the power of positive fishing with Adam reinforced and nurtured my willpower and offered a sounding board for honest feedback.

Although now was not the time to up and quit my part-time corporate job, I knew I was getting closer. I also understood the kind of commitment it took to write and research a nonfiction narrative like *Ten Hours*, and I knew I could do it again. For me the trick was learning to say no to anything that did not bring me joy, and instead channel that time into writing. I only said yes to my wife, my kids, fishing, and vegetable gardening. TV, alcohol, and many social functions got the big No. Surprisingly, over time, I realized I didn't miss them.

My literary agent was able to land me a contract for my next book about survival at sea, *Fatal Forecast*, and the advance for this book with Simon and Schuster was far larger than *Ten Hours*. Now all I had to do was write it.

I'd completed the research by flying out to California and spending a week with Ernie Hazard, the primary survivor in the story. Ernie will have my ever-lasting gratitude for opening both his home and his heart to me, sharing the details of his harrowing experience. (Of all the survivors I've interviewed over the years, Ernie might be the toughest of all.) Then I interviewed the other men involved in that devastating storm, and spent a few days at the National Archives. After six months the research was complete, and I stared at about four dozen files filled with notes and a transcriptions from my audio recordings. The amount of material was daunting but not discouraging because I knew from *Ten Hours* that if I just tackled one chapter at a time, I would not be overwhelmed about delivering a finished project. The power of little steps was my mantra.

In any substantial endeavor there is always an element of luck that can make the difference between failure and success. With both *Ten*

Hours and *Fatal Forecast*, that luck came in the form of timing. I could not have written *Fatal Forecast* without Ernie's cooperation, and he told me that for years he had turned down requests to tell his story in detail, but that I happened to call at a time when he was ready to set the record straight and share his survival ordeal and not holding anything back. A similar situation occurred with *Ten Hours* when I called the son of the captain whose boat went down in the blizzard of 1978. Timing was everything. Frank Quirk III told me that just a couple weeks earlier he asked a bookstore owner if they knew of any authors that might be interested in telling his father's story. Frank and his sister Maureen, like Ernie, were ready to set the record straight, and they wanted an author who was going to give 100 percent to uncovering every fact accurately.

Call it karma, good luck, or the success of manifesting my heart's desire, but I always felt that my past writing and research were preparing me for these sensitive stories of life and death.

For the writing of *Fatal Forecast's* most intense sections, I rented a little cottage in the month of October on a beach where Adam and I frequently shore fished. The good karma continued because while I was there a nor'easter blew in and shook that cottage to its foundation, making the writing of the *Fatal Forecast* storm just a bit easier when trying to imagine what Ernie and the other survivors went through in their ordeal. Of course, there was fishing involved as well, and I had some great luck casting into crashing waves in the pouring rain. Later when the weather cleared, my son, Brian, came down and stayed with me for a night and together we enjoyed more good fishing. One of the days was quite warm, and we put our bathing suits on, jumped in a nearby creek, and let the outgoing tide carry us into the ocean.

Now that I think about it, Brian has been the recipient of some tremendously productive days on the water, especially on the *Scout*. Adam and I had improved our skinny-water fishing and that increased skill, coupled with a few strong years of the striped bass population, meant we had wonderful days catching big bass. We had learned that in the right conditions, particularly in early June, giant stripers could be found in as little as one foot of water.

What I loved about fishing with Adam was that he would take his boat in the shallowest of spots during high tide, up along the edges of salt marshes where few other boaters dared to go.

I had Brian stand on the cooler with me and scout the water. Suddenly I pointed and said, "There, right there, off to our right, is a huge pod of keepers."

"What are you talking about?" said Brian.

"Can't you see them?"

"No."

"See that dark patch? Dark streaks against the sand?"

"Yeah . . ."

"Those are fish."

Brian looked a little closer. "Whoa . . . I thought that was seaweed."

"I used to think the same thing, but if you pay attention you can tell that what looks like seaweed is moving."

Adam shut off the motor and our forward momentum moved us closer to the bass. They had heard the boat and now they were moving away.

"Brian," I said, "quick, go to the bow and try to cast ahead of the direction they're moving."

He made a nice cast and as soon as his lure hit the water it erupted in spray.

"You've got one!" Adam shouted.

While his drag was screaming, Brian reeled frantically.

"You don't need to reel when he's taking out line. You can let him run," I said. "Just keep your rod tip up. As soon as he starts to slow down or stop, reel as fast as you can. Keep tension on the line."

Brian and I had been trout fishing in New Hampshire and Vermont for years, but he never had a trout take out line for more than a second or two. This big bass was off to the races, and I was probably more excited than if I had hooked it myself.

He played it like a pro and slowly over the next five minutes worked it to the boat. Despite my vow to use fish grippers to avoid getting hooks in my hand, I reached down and grabbed the bass by the lower lip and hauled it in. A beautiful thirty-six-incher.

Brian then thanked our captain. "Adam, I was wondering why you were going so close to shore. Now I know."

Over the next few hours as the tide fell, we moved further out, hunting for another pod of fish. We might search for a half hour or more, but when we found them we all enjoyed the type of fights with big fish like Brian had. Then the stripers would scatter, and we'd resume our hunt. (I recently asked Brian what he remembered about that day and he said, "There were acres of big fish—I think it was over a thousand. They were everywhere. And you were in your glory.")

A beautiful sunset prompted Adam to say, "Time to head in."

"Let's hunt on the way," I said. "If you go at about seven knots I think I'll still be able to see bass."

Brian was pooped after a long day on the water, catching and releasing fish from thirty to thirty-seven inches. Really a dream day.

As we were heading to the harbor, I saw a massive pod of fish, all keepers. "Stop the boat!"

I said it with such urgency, Adam slammed it in neutral and I almost went flying over the bow. "Big pod of fish at 11 o'clock," I said. "We gotta cast."

And so Adam and I let loose with long casts. That's when Brian made an astute observation, "You know Dad, you're like an addict, a crack head or something, you just can't stop."

Adam laughed. "What do you think I've been putting up with for years?"

"You're casting too," I said.

"Only because you are."

"I wish we had a fly rod. Today was one of those days we could have nailed them."

While I've been an occasional fly fisherman for trout over the years, and caught some fat twenty-inch rainbows out in Montana, my experience with a fly rod on salt water had just started a few weeks before the trip with Brian and Adam. I had the good fortune to have given a presentation on Martha's Vineyard when a gentlemen connected with a bookstore invited me to go out on his chartered fly-fishing trip the next morning.

The guide put us in his favorite rip, but the fish were skittish and my casts weren't very long. As with all good guides, he knew a couple tricks to help me. "I'm going to toss this plug without hooks far from the boat, and then retrieve it. You stand at the bow, because there's going to be fish following it back. When I say cast, make yours, and be ready for an immediate hit. Set the hook, but don't yank the fly out of the water."

Sure enough, three or four bluefish followed his plug. As soon as I made my cast and the fly hit the water a blue grabbed it, and I set the hook. You sure can feel the power of a fish with a fly rod. I used my fingers to slow the line going out and add resistance rather than letting the reel impart the drag. The captain didn't mind my technique, but he was watching me closely. He wanted me to catch a fish, but I was also using his fly rod, a beautiful lightweight rod that was now bent to the max.

I'm not sure how it happened but somehow the line that I was slowly bringing in and let fall to the deck of the boat got wrapped around one of my legs when the fish made a strong run. (I should have used a stripping basket.) What I'll always remember about this guide is that he wasn't overbearing. In fact, I didn't even think he knew about my predicament, but I glanced down and could see that if the blue kept up its run the line would close tight on my leg and fish would break the leader.

Somehow at the last minute I was able to raise my foot and the line slid off my leg while still keeping my eyes on the big blue. Some striper fishermen thumb their noses at bluefish, but not me. This fish made a couple spectacular leaps that a bass would almost never make.

When we landed it the captain congratulated me on my first large bluefish on a fly rod, and I felt sky high. The seas were kicking up, and we caught a few more fish before the captain said, "Better go in."

"How about five more minutes?" I asked.

Then he said something that reminded me of Brian. "You really are obsessed with fishing, aren't you?"

The man connected to the bookstore then piped in, "And this is the guy who is starting to write about survival at sea. He's so locked into the fishing, he doesn't even know we're getting hammered by big waves."

He made a good point. I was letting the fishing get in the way of common sense, and I sheepishly agreed it was time to head in. Since that day I try to let the weather dictate how long I fish rather than how productive the fishing is.

***

We knew our obsession with shallow-water fishing was risking getting the *Scout* hung up on a sand bar, but we were willing to pay that price. We tried to time our trips to our secret spots just a few minutes before high tide, and then move back to deeper water just a few minutes later. Still, we had our share of groundings. Usually all it took was the two of us to get out of the boat and push it to a deeper channel. There were one or two cold October days where getting in the water wasn't easy. On one of those trips we had Guong onboard, a friend of Adam's originally from Malaysia, and I can still hear his shrieks when we entered the cold water in our underwear.

Another grounding led Adam and me into a good-natured argument, that we still debate today. It was in the early days of our trips together and we had anchored the boat just a few feet from a long sandbar so we could hop out and wade along the sandbar while casting. Adam went far down the sandbar, but I stayed within sight of the boat, enjoying catching a couple schoolies. After an hour I noticed the *Scout* seemed to be resting on the bottom, sitting on the sand. I looked around for Adam but he was out of sight. I remember thinking the tide must be dropping, but Adam will be back and we can push the boat into deeper water. I was still a rookie operating his boat, so I was hesitant to try and push it into deeper water and reset the anchor. I made the dumb assumption that Adam knew the boat would eventually be beached and together we'd move it.

When Adam did come strolling down the beach a half hour later, he looked at the boat and then at me, and said, "Why didn't you move it?"

I said something brilliant like, "You didn't tell me to" or "It's your boat, and I wasn't sure you'd want me moving it."

My hesitancy to take action meant we were now stuck. No matter how hard we tried to push the vessel it wasn't going anywhere until the tide came back up. And so we wandered our sandbar island, lay in the sun, and waited.

"If I knew this was going to happen," I said, "I would have brought a book."

"You'll probably be able to write a book in the time we're going to be stuck here."

***

Our willingness to pay the price of going into shallow water was in sync with our mindsets toward our careers. We were not afraid to make mistakes, look foolish, or do whatever grunt work we had to move our projects along. You have to have a thick skin in the book business. Not everyone is going to love your work, some critic's reviews will cut to the bone, and in some books, like this one, you bare your soul. Same is true for a publisher like Adam—some of the books you publish will either be flops or die a quick death long before the first print run has sold through. Our attitude for both writing and publishing, however, was like the shallow water we dared to take the *Scout* in—the rewards will be worth the pain of our screw-ups.

In 2005, our rewards were coming more often than our failures, and my writing career was taking off. This was also the year Adam wrote and published two children's books that sold tremendously well. Both situations would lead to significant changes in our careers. I could visualize happy years ahead, with drug-free sleep and much more time for writing, research, and of course fishing.

But God chuckles when man makes plans . . .

CHAPTER 8

Bluefish

AG

Mike looked at me with his mischievous little-boy smile that soon grew into a full-fledged grin. We had just arrived out on the bay for a short evening of catch-as-catch-can.

"Let's go fish the channel!" he almost yelled at me.

The channel is one of our favorite spots. Tucked between two sand-flats that are covered by seven or more feet of water during high tides, but which are high-and-dry during low tides, it runs deep and holds water at all times.

"The witching hour," he half-yodeled when we got there. "Imagine all the people heading home from work in bumper-to-bumper traffic. How lucky are we?"

Mike's whole body communicated enthusiasm.

"It's hard to believe you were in Tokyo yesterday," he said. "I don't know how you do it."

"I can't believe I'm out here either. What a life," I said, attempting to echo Mike's cheer, but I felt less on the water than underwater. I was completely jetlagged. Tokyo is eleven time zones from the Cape, literally the other side of the globe. I had been there working on a book with a professor I had been introduced to through friends. It was a once-in-a-lifetime opportunity for me to coauthor with "Watanabe Sensei," so I had thrown myself into it and was working night and day. The book was based on his scholarship, with me performing the grunt writing work. Once again, the two-person team model Mike and I used sight fishing played out professionally.

I was well into my thirties then. Despite my many hopes and dreams, my mind constantly swam with contrary thoughts. They were like a school of predatory fish taking bites out of one other. I was grateful for the opportunity but felt overwhelmed, especially as I simultaneously continued to operate On Cape Publications.

Based in part on Mike's practice of manifesting and my study of Buddhism, I was trying to build something in both publishing and writing. Around that time my vision of stacks or books piling high morphed to include the idea that each was more than a book, each was a packet of positivity sent out into the world, inspiring messages in bottles floated out onto the sea of society. The problem with my visualization was that I also, quite simply, did not feel worthy of such a goal. At times I knew I could do it; at others I was sure I'd fail miserably. Sometimes I believed I deserved to fail. So it went with the sharp-toothed thoughts in my head.

My daughter and son were in preschool then. I tried my best to give them the time and energy they deserved, but I often fell short. For example, I loved reading bedtime books to them, just as I recalled my parents reading to me. But it was sometimes my daughter or son on my lap who had to nudged me awake when I started snoozing.

"Daddy, turn the page. Daddy? Daddy!"

I rarely, if ever, drank alcohol back then prior to their bedtimes. I knew deep down I had no business consuming it around them. My personality often shifted with alcohol. So I tried to confine it to odd evenings, mostly after the house had gone quiet or when traveling on business. But it was too often excessive anyway. No wonder I was so exhausted.

I did land one solid idea around that time. Reading to Miki and Jack helped me appreciate children's literature. A couple books had been favorites when I was a preschooler, *The Little Engine That Could* and *The Cat in the Hat*. I distinctly remember my mother reading to me and pointing out all the bright colors Dr. Seuss used in his illustrations. I also recall my father chanting the words of the little engine as it tenaciously fought its way up a steep mountain pass:

"I think I can, I think I can, I think I can . . ."

One night while kissing my children on their foreheads I said to them:

"Good night, Miki. Good night, Jack."

Then an idea came: *"Good Night, Cape Cod. That could be a nice children's book."*

My publishing business specialized in local titles, and we had recently published a children's book about a lighthouse called *Cape Cod Light*. I had learned authenticity was the key.

Right about that time Mike started writing "survival at sea" nonfiction books. When researching the *Blizzard of '78*, he had come across archived newspaper articles about a boat and crew trapped in a ferocious storm. The vessel was named *The Can Do*, a name that like *The Little Engine that Could*, resonated with what we now like to call the power of positive fishing.

I wonder how the very real fear both Mike and I felt during our infamous kayak incident influenced him toward the subject matter. Not to make light of the tragedies he has written on, but it seems no coincidence that just when he and I really got into saltwater fishing together, he launched a career focused on men floundering at sea.

When the *Scout* arrived at the channel, Mike lowered his rod behind him with two hands and then whipped it forward, propelling a hard plastic lure into a long arc.

As he retrieved, I cast a seven-inch soft rubber bait that comes in multiple sizes. I could just make out its splash in the bright glare of a low sun far downwind.

"What size are you using?" he asked me.

"Seven inches. Why?"

"If you say so, Adam. That reminds me, why are most men so bad at math?"

"Why?"

Mike held his forefinger and thumb about three inches apart. "Because they've spent their whole lives trying to convince women that this is seven inches."

"Dude, it says seven inches on the package. I'm not exaggerating."

"Sure you're not."

I retrieved my lure with the tip of my rod aimed skyward. I shook it to cause the lure to splash along the surface and let out a long, deep yawn.

"Did you sleep on the plane?" he asked.

"I slept," I lied.

But the lie wasn't as much to Mike as to myself. I had essentially passed out on the plane back to Boston after too much sake and sushi at Narita Airport.

Just then a swirl rose in the green-blue water behind my lure. Then my lure disappeared. My rod tip bent forward. I pulled up and back to set the hook.

"Fish on."

Then my rod tip popped up, all tension dissipated. I had lost it. I reeled in my line and saw half my rubber lure gone behind the hook, a sure sign a bluefish had chomped it.

"I got one!" hollered Mike. "Hell yeah!"

I could hear his line coming out in long jerks.

"Feels big."

"Probably a bluefish. One just bit off my lure." I plopped down on the cooler to watch Mike work.

"It's a fighter," he said, his rod bent hard.

The sky bled bright colors in the west. Mike's fish took still more line. When it slowed, he cranked it in, just a few inches at first, then a foot, then more. Then a bluefish exploded out of the water off the bow. The low sunlight lit it up. It reminded me of a coin thumbed into the air before a football game. It shook its head desperately as it rose, two, then three feet.

Mike pulled back, trying to keep tension between him and the hook. When lines slacken, hooks and lures are allowed to swing free and become dislodged. The fish slapped back into the water and made yet another determined run.

"I don't dare fight too hard with this light line," he said. "It'll snap."

A rod-and-reel combo does far more than just propel and retrieve a lure. The rod serves as a shock absorber, taking energy off the line. Reels also have a mechanism called the drag that allows the spool to spin backward and let line out. A reel's drag should be set in such a way that before the tension on the line reaches a breaking point, the reel feeds more out.

If a line is rated for ten pounds of pressure, it is referred to as "ten-pound test." When using it, one wants to set the drag on the reel such that line will be fed out with less than ten pounds of pressure on it, so it never reaches the breaking point. Of course, the greater the drag, the harder the fish has to fight to take it, and the sooner the fish will tire.

I knew it would be a few minutes before Mike landed his fish, so I shut my eyes, and felt the day's final rays on my eyelids.

Then Mike surprised me, because he's usually so hyper-focused with a fish on his line that he just grunts or swears. "You know, fishing and brainstorming have really helped me. We should write a book about fishing together."

"Okay."

"I'm serious."

"Okay."

When I lifted my lids, the sun was touching the horizon line, making a mess of dark purples, reds, and pinks above it. I believe bluefish mouths and jaws are relatively resistant to the pain of the hook. I'm not saying they don't suffer from it. They undoubtedly do. But how can they chew up different prey, day after day, including crabs, clams and boney fish, if their jaws aren't super tough? The way I imagine it, fish have to experience something even more terrible than the pain of the hook when they are caught. Probably for the first times in their lives, they can no longer swim freely. Some force they can't understand clings to them and tethers them, forces them toward the surface. One instant, a bluefish is a predator, ready to shred and consume what it desires. The next it is fighting for its life, against an unknowable foe.

It was one thing for me to talk to Mike about our careers. But to admit, even to myself, how confused I was about my own life was differ-ent. I seemed to have everything I wanted—a family, a career, even a boat. But I also had a sinking sense of dread and doubt those days. I felt so much pressure, so many pressures. All my actions, all my commitments, all my go-go-go, all the overeating, and drinking kept me distracted, kept me from an honest self-reconning. I was coauthoring a book about Japan while running a locally focused publishing company on the Cape. The two places are literally on opposite sides of the planet. Meanwhile, I was going through more and more fast-food drive-throughs, ordering more and more cheap Chinese food and pizza, getting fatter to the point that it embarrassed me. I was wearing my inner pain on my outer body.

"He's getting closer. Can you help me boat him?"

"Work him toward the stern," I said.

A lot of anglers use nets to boat bluefish. But I've always considered using my hands to get them in over the gunnels as part of the challenge. My favored technique is to grab hold of the leader and use it to ease the fish up against the side, then to lift its head a little above the waterline. From there, I grab tightly onto its tail and raise it out of the water.

Gripping a bluefish tail is not easy. They thrash and slap around. Fortunately, there's a small bony notch where their spines meet their tails. It makes for just enough of a handle to hold onto. This one was bigger than the usual we caught. I knew Mike would kill me if I lost it.

I got it onto the deck where it promptly starting flailing. It could no longer breathe and was clearly overcome with panic. With no tension on the hook, Mike's lure promptly popped out. Blood flowed from its wounded jaw.

I should say here that we rarely catch and release bluefish, as Mike and I both love eating them, and there are no size limits. We typically catch what we will eat, or share with others to eat, and then stop fishing for them. Currently, anglers are allowed three bluefish each, but that's more than we've ever wanted or taken.

Once Mike's blue calmed a bit, we measured it at 30.25 inches, whereas our average blue tended to be in the high teens or low twenties.

"My arm is killing me," Mike proudly complained.

"I'll dress him off for you then," I said.

We have tried different techniques for filleting bluefish. The simplest is to throw the whole fish on ice. Then, after the trip, take it out and fillet it on dry land. The problem with this method is that it yields the kind of bluefish meat that most people are used to. Mike doesn't mind the thick oily flavor of blues handled this way, but I find it nearly inedible. The flesh takes on a blue tinge and holds a strong fish-oily flavor. According to one bluefish cookbook, when a bluefish dies its brain sends out signals through its body that change the chemical composition of the meat. The book describes such meat as tasting like the fish's fear, and of having the flavor of its death.

The one way to guarantee bluefish meat is not oily is to immediately kill it, fillet it, and ice the fillets. The key here is the word immediately. The filleting needs to start the first minute or two after killing it. Anyone who has had it prepared this way will agree that it's completely void of oily taste and akin to other white fish, though flakier than cod or flounder.

It's also more humane to kill a fish quickly. But this brings up the question of how to do so. In recent years I've taken to stabbing fish through their brains with a sharp tool like an awl sometimes called a "fish pick," or just with a strong knife; but the method we used back then was to hold its tail with one hand and then hit it hard on the head just above the eyes with one of the wooden clubs my brother-in-law Richard and I bought for kayaking. He referred to it aptly as a "priest."

I can hear Richard's English accent in my mind: "Hand me the priest, would you, mate? It's time to administer last rites to this fish."

As I raised the priest, I became conscious Mike's bluefish was eye-balling me and recalled the term fisheye lenses from photography. I wondered how well a fish sees through the air. Is it like humans trying to see through water without goggles or a mask?

"Thud" went the priest. The blue's skull and face were dented and distorted from the blow. When I hit it the second time, blood spurted from its head, and its eye went dead.

As always, I was aware of my own brutality. The scent of blood was in my nose. Yet having killed hundreds of fish over the years, I rarely feel sympathy for them. Bluefish in particular are so aggressive with such sharp teeth, I think of them mainly as killers themselves. "Bullies of the sea," Mike once called them, which made me wonder what we are. In contrast, stripers seem almost tame with their sandpaper-like teeth. Stripers have an attitude when you catch them and lay them out on the deck like, "Hey, what did I do? What's going on? I was minding my own business." Bluefish on the other hand seem to be thinking something more like, "I want to bite something! I want to bite something!"

For me, it is somehow better to eat a wild animal I've killed myself, rather than a factory-raised and executed one whose meat I receive in exchange for a credit or debit card.

I suppose that the mess of butchering is one reason many anglers prefer to exclusively catch and release. But that begs questions about putting fish through all the traumas of being caught without the result of serving as sustenance. There is a lot to be said for not diminishing the fishery population. But most sportfish also live within an intensely violent environment of killing and being killed. So who is to say there is something wrong with we human beings engaging in that life cycle with them? Vegetarians and vegans avoid participating in the suffering of animals. But we anglers participate in it, whether catching-and-releasing or catching-and-consuming.

A good fillet knife is a fairly intimidating item. Typically six to nine inches, it tapers from about an inch and a half wide at the hilt to a point that stabs easily through thick skin. Ideally there is a gentle curve to the blade. The cutting edge should be very sharp. The blade is usually thin and malleable, so that one can bend and hold the handle at an angle while the rest of the blade is pushed flat and parallel to the cutting surface.

Both blues and striper have similar anatomies and are filleted the same. First, I cut behind the gill plate from near the spine down to the underbelly. Then I use the tip of the knife to make a long shallow cut down the length of the spinal ridge on the side I am filleting. Next, I remove the meat (the fillet) with a series of slices behind it, using the spine and rib cage to guide the knife while pulling the meat up and away from the ribcage with my fingers. A freshly landed bluefish will bleed a fair bit. It will also often spasm a little during the process. I typically say a prayer for the fish while cutting it up. All life is connected and prayers address that connection.

Once the first fillet is removed, I repeat the process on the other side. Unless it is to be saved for boiling into stock, the remaining corpse (sometimes called "the rack") is tossed overboard, a natural burial at sea where it is consumed by a myriad of ocean creatures. I then slice the skin off the side of each fillet and toss them into the water too. I wash the blood off the fillets and get them on ice. Then it's time to clean the knife, boat, and my hands.

"Those look delicious," Mike said solemnly when I handed him a ziploc with the two fillets inside. A gorgeous animal, glittering brightly in the waves just a few minutes previously—all vital muscle and bright scales—had been reduced to two pieces of plastic-bagged meat.

"I'm going to pan fry mine and eat it with sauteed onions and peppers from the garden. Snap peas and beans and strawberries on the side. This is the good life," Mike said.

Mike is probably an even better gardener than fisherman. It won't surprise me if one day he published a book called *The Power of Positive Manure* or something similar.

We started up the *Scout* and pointed her bow toward home.

"What a sunset," my fishing pal observed, patting me on the back. In spite of all the excesses of life in those days, I once more felt just a little more connected, both with the natural world and with a friend.

CHAPTER 9

To Fish in Your Underwear, or Not

MT

Several years had gone by since Adam first introduced me to striper fishing, and we had improved our craft of shallow water fishing while making strides in our writing and publishing careers. We still had a long way to go in both departments, but our therapist-floating-couch (the *Scout*) was proving to be a big help in our personal growth. Slowly we were spreading our wings in our quest for meaningful work that could also support us financially. Out on the boat we pushed and prodded each other to take more risks while at the same time bolstering each other's confidence.

Not all our therapy sessions were on the *Scout*. Sometimes we would do a little shore fishing, often walking a couple miles down various beaches of Cape Cod. We quickly realized our odds of catching fish from shore were poor in the summer but much better in the spring and fall, sometimes right up to November. We'd put the time in, often get skunked, but every now and then our timing would coincide with a school of stripers trapping bait up against the beach. Then we'd enjoy angler's heaven with a hook-up on almost every cast, and our tackle took a beating. Now that I think about it, so did our thumbs and fingers from sticking them into striper's mouths with their tiny sandpaper-like teeth. They call it "striper-thumb."

During our night fishing outings I was always glad to have Adam's company in case I got in a jam. More than one fisherman has drowned when wading out a creek mouth and then having an incoming wave fill their waders. Other tragedies occur when an angler wades out to sand-bars, but then coming back to shore, in a rising tide, steps in a trough now far deeper than before. Adam often tamped down my blind enthusiasm/obsession of wading further and further out with nothing more than a headlamp for light. Who knows, maybe he saved my life with his warnings. Even while our fishing friendship grew, I found myself so addicted to striper fishing that I started doing it alone whenever I could. I didn't own a boat, so I mainly shore fished. This was when I tended to take the most foolish risks and found myself in the strangest situations.

One night after a speaking engagement on the Cape, I stopped at a creek for a few casts just before midnight. The tide was rising, and the fish were following it right up the creek. I could hear the fish before I was in casting range: that unmistakable "pop, pop" as the striper's mouths inhaled bait fish driven to the surface. Such a sound gets my heart racing, and on my first cast I forgot to open my bail and my plug snapped off and sailed across the creek.

Tying on a new leader and plug is never easy at night, but it's especially nerve-wracking when you can hear stripers, probably over a hundred of them, slurping up bait fish on the surface. My hands were shaking in anticipation of the battles to come. Once my new popper was tied on I turned off my head lamp and waded into the river and cast away. A strange thing happened—nothing. I could hear fish all around me, but they were ignoring my small Gag's popper, which usually delivered for me.

Having so many fish at hand with no competition from other anglers is a dream come true—but what good is it if they ignore your offering! Frustration to the max.

Now I know you shouldn't shine your light on the water as it might scare the fish away, but I couldn't resist. Schoolie stripers in the eighteen to twenty-three-inch range were everywhere, one even swam right over my wading boot. In the next half hour, I tied on three different lures, and it wasn't until I put one on no larger than an inch and a half that I had some luck.

Then I figured I'd go after bigger fish at the mouth of the river. Nothing was hitting near shore, but I believed the big guys were out there somewhere. Concerned that a wave might fill my hip waders, I took them off and went out in my bare feet and didn't stop until I was in waist deep water. That was the ticket, and I caught a couple nice thirty inchers. It occurred to me that a thirty-incher from shore felt like a forty incher from the *Scout*, perhaps because I was down almost level with the fish rather than up high on the boat.

I'd be untruthful if I didn't admit it wasn't a little spooky out there at the creek mouth in the dark. Thoughts of sharks and rogue waves did cross my mind, so after battling the second fish, I dragged it to shore, released it, and then went to get my waders. But the waders were not where I left them, nor were they anywhere in the vicinity. Then it hit me—the rising tide carried them off! It was no fun losing them, and less fun walking back to the car barefoot on a mix of cobbles and rocks.

But losing my waders was nothing compared to losing my pants . . .

That indignity occurred on a summer's day on a beach in Buzzards Bay. A few homes were scattered along the shore and a couple sun-bathers were enjoying the summer sunshine before a predicted bank of rain clouds was due to arrive. I wasn't planning on fishing and had no backpack full of gear, but my rod was in the car and I could wade in my sneakers if I needed to go into the water. So I figured, no harm in taking a quick cast or two. I parked my car, grabbed my light spinning rod, and walked down to the shoreline. A little shot of adrenaline coursed through me as I looked to the left. Could it be? After an entire summer of no surface action in this spot, far down the beach I could see birds working over fish. There are few sights I'd rather see.

I had to figure a way to get to the feeding fish, and fast. Fortunately it was low tide and I was able to wade in knee deep water in front of five or six homes that had seawalls and docks. Slogging through the water I moved as fast as I could hoping the birds and fish wouldn't move off just as I arrived opposite them. My luck held. The frenzy was happening quite a bit offshore and it was directly in front of a house where on a previous trip the homeowner said I was on private property and that I must leave. I answered that I was walking below the high tide line and was fishing which in Massachusetts made my approach legal. He barked back, "Private, now get out!" I'm a pretty laid-back, mild-mannered guy, but when

someone is rude or a bully, a different Mike emerges. I answered, "F---
you. I'm not moving one inch." He went into his house and never came
back out.

Now, wading in front of his house I took a long cast with a Super-
strike plug but realized I was well short of the school of fish. But I did
see a couple bass partially come out of the water and they looked to be
about keeper size. That in itself was a rarity, because in this particular cove
I've probably caught two hundred schoolies but only one keeper. I had to
act fast. I was wearing jeans with my wallet and keys in the pocket and
quickly moved back up to the dry sand figuring I'd fish in my boxer-style
underwear. But when I took my pants off I realized I was in gray briefs
(aka almost tighty-whities) that probably would not pass for a speedo.
It was difficult to make a quick decision with terns crying out and dive
bombing the bait.

I thought of the man who tried to shoo me away from the area, and
how this time he might call the cops on me for indecent exposure. Is
fishing in your underwear a crime? I decided to put my keys and wallet in
my pants and hide them all in the sand, about fifty feet from the obnox-
ious guy's house on a secluded section of beach. I then waded out to my
armpits. But the fish had moved still farther out and to the left. I missed
the blitz! I calculated that I best get back on the beach and run to try and
intercept them further down the shore.

I soon had myself in a position where the frenzy was heading. This
time I was ready and waiting in chest-deep water. The birds were closer
now. I was about to place my first cast to land directly in front of the
school when a disturbing thought flashed through my pea-size brain . . .
the great white shark menace. I had just been explaining to a friend from
London who was visiting about how a great white was seen not far from
here. My friend was shocked and said he'd never step foot in waters
where these mammoth creatures lurk.

Now here I was in the ocean, almost up to my neck, with feeding fish
moving toward me. But as the school came closer, my attention focused
on fish slashing the surface, and thoughts of sharks vanished. The bass
didn't look as big as the couple of keepers I thought I saw earlier, but no
matter, I was in the moment and pumped. I made my first cast and as

soon as the lure hit the water a striper slammed the plug. It was perhaps twenty-three inches but still fun, and I caught two more little guys before the school moved out of casting distance. I couldn't help but wonder if I missed catching a keeper in the first spot by being indecisive about keeping my pants on.

As I mentioned, stripers tend to school together by size, so I consoled myself thinking that maybe I was mistaken about seeing bigger fish. By now the clouds had rolled in and the sky was darkening. I decided to ease back into knee-deep water and keep moving to my left to an area I hadn't fished before. The blitzing fish were gone but I soon hooked into a strong bass, thrilled by that wonderful sound of my drag briefly being pulled out. I landed and released the fish that measured twenty-six inches. It turned out the bigger fish were on their own, not with the feeding school, and ten minutes later I was into a striper of thirty inches. Normally, I would have kept it, but not wanting to call attention to myself on the way back to the car, I decided to let him go.

This had been one of my best days at this particular location and for the next hour I kept moving, often in water between knee-high and neck-high. A warm rain started pelting the water, making it look like diamonds dotted the surface. I caught a couple more schoolies and one bluefish that rocketed out of the water. The action slowed down, and I began to think maybe the best way to get back to my car was on the backroads through the neighborhood.

But wait a minute . . . I was in my underwear. Then another *wait a minute* thought—I had to go back and get my pants hidden in the sand with my car keys and wallet! The tide had come up a bit, and now I feared my pants would suffer the same fate as my waders did that night at the creek mouth. I had to move, and move fast. To save time, I swam across a shallow part of the bay, rod in my mouth sideways, while doing the breaststroke.

When I got to the spot where I thought my pants should be I came to the startling realization that all sand looks alike. So where the hell did I bury my pants? I walked the beach looking for a lump, but the sand was smooth. I tried to think exactly where I was when I took my pants off, and I remembered it was up by a patch of dune grass. That's what saved me. I finally found my pants and regained my pride.

***

My next mishap did not involve losing my waders or my pants, but something far more important—a fish I caught and put on the sand. I had been fishing without much luck even though anglers down the beach had caught some small bluefish. Finally I landed one, a little blue of about thirteen inches. I love the strong oily taste of pan-fried bluefish, so I kept him and tried to get another to make a decent meal. As I was casting for bluefish number two, bluefish number one went airborne. How could that be you ask? An osprey saw it flopping in the sand, silently swooped down on it, got it in its talons and through sheer power lifted it from the sand. It flew a few yards over my head, then lost its grip on the fish, and dropped it in the ocean right in front of me but beyond my reach. Could there be a greater insult?

The answer is yes.

While at the same section of beach, just one week after the osprey stole my fish, I saw birds working far in the distance. It looked like a large flock of seagulls were hovering near the shoreline where I assumed bass had bait fish trapped. *Oh yeah*, I thought, *if I get there in time this is going to be wild*. And so I threw my backpack on, and with a rod in each hand (if possible, always take two rods in case of equipment failure during incredible fishing), I set off on a run down the beach.

Loaded down and running in sand at my age probably looks to a young person like a turtle on its back flailing its legs and going nowhere. However, slowly but surely I was closing the gap, and best of all the birds had not left the area of the blitz. For a moment I thought someone had beaten me to the spot but it was a woman watching the birds, with no fishing rod in hand.

As I got closer, heart pumping, not wanting to have a heart attack until I had least caught a fish, I shed my backpack so I could move faster. The woman stared at me, startled that I was racing toward her.

Then it all became clear. There were no blitzing fish. The women was feeding the gulls and they were in a frenzy.

Just then she put two and two together, and said, "Sorry, to get your hopes up."

When I caught my breath, I answered, "You're not the first woman to say that to me."

***

Aside from the mishaps just described, shore fishing does have advantages over boat fishing. When I catch a fish from shore I feel more connected to the natural world than I do when I catch one from a boat. Walking, wading, and observing the most minute changes in the water—a ripple here, a change of depth there, or a dark weed patch—make me feel like one more predator in this natural setting of predator and prey. I could be a great blue heron, an osprey, or an eagle, slowly circling over shallow water. And when I hook into a fish, they always feel bigger from shore. Even the fight is different, because instead of diving down into deeper water, they tend to flee from the shoreline and take off like a torpedo. Landing the fish can be more challenging as well. Sometimes when the fish is struggling right at the shoreline, it uses the bottom for leverage and with a flick of its tail is able to get just enough slack in the line to shake the lure.

The underwear incident turned out instructive as well. From that time onward, whenever the water wasn't frigid—usually mid-June through mid-October—I started shore fishing in a bathing suit. I find it more pleasant than traipsing around in heavy waders, and—this is important—if the fish are far from shore I can wade out until only my mouth and nose are above the water and somehow manage a cast. (Yes, I love all things "water" and make a point to take my last jump in a lake in November.)

A couple times I've even swam for a short distance to reach a sandbar, trying but usually failing to keep my rod above the water, by doing a modified side-stroke. I never did this at night for fear of unforeseen drop-offs, currents, and sharks. But during the daylight this willingness to go the extra mile has paid off, so I always keep an old bathing suit in the car just in case.

With only water separating me from the fish I feel less like an intruder in their environment, and more like I belong. Sounds a little weird, but when a fish jumps from the water and it is at eye level with you, the adrenaline rush can't be beat.

In a bathing suit, I feel as close to the fish as a human can be not snorkeling or diving. There is a downside of course: the cold water. While in the hunt, though, I never seem to notice the chill, but on more than one occasion, about a half hour after leaving the water, mild hypothermia has set in, and I wonder why I am so obsessed with catching fish.

Some anglers use wetsuits, and one of these days I'll get around to giving it a try. Extreme anglers—even more driven than me—will use a wetsuit for buoyancy and fins for maneuverability for fishing in deep water. They call it "skishing," and before I turn seventy I want to give that a try. But only in a protected bay, because I don't want to find myself on a slow ride far offshore.

I certainly wouldn't keep a fish while bobbing in deep water because that seems too much like ringing the dinner bell for sharks. A shark can smell blood from almost a quarter mile away. And in my case sometime the blood is not from the bass but from me! Over the years I've had four hooks caught in my hand. The most recent time I was with Adam when I picked up a fish I just reeled to the boat and while extracting one hook from the fish, it wiggled out of my hand, and a second hook became embedded in the tissue of my palm. I was unable to pull the hook out because of the barb, so I pushed the hook through my hand so the barb was now exposed. Adam used a pair of pliers to try and blunt the barb and after three minutes of work was able to pinch the barb back so that it was flush with the shank. Then came the hardest part. I gritted my teeth and with the hardest yank I could give, pulled the entire hook out of my hand the way it went in. I then stuck my hand in the ocean to clean the wound. There was no serious damage to my hand that I could discern, so we were able to continue fishing, always a priority. Now Adam also carries a powerful pair of wire cutters with him for snipping hooks if need be. Something tells me the "need be" will be me.

The most severe of my self-inflicted wounds happened while fishing aboard my buddy Doug's boat. That one really hurt because the same hook that was in my thumb was also still attached to the fish that was thrashing around. Once I got the fish off I hollered to Doug to take a look, and he said we better motor to shore, fast.

The fishing had been going really well, and I didn't want to leave. I held out my hand and said, "You yank it out."

Doug looked at me like I had three heads, and said "No way."

"Why not? I don't want to go in just yet."

Doug had a thoughtful comeback. "It's embedded in your thumb," he said, "and if I screw it up, I'll also screw up your writing career. You won't be able to use the space bar on your computer. Just think of what your sentences will look like without spaces between each word."

Iguessthey'dlooklikethis,soI'mgladItookDoug'sadvice.Aren'tyou?

***

One improvement I need to implement in order to take my bathing-suit fishing to the next level is to reduce the number of lures I carry. I've got more lures than Imelda Marcos had shoes, and for some dumb reason I feel the need to take as many as I can with me in a bulging backpack. And even though I have thousand of lures, I still buy more. (And we men make fun of women who buy too many clothing items.) To show this tackle madness in all its futility and absurdity, I once counted the number of lures that I bring on Adam's boat each trip. The count was ninety-seven. Guess how many I actually use on most trips? Four.

So why continue to lug a giant tackle bag from car to boat? The reason is simple: the *what if scenario*. What if bass aren't biting and we have to fish for flounder? (We've only done that once in over two decades of fishing together.) What if bluefish chew up our soft plastic lures and we have none left? (We never let that happen because if blues are around we'll switch to a hard plastic popper.) What if the stripers only want a certain color? (Five lures in different colors should suffice.) What if there is bait everywhere and we need to catch it? (One weighted treble hook to snag the bait does the trick.) And the biggest "what if" I use to justify all the lures is what if there are tons of fish around, and I want to experiment which lure works best? (The blitzing fish rarely last long enough to try two lures before the bite is over.) You get the picture . . . I'm nuts!

Chapter 9

***

To all you women out there who are non-anglers but married to one, please don't go waving this page of the book under your spouse's nose. You can be sure I'll hear about it whenever I do a presentation. Instead, let me do my best to explain why some of the more unbalanced types like me fish.

First there is the joy of being out on the water or in the surf. Then there is the excitement when we actually catch a fish. These are the obvious answers to the question, but they don't get at the heart of the matter or examine the compulsion. For me, fishing is about focus. I am locked in to the hunt, the presentation, and the expectation that at any moment I'm going to be battling the biggest fish of my life. This single-minded focus alters the normal passage of time. When the fishing is good, time passes by at warp speed, and when it's slow, time crawls, but I'm still concentrating on how to find the fish. More importantly, at least for me anyway, fishing is one of the few pastimes where I'm in the moment, and no outside thoughts enter my head. I'm either thinking about how we can catch more fish or trying to figure out why we aren't catching any. Every time my lure comes back to the boat or the shore, my brain is considering the next cast. And that's a good thing, because there is no room for the problems of daily life to enter my head.

I also think it's coded in the DNA of some of us more strongly than others—that age-old need to be a hunter-gatherer. Sure, I could buy a fish at the grocery store for far less money in and in far less time than I can prowling the ocean. But that feeling of accomplishment wouldn't be there. Even though an angler like me spends a ton of money on the sport, when I bring a fish home for dinner, I have it in my head I found it and caught it for free, and therefore I'm a wonderful provider. The closest comparable hobby to this is vegetable gardening. Time flies doing garden work, and the pride of growing your own food knows no bounds. (Don't even try to make the comparison between fishing and golf. Okay, both involve swearing. But I've never seen a fisherman throw their rod in frustration, yet how many times have you seen a golfer throw his club to the ground? I'll bet the answer is "many times." Which means you have watched me attempt to golf. Also, I defy anyone to serve golf balls to their family for dinner.)

My style of fishing is not, I repeat *is not*, relaxing. You might have an image in your head of man smoking a pipe, sitting comfortably, waiting for a fish to find his bait. I've tried that, and I can't do it. First of all, I only use bait as a last resort, and second I'm fidgeting the whole time. So bait fishing is not my cup of tea. Instead, I need to be *doing*, and that means casting in all directions to cover as much water as possible, or taking over the wheel of Adam's boat and going hunting for birds diving on bait fish driven up by stripers.

Don't misunderstand my lack of relaxation as impatience. I can be the most patient guy in the world if I believe that sooner or later I will find fish. This probably comes from my days of trout fishing on rivers, where in the course of day I might easily cover four or five miles of a river, wanting to see what's around the bend, always believing a beautiful brown or rainbow trout is waiting for me if I just push on a little farther.

Likewise, I will stay out on Adam's boat from dawn until last light, hunting for fish, totally invigorated by the environment. I never feel tired when fishing, whereas at home I take a nap most days about 2 p.m. Although I'm not tranquil when fishing, I find being outdoors energizing. Emerson said it best: "The lover of nature is he whose inward and outward senses are still truly adjusted to each other; who has retained the spirit of infancy even into the era of manhood. His intercourse with heaven and earth becomes part of his daily food. In the presence of nature, a wild delight runs through the man, in spite of real sorrows."

All true, but more so if there are fish around.

Just because I'm not relaxed when I fish, doesn't mean the sport doesn't yield healthy benefits for both body and mind. The word I would use for my mindset when fishing is *engaged*. And in this modern world with a distraction every minute, the simple act of trying to find a fish becomes, well, all important. Sure in the scheme of one's life it means little compared to family, friends, and work, but while you are angling the search for fish and the setting become your world. And a trip is enhanced, as it sometimes has been for me, by seeing something unusual, such as an ocean sunfish, a basking shark, a spiraling pod of dogfish, a breaching whale, an unusual cloud formation, even pelagic birds on the ocean in the fall.

Unfortunately, a near miss—when a striper goes for my lure and misses it (or I yank it out of its mouth in excitement)—will cause me to go apoplectic. Adam once brought his friend Mark on the boat with us, and after Mark witnessed such an incident I heard him say to Adam, "Does he always swear like this if he doesn't get a hook up?"

"Not always," Adam answered. "I've seen him cry like a two-year-old when he misses a really big fish."

CHAPTER 10

Fatherhood

AG

Even when it's just the two of us out on the water, Mike and I feel the presence of our children. Fatherhood has a way of at least partially defining guys like us, of factoring into virtually everything we do. We continuously carry the responsibility. In many ways, the facts of fatherhood are emphasized even more when we fish without our kids than it is trumpeted when they do come along.

My daughter, Miki, and son, Jack, each learned how to work a rod and reel long before they could ride a bike. None of our children have developed into fishing fanatics, though all four have deep connections with the water. My favorite image of my kids' childhoods is of the two of them sitting together at the bow of the *Scout* while she cruises along, the water whipping by in front of them, sunlight glittering, the strands of their fine, blond-brown hair whipping away.

The only time I regretted taking them boating was when Jack reached the age when many boys start to spit. Sure enough, as we cruised along at twenty mile per hour, he decided to hawk a wad from the back of his throat and then inexplicably spit it straight up in the air. The glob instantly shot toward the back of the boat, just above the small windshield, smacking me squarely on my nose and splattering goo-ily and warmly all over my cheeks, sunglasses, and—yes—my lips.

Jack and I had a little discussion that day about what Mike calls "boating etiquette."

We also took Mike's kids with us from time to time, Kristin and Brian. We have even held a few annual father-daughter trips with Kristin and Miki, and hopefully will have more in the future. Over the years, the girls caught quite a few fish. But probably my favorite trip was when it rained on us straight for three hours. Neither of them complained a single time and in fact thanked us for the trip afterward. Now those are two fine daughters.

Partly because Mike's kids are older than mine and partly because my father died when I was young and I didn't have a role model, I watched him closely to see how he handled being a dad. The thing I noticed most is that he seems to accept both his kids for who they are and that he holds few preconceived notions of how they "should" be. For instance, when she was young, Mike focused on Kristin's passion for the outdoors with hiking trips and similar adventures. Yet when he noticed Brian's talent for sports and sports analysis, he signed up to coach his basketball team and then established a tradition of actively watching games together on TV, always hashing out the strategical intricacies of pro sports together.

Mike still teaches me with his parenting approach that it's far better to try to guide than to try to control. One fishing season after another, he shares stories where he encourages certain behaviors from Kristin and Brian while avoiding forcing things.

The one time I forced Jack to do something he truly did not want to do, I created a lot of negativity. It was the summer before his senior year in high school. I threatened to take away valued privileges if he didn't attend a certain college preparation course that he tried to explain to me was not right for him and that he hated with all his heart. Oddly, it was around that time he lost interest in fishing too, at least for a few months. Later when I saw pictures of a trip that summer he made without me to Mike's cabin in Vermont, he and his friend were framed with broad grins holding big freshwater fish. Of course, Jack hadn't lost interest in fishing at all. He had just lost interest in fishing *with me*, the guy who was forcing him to do something he loathed. Once I finally understood his perspective, I apologized and explained that some of us parents are harder to raise then others.

Mike's daughter Kristin is probably the most productive angler in both our families, including Mike and me. What I mean is that she has probably caught more big fish per hour of fishing than any of us. Her schedule has meant that she hasn't gotten out with us as often as we'd like, but when she does, it seems she always lands a whopper, the kind of fish that the whole group wants to get photographed around. Even at Mike's cabin, Kristin holds the record for largest fish. To be accurate, I should say that she "held" the record independently until I learned the details of where she caught it, and with what lure, and then copied her the next season. As a result, I'm pretty sure I landed the very same pickerel and am now co–record holder. (She really should not have written down all the details in the cabin's log where just anyone could read them.)

I'll never forget that pickerel. It slammed the imitation frog lure as if grievously offended that the frog had dared enter its domain. The fish positively emanated aggression. Maybe it was still mad at having been duped by Kristin the year before. Although she now has a successful career in business, she has made the time to coauthor a humor book with her dad, *The Cringe Chronicles*, that recalls many embarrassing moments she experienced as the daughter of Mike Tougias. (For example, when Mike insisted young Kristin carpool with other kids to an activity in order to save on his driving, yet when it was his turn squeezed everyone into his car already over packed with smelly fishing rods and well-worn gear, not to mention boxes of his books and a slide projector.) Eventually, after *somehow* surviving and even thriving into adulthood under such cringeworthy circumstances, Kristin wound up living and working in Hong Kong for a time. This provided her with the material to write the children's book *Good Night, Hong Kong* for my company as well.

The most memorable fishing interaction with my own daughter, Miki, began prior to the third season we had the *Scout*. It was the start of March, and she had just turned five. She came to me with intense excitement in her little girl's voice.

"Daddy, can we go fishing?"

"Sorry, honey. It's too cold this time of year."

"Can you catch me a fish? I want to see a fish's heart. Can I see a fish's heart?"

Valentine's Day wasn't far behind us, so I assumed my little cherub envisioned a classic candy heart. I tried to explain that an actual fish's heart isn't so pretty, but she would not be placated.

"I want to see a fish's heart."

"Okay, okay, next time I catch a fish, I'll save it for you."

When May rolled around and I mentioned that I was fishing the next morning, she piped right up, "When you catch a fish, I want to see its heart."

In all the excitement of my first day back on the water, I forgot entirely and returned with fillets to fry but had discarded the "racks" (their bodies) along with their internal organs. (Did I ever say I was a perfect father?)

"I'm sorry, Miki."

"You promised!"

On my next outing I didn't catch any fish big enough to bring home and found myself in even more trouble with my preschooler.

"Why can't you catch me a fish?"

Yes, indeed. Fatherhood and fishing are two of the great humblers of men.

Finally, on my third trip I came home with both a bluefish and keeper striped bass. I promptly brought both, along with Miki, to the picnic table we used as a carving station. Before I did anything, I reminded her that we needed to be respectful toward the fish whose lives I had taken and offered a small prayer to them in front of her. Then I explained I would butcher them and take out their hearts for her to see and learn about. But I emphasized, she needed to stay back away from the knife.

"It's very sharp. It cuts right through skin and muscle and bones. Do you know what our hands are made of?"

She just looked up quizzically.

"Hands are made of skin and muscle and bones. That means this knife can cut us just as easily as a fish."

I distinctly recall her steadily edging closer as I worked on their bodies which were cold from being on ice. She reminded me of a puppy nosing into its dish while dogfood is still pouring out of the bag. Eventually, I had to move her back in her chair.

The hearts of both species are located up inside their rib cages, so it takes a little doing to get to them. Her face lit up when I finally handed her the first heart about the size of a marble. She was even more excited when she inspected the intestines and found undigested minnows. And she was downright awestruck with a fish eyeball I cut out and handed her. She thoroughly examined their scales, skin, mouths, tails, bones.

It reminded me of our having decorated Easter eggs a month previously, only this morning there was just one color dye, and it wasn't a pretty pastel. It was the various shades of blood red, and it was all over her little fingers and palms.

Eventually two-year-old Jack joined us. He was naturally curious about his sister's excitement. He looked over the gutted fish on the newspapers but kept a wary distance. Then his sister reached out to him with a fist full of guts.

"Do you want to hold them, Jack?"

He screwed up his face in an unmistakable *Yuck!*

It's wonderful how kids born and raised by the same parents can have such different personalities.

A few weeks later in June, Mike and I had a banner day in the bay. We caught two keepers each, then the daily limit, and a beautiful bluefish as well. We got home towing the *Scout* and laid the five large fish on the picnic table, dragged the hose over, and got to work filleting, skinning, bagging the meat, and setting their racks aside.

Because Mike was going to bring the bluefish home for himself, we hadn't bothered filleting it out on the boat, as is my preference. We took turns filleting. Not long into our work, Miki came out and started watching. I hosed off the boat, cooler, and rods.

"Hi, Miki! How are you?" Mike asked her.

"I'm good. Do you want to see a bluefish heart?"

"Sure." he said. "Just don't get close to me while I'm using this sharp knife. Okay, honey?"

"Okay. It can cut our hands as easy as fish," she said. A few minutes later she called to him, "Mike, Mike!"

He looked up and saw my five-year-old with blood up to her wrist, her right hand extended, a small purply-red bluefish heart in her palm.

She had walked over to its rack, dug into its cut-up corpse with her fingers, and literally tore its heart out.

"Adam, did you see this?" he called to me. "Your daughter is going to grow up to be either a doctor, or some kind of a gothic chick."

While she has never been a "goth," Mike was partly right. Miki is studying to be a veterinarian, and has worked in animal clinics for years. Interestingly, she also decided to stop eating meat and fish, on humanitarian grounds.

Mike has already mentioned the first trip we took with his then teenage son Brian. It was the first time that I saw what distinctly struck me as "a herd" of keeper-sized stripers in shallow waters. They meandered slowly toward us, just below the surface. I say "herd" because that's how I perceived them. There were perhaps thirty fat-bodied fish, swimming slowly together in a loose formation. They were close enough to the *Scout* that I could literally see the whites of their eyes. It sounds odd, but they reminded me of bison I once witnessed roaming across a field in Yellowstone National Park.

Brian picked up on our instructions as soon as we got out there and began hooking and landing fish right off. His first was a thirty-six-incher. He was a natural with a rod and reel, and like many teens, he was also adept at teasing his father.

"Whoa! Whoa! This thing is a monster. Holy cow!" hooted Mike on one of his first big keepers that day.

"Dad, chill out. You're going to have a heart attack," Brian admonished.

Half an hour later, I heard Mike almost whisper to Brian, "We have to savor this. We may never have another day like it."

Mike and I had many fishless days under our belts by then, so we appreciated what a special situation we were in. In a way it was almost unfortunate for Brian, as it can be difficult to "start at the top" on a bountifully fishing day like that.

Part of the power of positive fishing for Mike and me is that we both know and often recognize how privileged we are to be saltwater fishing at all. Neither of us grew up in fishing families, nor in families that had the kind of abundant time and resources that the hobby can demand. We know we are among a relatively tiny minority of people worldwide who are lucky enough to be able to ocean fish in a motorboat for pleasure on a regular basis.

When the sun started setting, our cooler holding three keepers, we motored toward the harbor and saw the sky aglow with soothing oranges and yellows.

Brian was fished out from a long day on the water and looked tired. But Mike wanted us to stop and take his fabled "one last cast." It was about then that Brian told his father that his fishing rod was like a crack pipe and that he was "a fishing crackhead." Brian let out a long loud laugh when he said it, and we joined in with him.

Brian pegged us both, actually. It was selfish of us to keep him out too long. No matter how healthy an activity fishing can be, it can be taken too far. Brian helped me realize that for me at least, it isn't always a benign hobby. Just as fishing has helped create connections with my family members, it has also served as a way for me to *not* think about them.

The irony of Brian teasing Mike is that today as an adult himself Brian has adopted a profession that seems potentially more addictive than fishing. Brian is a full-time professional poker player and has been for several years. So far, he has earned a respectable income, accumulated a decent bank or reserve of funds, and even won a couple of international tournaments. I have to give Mike credit there too. Rather than try to discourage Brian's passion, as many fathers might, he has combined being supportive with encouraging his son to hedge his bets, build savings, and watch his back. Perhaps it's Brian's ability to *not* "take one more cast," and to keenly observe the obsessions of others, like Mike and me, that serves him best as a professional gambler.

CHAPTER 11

Navigating Rough Water
Divorce, Job Loss, and Insomnia

MT

Every now and then Adam and I would see Jon Hyde the fishing guide coming into the harbor while we were going out or vice versa. Invariably his eagle eyes would latch onto one of our rods, and he'd shout, "I thought I broke you guys of that bad habit! The next thing you know you'll be trolling umbrella rigs!"

He was referring to the one heavy boat rod loaded with metal wire instead of monofilament or braid, which we used for a style of fishing he looked down on as too unskilled.

Okay, I admit it, we sometime jigged off the bottom, trolling at 2.5 knots, instead of sight fishing and surface casting with light tackle. We used the rod with wire as a last resort, when a day of scouting and casting in shallow water didn't produce decent fish. I'm not so much of a top-water purist, to occasionally go deep.

The problem with the heavy rod with wire is that when you do catch a fish, you don't feel the fight like you would on light tackle. Instead of battling the noble striper it feels like you're cranking in an old boot, or maybe some fool's waders that he let the tide carry away. The only thing worse than using heavy tackle, however, was spending a whole day on the water and not catching a striper of size. Though in Adam's defense, it was usually me who said, "Bring the wire, just in case."

Most days we never touched that rod, and it just took up space in the rod holders, which I usually filled by bringing more lightweight rods than needed. Adam often asked me if I really needed to bring so many rods, and I'd say, "Remember the day keepers were blitzing all around the boat and my tackle took such a beating that the reel broke."

"I know, I know," Adam would answer. "Back-ups."

"Exactly. You never know when a reel is going to crap out or a rod break."

Actually, it happens quite frequently to me. Not because huge fish damage the equipment, but rather the way I haphazardly care for my tackle. My theory is that because I fish every chance I get, I'm going to drop a rod, close a car door on a tip, or hopefully (in my dreams) get spooled by a giant fish making one long run. With those issues in mind, I purchase equipment in the mid-range price, so I won't succumb to tears if my tackle is damaged or God forbid, goes overboard. This last scenario has happened to me while kayaking, when a blue fish pulled the rod right out the holder. It has also happened with my son out on the *Scout* with Adam, when we were passing a rod between us and dropped it. We watched rod and reel spiral down into the depths. Instead of screaming and cursing, I just said, "Oh well, an offering to the fishing gods." (Well, maybe I cursed first and then became calm, it's hard to remember . . .)

There are some days when the stripers are lazy—probably because there's not much bait around—and the bigger fish are just lying on the bottom, not willing to venture into shallow water. This is usually the case on sunny days, and often in the midday hours rather than dawn or dusk. That's when you need to get your offering down to them. Adam has his special spot about a half mile off the coast, in about twenty feet of water, where one of us guides the boat while the other uses the rod with wire and a metal jig fished on the bottom. Then we do the backbreaking jerking of the rod so that the jig disturbs the sand. A striper on the bottom is first attracted to the sand kicking up and then spots the jig. In the striper language he says to a buddy, "Say, that's an easy, slow-moving meal, don't mind if I do."

Using wire saved more than a few days from being skunked. It is also a deadly way to catch big fish. But here's the thing—we never felt proud about it. We realize any angler could catch a fish this way if their shoulders held up from jerking the rod. No pinpoint casting, no imparting a secret motion to a top water lure, no setting the hook, and no deft boatmanship needed.

In recent years we replaced the wire jigging with a tube-and-worm fishing as a last resort. As described by Adam earlier, this rig consists of a colorful, foot-long tube with a hook on the end to attach a sea worm. The thin tube—usually red or orange—doesn't really look like any prey that I can think of, but it is so large that any bass with a smidgen of curiosity simply would have to swim over and take a look at it. (Maybe they think the tube is an eel with a pigment problem because of the way it undulates in the depths.) Once the fish gets close, that's where the worm kicks in; its scent is strong enough that a bass or a bluefish can't resist having a snack.

Like bouncing the jig off the bottom, we viewed this method of one step up from trawling a fifty-foot net behind the boat to catch fish, and we weren't particularly proud of it. But I vowed to write an honest book, so I feel it my duty to say yes, I'll resort to these methods if nothing else is working.

I viewed our heavy rod with the wire as similar to an emergency cash account that financial advisors are always urging us to keep in case of an unexpected crash in the economy or our personal lives. I'm glad I listened to those advisors because both happened to me in a relatively short amount of time. Fortunately, I had the finances to ride out the storm, and the friendships to help keep my spirits afloat.

The first of the double whammy was in my corporate job, where I was given a nudge out the door, three years before my planned escape. There were a couple options for me within the company but they were full-time positions rather than part-time. In essence, just when I thought my writing career was going to the next level, I'd be giving it up for a few years to work in a mind-numbing job, caged like a rat in a cubicle, staring at a computer screen for hours on end. The department I was in seemed to value "yes men" more than honest give and take, and I was a lousy Yes Man.

After consulting with Adam and people close to me, I knew I simply could not take the step backward. I kept hearing Thoreau's "the mass of men lead lives of quiet desperation" whenever I thought of the cubicle choice. Thoreau encouraged me a bit more when I thought of trying to make a go of full-time writing: "If one advances confidently in the direction of his dreams, and endeavors to live the life which he has imagined, he will meet with a success unexpected in common hours."

In making the decision I drew up a list of pros and cons, but in the end ignored it, because the list indicated I should stay with the company three more years. Financially, it was clear that made the most sense. But I'm a big believer of listening to your gut and it said, *The time is right to fly away*. Seeing Adam take chances in his life also gave me confidence.

I was working on three book projects at that time, and I felt like each one not only had potential but that I'd also be letting the people down who I was writing about. My projects were *Overboard!*, *A Storm Too Soon*, and *The Finest Hours*—they felt like my children and I couldn't compromise them for three years. *The Finest Hours*, which occurred in 1952, was the most challenging. While there was plenty of material on one of the ships in the story, the *Pendleton*, the other ship, the *Fort Mercer*, demanded painstaking research. Much of that research was done over a four year period at the Boston Public Library, pulling up microfiche of old newspaper interviews with survivors. (Newspapers around the country covered the event, and did interviews with survivors from their readerships.) At this time I had not yet reached out to a coauthor, because I wasn't sure where the research would take me, or if there was enough material to sustain a book.

I felt that if I put all three projects on the back burner for three years, I might not be able to recapture the momentum.

In the end, the passion for these projects was stronger than the financial security of a stable job and pension, so I walked away from the corporate world forever. I recall on my drive home after emptying out my desk that I threw my tie out the window, and watched the breeze blow it across the Massachusetts Turnpike highway. For better or worse, I was like my tie, untethered but free.

I remember thinking, *Well at least it's going to be an interesting path I'm taking. I'll bet my insomnia issue slowly fades away. I'm in control of how I spend my days, and with clear sense of purpose, I'll enjoy deep sleep.* I was right about the interesting path. But I was dead wrong about the sleep.

A few months later, storm number two hit, in the form of the great recession and divorce. The great recession knocked the stuffing out of my speaking business, and it accelerated the demise of many of the print magazines I was writing for. I had no idea what it meant for book contracts, but I knew it couldn't be good. Anyone who lived through that time surely remembers seeing many of their assets and their freelance work shrink dramatically in the course of just a few months: house prices plunged, the stock market crashed, and layoffs were widespread. All I could do was tighten my belt, keep plugging away with the writing, and run various ideas for expanding my income stream past Adam. I learned the power of positive fishing is not just for goal attainment but also for keeping your sanity by having someone in your corner who is brutally honest with their advice and ideas and an energy builder rather than a drainer. That's what Adam and I both tried to be for one another.

Although the divorce was a mutual decision, that didn't make it any less painful. Only people who have gone through a divorce can fully understand the emotional toll it can take. I only have one piece of advice for those reading this book and contemplating a divorce: do what my wife and I did and see one divorce attorney who specializes in mediation. They will hammer out a fair separation without undue bickering and ever-rising legal fees.

One curious aspect of the divorce is how some friends pulled away from me, as if I was contagious in some ways. Fortunately new friends stepped in. The first—you guessed it—was a fellow angler.

After the divorce I moved to a small cottage in Plymouth, and by good fortune a neighbor came forward and assisted me in many ways. Paul first helped me with the repairs the cottage needed—he was the most innovative problem solver I've ever met. Of course the bigger benefit was his companionship. He was never intrusive but every day we would chat for a few minutes, and in the dead of winter, sometimes Paul was the only person I spoke to all day. He and his wife Jane frequently had me over for dinner, or Jane would send over food as a surprise. My gift to Paul was to rekindle his interest in striped bass fishing. He was a native Cape Codder, who had fished Cape waters for many years, but now, living in Plymouth his fishing trips were few. I told him that my daughter and I had caught some decent-sized stripers in a nearby bay, and he dusted off his rod, and we fished it together from shore. I've never seen such a transformation. He went from a take it or leave it attitude on fishing to all-in. Before I knew it he was building his own rods, crafting his own lures, tying his own flies, and consistently out-fishing me. It was a beautiful thing to behold.

We fished often and hard together. Our styles were different, however, as Paul would pick his spot and then patiently work it, varying his retrieve and switching among his homemade lures and flies. I, on the other hand, would fish alongside him for five minutes, and then move on down the shore thinking the spot we were in was fishless. An hour later I'd walk back to him, and we'd compare our luck. He usually did just as well or better than me by staying in one place. That was never enough to make me stay put, however, and as one of my trout fishing buddies, Booge, will tell you: "Toug is a speed fisherman, he likes to cover ground, and misses some nice fish in the process."

Often, after Paul and I left our favorite spot we'd be driving home, and just like on Adam's boat, I'd say, "How about we try one last place." That place was usually a channel. And almost every time we did that Paul would walk down to a "Paul's Rock," make one cast and land a small bluefish, which I gladly took home to eat. Then we would both cast for five minutes and not catch anything else. I can't tell you how many times that happened. But I can guess why it happened—I think Paul was sneaking out at night and feeding the bluefish, or maybe talking to them, convincing them that if they gave up a little guy to his lure we would not catch the big ones.

Paul made me multiple lightweight spinning rods, and when friends saw them in action, they commissioned him to make them rods of their own. Paul preferred shore fishing to being out on a boat, but all my fishing buddies from the past got to know him over ensuing years. The brotherhood of fishermen was expanding. Adam had given me striper fever, now I was rekindling it in Paul.

***

My sleep issue plagued me at this time. I'm not sure insomnia is the right word, because it seemed like I did get eight hours of sleep most nights, although it was fitful. Whatever was happening at night was not deep REM sleep, and I'd wake up many mornings feeling like I was hungover, even though I rarely drank more than one beer. I wondered if the underlying cause was depression, but I couldn't be sure. Certainly those years, 2007 and 2008, were stressful. My ultimate conclusion was that my problem was not depression, because whenever I took an afternoon nap I felt like a million bucks afterward. If there was depression I felt it was primarily the result of poor sleep rather than it causing the poor sleep.

I quickly learned that morning exercise was key to having a productive day. The endorphins kept that hungover feeling at bay for awhile. Another technique that helped me—and I hope helps any reader with a struggle—was not to let how you feel define you. I was determined not to blab to anyone who would listen the details of my problem.

Pick your spots on who to confide in. For me it was Adam, my two buddies from elementary school, Opie and Cogs, and now Paul because I saw him every day. In fact, on those mornings when I really felt like crap, I became even more determined to spread cheer rather than gloom. The simple interaction with a bank teller, a gas station attendant, or anyone else I crossed paths with was an opportunity for me to smile and be friendly. My motto was "You become how you act," and I wasn't going to allow myself to become a cranky old man.

Looking back there were some light-hearted moments because of my sleep struggle. Adam knew that if we were going out evening fishing, that I'd want to take a quick cat nap before we departed. He'd throw a sheet over one of his kid's beds, and I'd fall asleep to the sound of Adam doing his Buddhist chants in the adjacent room. His son Jack would come home from school and Adam would say, "You can go in your room as soon as Mike wakes up." Jack was always good natured about it. He had a wisdom far beyond his years.

On the *Scout*, Adam would ask me what my latest effort was in my quest for refreshing sleep. I answered that I think I'd tried them all and run out of new ideas. I'd already had sleep apnea ruled out, and I gave every remedy a shot: acupuncture, holistic therapies, witch doctors (kidding), neuromodulation (including strange tapping of my head and wrist holding, which actually helped my sleep a bit), every change in diet under the sun, hot yoga, cold yoga, yogurt immersion (kidding), anti-depressants, a sound machine to mimic the ocean, sounds to mimic a brook, sounds to mimic shouts when catching a big striper (kidding), sounds to mimic seeing a striper or even a stripper, every sleeping pill ever made, tart cherry juice, sex therapy (wishful kidding), warm baths, and a million other potential remedies that did not work.

The only thing that helped was the diazepam, and it didn't sit right with me that I needed a prescription drug to help induce sleep at night. Here I was growing much of the food I ate in the warm weather months in a giant organic vegetable garden, yet I was taking this chemical every night! It really pissed me off. I knew the drug was highly addictive, so I stayed at small dosage, but could not eliminate it entirely.

Later, during one of our brainstorming sessions on the boat, Adam and I decided I should try marijuana. I certainly had smoked enough of it in college, but that was years ago, and maybe it might help my restless brain to shut down. Medical marijuana had just been approved in Massachusetts so I gave it a shot.

The dispensary where I bought my pot was called Theory Wellness, and it felt like I was walking into the future when I entered the building. A line of people of all conceivable ages waited their turn to talk to one of five consultants. The buyers (medicinal users all, I'm sure) would chat for a couple minutes then present their credit card and walk off smiling with a goody bag of herb, as we called it in the old days. It felt strange at the time that this was all state sponsored, when a few years earlier you could go to jail if you were caught with a large bag of pot. I envisioned a future where the government, in conjunction with big business, conspired to keep us all placated and docile in our crappy jobs by encouraging us to self-medicate ourselves with state-grown weed. I almost turned around and walked out, but then I remembered Adam saying I should leave no stone unturned in my effort to solve my sleep problem, and that he'd be chanting for me.

My "consultant" was a woman about twenty-two years of age who steered me toward "Sunshine Daydream," a strain of pot that she said would affect my whole body and not just my head. She showed me a joint, suggested I take only one or two hits the first night, and even recommended how long I hold the inhalation in my lungs. It wasn't lost on me that I was taking pot smoking instruction from a twenty-two-year old—it was like having a kid fisherman tell me how to catch stripers on the flats. I had to bite back the urge to say, "Do you know who you're talking to? At St. Michael's College in 1975 it was almost impossible not to get high." But I kept my mouth shut, not wanting to sound like some old geezer, saying "When I was your age . . . " I simply asked, "Will it make me relax?"

"Absolutely," she said. Next she recommended I try a little "Soulmate," followed by "Samoa."

"I'll take them all," I said.

Then she threw me a curve by asking me if I wanted them by the joint or in edibles called "infusions." I almost ordered the edibles but I remember my son telling me he had a terrible experience with pot-laced food because it had a delayed reaction, and he probably ate too much. There was no way I wanted that to happen; I clearly remember the time paranoia put me on the edge of almost checking myself into an emergency room. I was about twenty-five years old, living with two roommates in a home outside Boston. I had smoked a little weed while I fixed a big dinner, of which I was quite proud as it included vegetables I grew and a trout I had caught. The trouble started about an hour later when I was watching TV in the den and said to one of my roommates, "I can't believe I'm still hungry after that dinner." He responded by saying, "But you haven't eaten anything."

I swore I had eaten the fish and vegetables, but being as high as a hawk soaring near the clouds, I was unsure and decided to go back to the kitchen and investigate. The evidence was there: a dirty frying pan, a cutting board, and even a vegetable steamer. *Well,* I thought, *whatever happened, I'm still hungry.* I figured I'd have a piece of pie. I opened the cupboard where we kept our dishes, and that's when the mystery was solved. Sitting on the shelf was a plate filled with a cooked trout, snow peas, carrots, and sautéed onions. Next to it was a big bowl with a garden salad in it, complete with Ranch dressing on top.

That shook me up a bit and I lost my appetite. *Damn, I'm so high I cooked the entire friggin dinner and then put it neatly away in a cupboard.* I felt I had lost control—always scary for a Type A person like me—so I decided just to lie down in my room and let the effects of the weed fade. Unfortunately, there was no fading, but instead a few heart palpitations and a paranoid thought that perhaps a stronger drug was laced into the pot I smoked. *Okay, calm down. Just lie here for half an hour and you will feel better.* I looked at my watch and noted it was 8:15 p.m. Time seemed to crawl. I turned the radio on but couldn't focus on the music because of strange sensations buzzing both my body and my thoughts, so I turned it off. I waited, and waited and waited. Finally, I figured a half hour was up and I looked at my watch. It was 8:16. *Oh no,* I muttered, *I'm in a time warp. Something is terribly wrong.* I carefully made my way downstairs and found my buddy Dale on the couch. We were friends since seventh grade, so if I was going to confide in anyone it was going to be him.

"Dale, do I look ok?"

Dale glanced from the TV to where I was standing, holding onto the door frame for balance and support. "You look fine," he said.

"Well I don't feel fine. Time has stopped. We're in trouble."

I got through the ordeal, but after all these years I clearly remember that chilling feeling that I'd never come down from the high. This time I'd be careful. I certainly wouldn't smoke the pot on the *Scout*, knowing I did enough bone-headed things without involving marijuana. And I needed supervision. I volunteered my girlfriend at the time to be my caretaker should things go wrong.

Before I lit up, she relayed a cautionary story told to her by a cop friend several years before. Three men in their forties thought it was time to relive a little of their college days and get stoned on pot. Soon after smoking a joint, they became so paranoid they thought they'd get busted at any moment. This was despite the fact that they were in one of their suburban homes and had no cause to leave. The paranoia, however, became so strong the men finally decided that the best thing to do was to turn themselves in to the police. They actually called the police department and reported themselves. The cops came to the house, reassured the men they would be fine, and with a straight faces thanked the men for doing the right thing.

My experience with the "Sunshine Daydream" wasn't as dramatic as those three men, but the same sensation of time slowing that I experienced when I was in my twenties and I put my cooked dinner in the cupboard returned. I became very self-aware, perhaps even self-conscious, and noticed how long it took me to complete a sentence when I spoke. But at least I knew that the marijuana I had was natural and not laced with any other drug, and that offset any creeping suspicion that something was amiss.

There was one other problem—I didn't feel sleepy. So I watched a PBS special about how birds fly, and I ate all the chocolate in the house. I went to bed at 4 a.m.

I blame Adam for that sleepless night.

CHAPTER 12

Lobstering

AG

It was New Year's Day, and I woke up hungover as hell. I wasn't throwing up, but I had a definite drowned feeling. Back in those days, I loved alcohol. I loved the bottles, whether beer, wine, or liquor. I loved the flavors, sweetness, bitterness, heat going down, above all the feelings alcohol produced. Drinking was nothing short of euphoric. It was as if my mind had been a long shuttered-up room, dank and musty, with heavy drapes and no air. Like I had mildew in my mind. But as soon as the booze hit my bloodstream, it was like throwing wide all the windows, letting streams of sunlight and fresh air rush in. Negativity vanished, at least for the short term . . .

"Great way to start the year," I grumbled to myself that morning.

Our Christmas tree was still lit up in a corner, draped in tinsel and homemade ornaments, but with plenty of dried needles on the floor. The fish tanks Santa brought my kids were in the middle of the living room still, zebra fish and goldfish doing their rounds, aerators buzzing. I held six-year-old Jack up high enough for him to sprinkle food into each. Then I kissed nine-year-old Miki on her forehead and was out the door.

I was off to lead a "Thoreau walk." I had been leading these combination nature-history-literature guided walks for several years. I brought tourists and locals along trails and beaches, stopping along the way to read and discuss his observations and insights when he visited Cape Cod in the mid-nineteenth century. Essentially, I was making money by dispensing Thoreau's wisdom.

"Simplify. Simplify," he had urged us all through his "economic experiment" at Walden Pond and with his determination to "suck the marrow out of life." In direct contrast, I was not "living deliberately" but had without realizing it defaulted to the pursuit of the American Dream. I operated not one but two book publishing businesses while trying to be a professional writer. In fact, at that time I was in the process of going through a major expansion from three employees to a dozen. This meant more office space, phone lines, computers, payroll, accounting, health care, and on and on. I remember asking Mike's advice about hiring more staff and his suggesting: "Keep it small and keep it all, Adam."

However Thoreauvian my words may have been, my actions declared that "bigger is better."

It was easy enough for Thoreau to "simplify, simplify," I thought. He stayed single and didn't have any kids. I was married "with lawn furniture," as a character says in the TV show *The Wire*. We also had two cars, an eighteen-foot boat, a garden, six chickens, a dog, two cats, two guinea pigs, and now thanks to Santa Claus, two fish tanks. I led Thoreau walks. I volunteered numerous hours most weeks. In my "spare time," which mainly came while driving more than thirty thousand miles a year, I listened to inspirational speakers who, quite frankly, I hoped would teach me how to be more "successful" (codeword for "make more money").

Mike also continuously encouraged me to pay off all debt and focus on building reserves and equity. Instead, I carried loans against both cars and the house.

Simplify, schmimplify!

I called Mike that New Year's Day on my way home from the walk. He was living in his cottage on a lake in Plymouth after his recent divorce.

"How are you enjoying your new waterfront bachelor lifestyle?"

"The lake is pretty grey this time of year," he said. "Did you know that half of the Pilgrims died in Plymouth during their first winter of religious freedom?"

"Ha. More than half, actually. I'm sure you are making the most out it," I encouraged him. "You know sometimes I'm jealous of you single guys."

"Doing all the chores and sleeping alone every night isn't all it's cracked up to be. But I'm chipping away at a new book about an offshore lobsterman who survives a deadly storm in a life raft. What are you up to?"

"Wow, we're in rhythm with one another. Guess what I found on the beach today?"

"Pirate treasure."

"Close. I found a lobster trap. I was leading a Thoreau walk and it was on the beach in good shape. There is no tag on it that I can find, and no buoy, so there's no way for me to return it to anyone. It must have washed ashore over Christmas. I'm bringing it home now. We're going to be lobstermen, buddy, near-shore ones."

Mike sounded a little hesitant, "Okay? Lobstering, huh? I just thawed out my last piece of vacuum-packed striper the other day. You don't think we should stay focused on stripers and blues? Less can be more."

"Nah," I said. "Less isn't more. More is more. More is always more, especially when it comes to lobster. More is definitely more. That's why they call it more."

"You got a point, I guess?" He sounded unconvinced.

(Note: I've since learned that it's illegal to take lobster traps found on the beach.)

***

Six long months later, in June, Mike said to me, "Okay, I've got the bait in and the lid closed. This looks like a good spot."

"Over she goes," I cheered, and Mike dropped the pot into Cape Cod Bay, not too far from a harbor entrance, so we'd have easy access to it. Most people with residential lobster permits have multiple traps, but I figured one was enough for our first season.

About a week later I returned to the spot with Miki and Jack and their mother, my wife at the time.

"This is our lobster buoy, see it here with the yellow stripe and the number thirty-nine? Remember that you guys, yellow thirty-nine. That's us. Okay?"

"Can I pull it in? Can I pull it in?" They both clamored to help, so I let them essentially pretend to help me pull up the pot.

This being the first time I'd hauled it up, I made the mistake of putting the buoy and its line inside the *Scout* as I brought them up. I soon learned that it's much cleaner to leave the line and the buoy in the water while retrieving, because the line is usually dirty and slops seaweed and gunk into the boat.

The *Scout* was designed for sportfishing, not for lobstering, so the process wasn't smooth. There wasn't enough room on her deck to comfortably bring the whole trap in and still walk around it. This meant balancing the trap on the gunnel while inspecting it. But no matter how much effort was made, or where the trap was set, a lot of mud and brown water wound up inside.

"Something's moving!" Miki squealed.

"Crabs!" Jack exclaimed.

Sure enough. The bait Mike and I had left inside was gone. But instead of plump lobsters, there were crabs scurrying around, two green crabs and four spider crabs. The spider crabs were an ugly mud color with large round bodies of a size somewhere between that of a baseball and a softball. Out of each roughly spherical body jutted ten arachnoid legs each the better part of a foot long. I had heard they were no good for eating, though once dead and dried out, they'd probably make wicked haunted house decorations.

I found it challenging to extract them from the trap. Their arms and claws kept getting entwined with the mesh netting.

Miki kept asking me if she could touch them and hold them and bring them home as pets. In contrast, Jack made a sour face and went to the bow to sit with his mother. He ate crackers, sipped his juice box, and eyed the situation with more than a bit of suspicion.

The lobster trap was a four-foot long cube constructed of strong rubber-coated wire mesh of about one-inch squares. On the bottom were two wood slats called "runners" meant to keep it from sinking into the mud.

The inside of the trap included two bricks wired into the bottom to keep it from floating away. The interior was also divided in half. The first side of the trap encountered by a lobster entering it is called the kitchen. There are two "entrance heads" for lobsters to get into the kitchen from the outside, one on each side. These entrances have funnels made of tightly stretched nylon netting. The funnels are larger on the outer edge of the trap and smaller on the inside, so lobsters find it easy to crawl in but nearly impossible to get out. The other half of the trap is connected to the kitchen through a third nylon funnel. This half is called the parlor. Despite these domestic euphemisms for the two halves of a lobster trap, I doubt many lobsters lounge or otherwise feel at home inside. Videos online of submerged traps show lobsters scurrying around and around the parlor area trying, beyond all hope, to escape.

Lobsters (and in this case crabs) are lured into the traps by bags of bait, usually placed in the kitchen half of the trap. One can use pretty much any kind of bait, but its best to use something that will break down relatively slowly in seawater. Mike and I used the remains of the stripers and blues that we caught, if only because they were convenient.

It took some time, but I eventually removed all the crabs, re-baited the trap, and dropped it back into the bay, its yellow thirty-nine buoy bobbing maybe thirty feet above it. By then my family was more than a little disappointed and bored with the trip. Even Miki was put off by the stench of the mud.

I remember my then-wife asking me if the *Scout* was going to get swamped every time we went boating, now that we had a lobster trap.

"I really don't know," was all I could say.

There was a distinct coolness and quietness on the boat I couldn't admit to myself. In retrospect, I realize I wasn't even capable of consciously considering it. Instead of being honest and direct I just pushed anything that felt uncomfortable out of my mind, pretending everything was fine.

If I had let myself stop and think about things back then, I would have had to admit that many people close to me had commented on how overweight and out of shape I had become, how tired I always looked, and on the fact that I was always "too busy." I was trying to be a good person, yet I always had a sinking feeling I was failing.

The rest of the summer Mike and I checked the trap regularly. We moved its location twice and tried different kinds of bait, including chicken and mackerel, but we kept coming up with nothing but crabs and muck.

"I hear it's a terrible year for lobstering in the bay," Mike said, as we pulled up to our buoy in mid-August.

"Zero lobsters is a pretty bad year for lobstering."

We heaved on the line until we finally saw the weedy, mucky trap breaking the water.

"Hey, a lobster."

We measured the tail and saw that it was undersized by just a couple of millimeters. I kept checking and rechecking it, but it just wasn't there. We'd have to release it.

"Poseidon knows we are putting the work in," said my positive friend. "We're getting closer."

Our next trip was the week before Labor Day, end of the summer on Cape Cod. After a long day of fishing, Mike and I went to check the trap.

We motored around for a while but couldn't find it.

"Where the hell is it?" Mike asked.

"I don't know. I thought it was right here."

We spent more than an hour that evening looking for the buoy. There were hundreds afloat in the surrounding waters, and it felt like we checked every last one of them. Eventually, it started getting dark, so we called it a day and cruised in, concluding it was lost. The best we could surmise was that the buoy or rope had been destroyed by a boat propeller that inadvertently hit it. Such losses happen, we heard.

Little did I know I was in for a much greater loss. One week later, my marriage was over. We had become different people from the pair that had met two decades previously. The marriage had not gone well for some time. Someone explained to me around then that divorce can feel like a death—the death of a dream. Certainly, it was the end of a family structure, the end of a way of life. While I tried to accept it, it hurt intensely. I was in pain and no longer wanted to live the way I had been.

It hurt so much, for the first time since I had been a boy, I stopped. I simply stopped. I stopped rushing, stopped chasing my tail.

I also stopped drinking. I stopped overeating. I stopped volunteering and traveling for work. I even stopped fishing. I cut way back on my hours in the office. I did the minimum I needed in order to keep my business, and I just got quiet.

I called Mike. "I'm sorry, buddy, I'm not fishing anymore this fall, maybe even next year."

"What?" he asked. And I unloaded all the details of my situation on him.

"I'm sorry," he said. "Looks like I'm about a year ahead of you in this crappy divorce business. It hurts. Hang in there. There is life after divorce though. You'll see."

"It feels like everything in my life is upside down," I said. "Not only am I on my own, I'm not even sure the business will make it. I hired too many staff and have debt. I don't know what's real anymore."

"You know what's real," he said. "The kids are real. Our kids are real."

I felt like I had been hit in the head with a priest.

"Right."

I had two examples of parents growing up. My father had died. But my mother was able to hang in there and raised us the best she could. What was I going to do?

I decided to focus on my responsibilities to my kids. I wasn't going to leave them the way I once felt my father had left me. It was a difficult time. Lying in bed waiting for sleep was one of the most difficult things of all. I finally knew firsthand how Mike's insomnia felt. Thankfully, the condition wasn't permanent for me, though it took many long months before a normal sleep pattern returned.

Slowly I realized that if I was going to care for my kids, I also had to care for myself. I had lost my appetite for the first time in my life, and when I finally started getting it back, I ate much more healthily, eventually eliminating processed sugar entirely. I also took up exercising, especially long nature walks. "Adam walks," not Thoreau walks. I even started reading books for pure pleasure again not just for work or for so-called self-improvement.

Oddly enough, my mother became very sick around that time, with an undefined illness, so I started spending more time with her as well, taking her to doctor's appointments and the like. It wasn't the best situation for either of us, but it was rich, quality time. Slowly, ever so slowly, I started experiencing my own sea change.

I also followed Mike's advice in another area. My soon-to-be ex-wife and I hired a mediator, so we could work things out as amicably as possible. I did everything I could to avoid our having to hire separate lawyers to fight things out.

I only made one more trip out on the *Scout* that autumn, but it wasn't with Mike. It was with Miki and Jack in mid-October. We motored along the shore about five miles from the harbor, to one of our favored fishing spots. We cast around a while, but neither they nor I caught a thing. It was cold out. All three of us were struggling. They were now living between two homes. That was the biggest heartache of divorce for me: knowing I would no longer live full-time with my kids. It would mainly be half-time for us from then on. My only hope was to learn to be more present and available when I did have them. Who knew? Maybe being fully there with them half of the time would be better than being distracted on a full-time basis?

As time passed, I learned that parenthood is a full-time proposition no matter the physical proximity or custody arrangement. I'm always their father, and they are always my children.

"Maybe we should try to fish near those birds," Miki suggested, pointing west.

"We can, but they aren't on fish. Those are ducks that live out at sea in the summer. They come inshore this time of year for the shelter, but they don't show the way to the fish like seagulls."

Then Jack started saying something, pointing off the port.

"What, Jack?"

"Yellow thirty-nine."

"What?" Miki repeated.

"Yellow thirty-nine!"

Sure enough. There was a lobster buoy with a yellow stripe and number thirty-nine. It was ours. Jack had found it more than six weeks after it had gone missing, many miles away from the spot Mike and I had dropped it.

"Nice job, Jack! We got our lobsterpot back," said Miki.

The three of us hauled it up and on board. It was completely empty. It didn't even have any crabs in it. We didn't care. The dirty old thing was like a summer friend come to visit us in the offseason.

We never found out how it got five miles from where we left it. The ocean is a mystery.

"This is the biggest thing we ever caught," Jack said when we returned to the landing.

"Not bad," Miki said, smiling, "even if it was ours already."

"Next year I bet we catch a lot of lobsters," Jack insisted.

But I never wound up dropping the trap back in. It spent the next year as a lawn ornament before I gifted it to a friend. I no longer knew exactly who I was anymore, or even who exactly I wanted to become. I only knew what I didn't want. I didn't want to be distracted from my own life anymore. And I didn't want to be a lobsterman.

CHAPTER 13

On My Own

MT

The Great Recession did have an impact on speaking, but my speaking career goes back to 1991 when I took whatever gig I could get. So if that's what I had to do, so be it. And there was no shame in taking a step back with the economy in shambles.

I once heard an interview with Bruce Springsteen, and he described how in order to launch his career he'd play anywhere, including a psychiatric hospital! Springsteen recalled how before he started to play there, a man got on the little stage to introduce the singer. The introduction went on, and on, and on. Then Springsteen said two staff members took the man away.

While I can't top the Boss, when I started out I too was happy to speak at any venue that would pay me even the smallest fee. I spoke at birthday parties, a prison, family reunions, on a boat, at a kindergarten, and nature parks, in addition to the more typical places such as libraries and historical societies. I enjoyed every event, as long as people showed up. But I do recall in the early days I once had an audience of one and another time an audience of two (one of which was my brother). Those were not fun but they were good training. The show must go on, and my philosophy was that whatever group hires me deserves 100 percent, no matter the circumstance.

Now that I think about it, the audience of one led me to many future gigs. Lee Blackburn was the sole person who showed up, and we hit it off and had a great time talking. Little did I know that Lee was connected with a boating organization called U.S. Power Squadrons, and through Lee I probably have landed ten different gigs.

I relate these early days so that anyone going out on their own understands that most independent contractors, and writers in particular, succeed through the power of little steps, rather than one big hit that leads to all sorts of great opportunities. For me, the speaking engagements kept coming mostly through word of mouth, and I've enjoyed speaking to small groups and large, with a couple audiences over six hundred people. Some of the best gigs were in the Midwest or on the West Coast, and the hosts would fly me out there, put me up in a grand hotel, and then have a large, enthusiastic audience that energized me. Many organizations had me back year after year and I became good friends with the planners. I learned that if you are sincere, down to earth, and give 100 percent, people will go out of their way to recommend you to other groups—they want to see your career flourish. And as an added bonus, I met the occasional angler, and we'd make arrangements to fish together.

On the other hand, many authors start to think they are something special, and if that comes through in their talk the audience picks up on it and they are not invited back. Meeting planners have told me they avoid prima donnas and unreliable authors at all costs.

Later in my career I started giving inspirational talks for business groups, and over time I spoke at a few Fortune 500 companies and for awhile was represented by two first-class lecture bureaus. Yet I still mixed in a talk at an elementary school, a small venue, or church group, and later in my career would do the occasional talk gratis for a worthy cause. But I'm getting ahead of myself. When the Great Recession began, I was pleasantly surprised that speaking opportunities, usually small ones, still came my way. Besides the income, they offered so many other dividends. I often have direct contact with people who have just read my book (because they knew I was coming to speak), and they weren't shy about letting me know what they liked and didn't like. I am always on the lookout for trends in feedback, and my one takeaway was a frequent comment, "I read your book in two nights" or "I'm not much of a reader but I read your book cover to cover in just a few days." That's when I knew my niche was fast-paced books, and that I should stay with that approach. It's what I enjoy writing, and more importantly, it's what my readers want.

Staying in one book category, however, was never a goal of mine, and I made it a point to branch out, and let whatever lit a fire under me be my next project, even when I knew it might have a small readership. I didn't want to be pigeon-holed as the history author or the sea disaster author, but rather I sought to be one of the most versatile authors on the market. And so over the years I've written books of all types including narrative nonfiction, fiction, history, humor, guidebooks, biographies, nature, travel, self-help, middle-reader ages, children's chapter books, and of course the preschool board books *Goodnight Vermont* and *Goodnight Coast Guard* with Adam.

Many of these books from diverse categories had one thing in common, and that was water. I never planned it that way, but a reader I met at a lecture once said, "Most of your books feature the ocean, a river, or a lake, or the setting is by the water. Was that intentional?" Until that reader pointed it out I wasn't even aware of my gravitation in writing to have water play such an important role. It shouldn't have surprised me however, because I love all things to do with water, including a simple swim. Which brings me back to the power of positive fishing. The friendship component could have been in another setting, but something tells me that men don't open up the way they do on the water. I don't think there could be a successful "The Power of Positive Bowling." However, an outdoor setting, such as hiking, probably does lend itself to deeper conversations, especially when you throw off your sweaty backpack for a rest and look skyward. Nature opens us up.

In my experience the conversations men have are usually the by-product of an activity rather than the reason for getting together. It's rare that I'll call a male friend and say let's have coffee and talk. Men, I believe, need a common interest to get together, and it's during the *doing* that the conversation happens. Women don't seem to need the excuse of a pastime or hobby to communicate, but I could be wrong.

My guess is that most women communicate face to face, but men talk side by side. I'd wager most of my conversations with Adam occur when we aren't even looking at each other, but instead are in the process of casting or scouting for fish. And our conversations are deeper on a boat than they are when shore fishing.

Think about it. On a boat with one other person, you are essentially trapped for the day. Very quickly, a fisherman knows who is a good companion and who is not. I've found that fishing skill has nothing to do with having a great trip. If the captain of the boat is not a fisherman, I generally know enough to get us into fish. But far more important is the conversation or the lack of conversation—and the mix of both is ideal. You don't want to be stuck on a vessel with a know-it-all. You don't want someone who ignores the weather or safety. The ideal angler on a boat knows when to just enjoy the spectacular surroundings, be comfortable in silence, yet engage when it's time to talk.

On just about every boat I've ever been on, I'll ask questions, lots of questions. Not just about the fishing in that particular area but about the person's life. I figure if they don't want to discuss something they will say so or gently move the conversation in a new direction.

Men, more than women, in my opinion, are reluctant to share emotions, and put on a stoic front. That's a problem. I've read men are three-and-a-half times more likely to commit suicide than women. Psychologists also tell us men do worse than women after a divorce. (That is quite understandable, because most men have fewer friends than women, and for some men their spouse is their exclusive confidant.) Divorce is never easy, and only men and women who have gone through it know how challenging it can be. But Adam and I had our floating therapist couch—the *Scout*—and were able to talk openly about the transitions we were going through. With a good friend you can explain any pain, be vulnerable, and not go through the charade of being a tough guy. (I joked to Adam that we don't fit the mold of macho-men because we couldn't even be lobstermen—a six-year-old had to find our trap for us! The mere mention of yellow thirty-nine puts us in our place.)

During a recent NPR broadcast, psychologists discussed how a majority of men think they should conquer all their problems on their own, and anything less is seen a sign of weakness. In my younger years I certainly fit that mold. But with age comes wisdom, and I realized its okay not to be okay. It's okay to tell a friend. I encourage everyone to be more open, seek professional help (I did in my forties, and the therapist helped greatly.) The development of deep friendships is just as important. For me, the friendship part was aided by my passion for fishing: besides Adam and some new angler friends, I have three who I've known since elementary school! Fishing has been the glue that has kept us together more than half a century now. I'm sixty-five as I write this, so that's 165 years of combined brotherhood with those three school friends.

One of my friends illustrated this phenomena when he described how the angler he spent the most time with would only talk about his terminal cancer while fishing on his boat. Makes me wonder that if he didn't own a boat would he have kept things bottled up inside? Would he have suffered in silence? It's our job as friends to pick up on clues from others who only hint at their pain and then find the right setting to ask if they are okay, and let them know we care. Time and time again, I've found the ideal setting to be on the water.

Adam and I obviously talked about the big issues we were dealing with such as divorce and our careers, but what else do men talk about when they are alone at sea? Inquiring minds—perhaps female readers of this book—might want to know. Surprisingly, discussions about fishing, family, finances, and even sex, often take a back seat to conversations about our health. And here's how I know Adam was listening to me during one of our health talks: two weeks later I received a package in the mail that contained six different supplements, ranging from pumpkin seed oil to stinging nettle root extract, all "For a Healthy Prostate." Adam was either truly concerned about my health or he was getting pissed off by how I pissed. He may have found my frequent, and lengthy peeing put a crimp on his fishing. So, before I put Adam on a friendship pedestal, I'm going to hook him to a lie detector and ask him what his true motivation was.

***

I believe we are a product of all the interesting people we've gotten to know. We take a person's particular strength or a person's personality trait that we like and bring it into ourselves. When people speak of someone who has passed away and they say, "He'll always be with me," I interpret that to mean that they'll never forget that person's special qualities. In my case, I think I subconsciously adopt another's perceived strength and try to make it my own. That's why you might hear me say, "Geez, I sounded just like my father."

We become a mosaic of all the interesting people in our lives, and through my speaking, research interviews, and many fishing partners, I've felt I was blessed by crossing paths with so many diverse people.

One lesson that has stayed with me after observing how individuals handle problems is that there are essentially two kinds of people: those who manufacture problems and those who downplay troubles. I believe the manufacturing of problems comes from having too much time on your hands and that to fill the void they obsess over a small issue. On the other hand, those who downplay problems decide early on not to give the tribulation too much energy, because they have so many other things they want to accomplish. Early on in life I decided to be one of the latter. Perhaps it came from my father. When a problem came along he had this gesture as if the problem was on his shoulder and then he flicked it away like you would a piece of lint.

As you have read in this book, I'm not saying I master all the struggles that come my way, but like my father I developed my own technique for managing challenges. I simply say, *Mike, it's as difficult as you want to make it.*

Ultimately, I decide to first reduce the "big" problem into a mere nuisance, and then solve it quickly—it leaves me more time to go fishing!

This approach served me well in not just my personal life, but also my speaking career, because inevitably there are unanticipated challenges—often when I am onstage in the middle of my talk. I can let an interruption throw me totally off my game, or I can flick it away like so much flotsam and steam ahead.

***

Looking back, I'm glad I spoke at some of those odd places, because I like the odd and unusual. And the ocean has provided me with more than a few peculiar creatures to observe. One of those instances occurred many years ago at the Cape Cod Canal when I was relatively new to saltwater fishing. I'm not a big fan of the canal because it can get crowded, and my rule of thumb is to always bring my bicycle, ride the seven mile length, and only cast if I see birds working or a fish breaking the surface. I know I miss catching a lot of fish by this approach, but I just don't have the patience of the "canal rats"—those who are usually willing to stay in one spot.

More than once I've sarcastically suggested that the canal be filled in; it would eliminate the traffic jams on the aging bridges and perhaps force more stripers to mill around Bourne and Onset, where I prefer to fish. Of course as soon as I someday catch a giant striper on the canal, I'll change my tune.

Of course you don't need a bridge to get out to the Cape—just ask the black bear that likely swam across the canal in 2012. Seen ambling around in several backyards in Barnstable the bear caused quite a buzz. He wasn't done with his travels, and eventually made his way all the way to Provincetown. The question I ask is why would the bear brave swimming across the canal in the first place? Imagine fishing on the canal at night and being in the spot where the bear swam ashore . . .

The canal also likely hosted the first manatee to make it into Cape Cod Bay. Somehow it made it all the way to Sesuit Harbor in East Dennis. This occurred in 2008, causing traffic jams of people swarming the harbor to catch a glimpse of it. I've snorkeled with manatees in Florida, but nevertheless wanted to glimpse this one that traveled the length of the Eastern Seaboard. By the time I made it to the harbor, however, rescue crews had captured the "sea cow" and were in the process of bringing it back to Florida. Sadly, the manatee died before reaching the rehabilitation site in the sunshine state. That was the same year I had my own incident on the canal, with a "thing" that survived.

The day I saw the oddity was one of the few days that I actually caught a fish on the canal. A ripple of fish chasing bait had me off my bike and casting a plug that was quickly engulfed by a big blue fish. Between the strength of the fish and the incredibly powerful current on the canal, it took me forever to get it to the bank, navigate my steps down slimy rocks, and then land it. I put my rod down, knocked the blue over the head with a rock, and brought it up to my bike where I put one end of the handlebar through its gill, having no other way to transport it home. Then I gingerly descended the rocks to get my fishing rod. That's when I saw what almost gave me a heart attack.

A giant fin sliced the water just six feet in front of me. My jaw dropped, my heart quickened, and I took a wobbly back step or two. Has a great white shark ever plucked a fisherman right off the shore? With my luck, I'd be the first. Then things got weirder—a giant head partially emerged from the water, and the creature stopped swimming. I swear I saw one of its giant eyeballs looking directly at me.

It didn't look like a shark. Maybe a small whale? It certainly had size—bigger than a refrigerator and almost the same dimensions as my car.

Now it turned and I could see its entire upper half. My brain was trying to process what I was seeing. Even though I could have reached out and touched it with the tip of my fishing rod, I still had no idea what it was. The "thing" floated on the surface, and the fin flopped over. Then the situation got more bizarre: it seemed like the lower half of the creature's body was missing. For a fleeting second I thought it was a whale and that the mother of all sharks had bitten its tail off!

Then the "thing" let the current take it closer to the rocks just downstream of where I was standing, and it rolled slightly so that a different fin came out of the water. I felt like I had smoked some really powerful pot—maybe some of that "Sunshine Daydream" strain—and reality was taking strange forms, messing with my mind. Then I heard a voice, a real voice. An angler up on the path above me said, "It's an ocean sunfish. Strange looking, isn't it?" That was an understatement!

I hopped on my bike and started pedaling back to my car to get the bluefish on ice. People stared at the big bluefish hanging from the front of my bike; I looked like a kid bringing home a fish to show my mother. I stopped at a wooden pier next to the canal where a couple guys were fishing and struck up a conversation. One of them said, "You should have been here an hour ago. A giant fin went by. It was the first great white shark I've ever seen! We got a picture and everything."

I didn't have the heart to tell him otherwise.

That night I looked in the *World Book Encyclopedia* (remember those?) and it said, "The Ocean Sunfish (genus *mola mola*) is a grotesque-appearing fish which has the habit of resting on the surface in sunny weather, with one fin above the water. The body is scaleless, silvery and clumsy. This fish seems to consist of one great head." So I wasn't smoking pot. And if I was, the munchies should not be satisfied by trying to catch the ocean sunfish, because the encyclopedia went on to say, "They are never eaten." Unfortunately, this last line is incorrect. They are eaten by people in Asian countries, and consumed at sea by sharks, sea lions, and killer whales. However, I'm guessing the sharks are not fond of them or their thick skin, because they would be easy pickings.

The ocean sunfish in turn eats small fish, crustaceans, and squid. Besides their unusual appearance, they have other stand out qualities, particularly females which can produce almost 300 million eggs at a time. Despite all those eggs, they are considered a threatened species, so please pay close attention when boating in late August and September when the waters off Cape Cod are at their warmest and attract these natives of more temperate and tropical waters.

If you want to see a hilarious video of two guys from Boston out in their boat encountering an ocean sunfish, check out the Youtube video, "Boston Fisherman Freaks Out About Fish." Their reaction was much the same as mine, except I had no one to talk to. To watch the video is pure joy—first they think it's a sea turtle, then a tuna, then a whale, and finally one of them says, "We're seeing some shit we ain't seen before, kid!" There are plenty of F-bombs, boneheaded lines, and idiotic observations. My favorite line comes after they try to hook it with standard striper gear: "Ah man, we need f---ing help buddy. Oh my God. That is still good meat on the f---ing fish. Am I lyin'?"

And now that I have you on the internet instead of the *World Book Encyclopedia*, Google the ocean sunfish and take a look at what they are called in other countries. Most of their names are better than ours and my favorite is Schwimmender Kopf, German for "swimming head." A close runner-up is the Finnish term that translates to "lump fish."

Since that day I saw my first ocean sunfish, every September Adam and I seem to see more of them. They can weigh in excess of 1,200 pounds (the largest ever recorded was 4,927 pounds), and they certainly do look clumsy. But here's the thing, these blobs can come breaching out of the water. Why and how they do it, I'm not sure, but the first time one leapt from the water it crashed down with such force that it seemed like a boulder was dropped from the heavens. Adam and I weren't sure what we had witnessed, but a few minutes later another one did the same thing farther away from the boat. (They may jump to rid themselves of parasites, but no can tell me that they don't also do it for fun. Yes, fun. I've seen many creatures do things in the woods that I can only categorize as "play.")

When they breached, Adam and I just laughed and shook our heads. How the least streamlined creature in the world could clear the water was a true marvel. We couldn't wait to get our kids on the boat and share the experience of seeing a "lump fish" up close and personal. I also recall telling Adam about a friend who was waterskiing off Dennis and he wiped out. The people in the boat heard frantic screaming, and raced back to pick him up. All he could stammer was that there was an extremely large fin nearby and he thought he was a goner. I would have needed a new bathing suit . . .

Perhaps global warming is bringing more ocean sunfish to the warming waters off Cape Cod, but whatever the reason, when people see one for the first time, the reaction is always the same: "What the heck is that?" In fact, in October 2020 so many people saw the creatures, and not knowing what they were seeing, they swamped a local police department with frantic calls. Town officials finally put a plea on Facebook: "Please stop calling the Police Department about this sunfish!" The town's harbor master added, "Calling 911 isn't a good avenue to report fish that are swimming around."

Surprises on the ocean are just one aspect that make it special; you leave your land world and enter a new domain. The more time you spend at or by the sea the more you discover. (The average American spends 93 percent of their time indoors, so to experience more means getting outside more, or put another way, be a participant rather than a spectator). Sometimes the surprises are not pleasant, as you will read, but that comes with the territory of connecting with nature.

It took me many years to encounter a creature of the sea that was as odd as the sunfish and as breathtaking as the basking sharks described later in the book. I was fishing aboard Doug Bernhard's boat with a companion just a half mile off the Florida's southern Atlantic coast when we spotted a commotion on the water's surface. Thinking there was a blitz of fish stirring up the water we started the engine and motored over for a look. What we saw first was a massive, wide open mouth, about two feet across.

A whale shark, covered with its distinctive white dots, approximately thirty feet long, lazily swam along the surface. We pulled up nearby and cut the motor. Incredibly the whale shark (it's actually a fish, not a member of the whale family) came closer, its open mouth like a giant vacuum, sucking in plankton, and filtering the particles from the water. Our mouths were open too—in wonder.

We could see small fish racing around in front of the shark, but it was hard to tell if the shark was filtering those as well. Because the shark's mouth is at the front of its wide, flat head, we could look right inside it. I quickly told Doug that I wanted to swim with it, and he quickly reminded me of the hammerhead shark we had both seen nearby a week earlier. I dropped the idea and enjoyed the show.

Just to know that our planet can still support a creature that large gave me hope. We still have time to change our ways of multiplying like rats and driving other creatures to the brink. The ocean sunfish, the basking shark, the whale shark, and all the rest have as much claim to Earth as we have.

***

Back on Cape Cod Bay on the *Scout* I told Adam about wanting to swim with the whale shark and how we had to find one. He reminded me they are a tropical fish and don't inhabit waters in the northeast. I then went to plan B, saying we needed to motor off Provincetown to Stellwagon Bank to see whales, and we talked about dates.

We then got philosophical—or at least as philosophical as one can get while casting and peeing at the same time. I got on my soapbox (the cooler used for scouting) and explained how the surprises on the ocean are a good metaphor for those in life.

Most surprises in day-to-day living are not welcome because we fear uncertainty, and if we truly want a better life we need to realize uncertainty is a part of life, just like fishless days are part of angling. While I'm not about to embrace either, I've learned to accept disappointments, roll with them, and move on. To do otherwise, and shun situations where uncertainty and risk are present, would be living our personal lives in a shell seeking not to get hurt. And to remove uncertainty from fishing would mean we'd spend all our angling trips on charter boats for the near certainty of catching fish. It's a hell of a lot more satisfying to figure the fish out on our own, despite hooks in hands, rods slipping overboard, getting lost in the fog, and conversations about divorce and prostates. But if you are really lucky, you might get home after a long day of fishing and find a bottle of stinging nettle root extract in your mailbox.

CHAPTER 14

The Bahamas

AG

It was a grey day in October the autumn after our failed lobstering experiment. I stood on the bow of the *Scout*, rod in hand, Mike casting from the stern, a chilly wind blowing. It seemed most all the stripers had headed south to warmer waters. Instead of seagulls and terns, the bay was loaded with ducks and seabirds. That day in particular, there were hundreds of white gannets continuously divebombing the water. They'd fly up and then shoot straight down, beak first, sending up huge whitewater splashes over and again. Unfortunately, their aerobatics had no relationship with stripers or bluefish. If anything, their presence portended the end of another fishing season.

My day in divorce court, finalizing everything, had been just three months earlier, ironically the very week my mother died. The illness that had plagued her turned out to be pancreatic cancer. By the time it was identified, it was beyond treatment. She had a tough final few months, wasting away with bouts of intense cramps and unrelenting fatigue, her body weight dropped to a mere eighty pounds.

She finally died at dawn in a hospice center on the Cape with me and her niece, my cousin Diana, holding her hands. Surprisingly, despite all her suffering, she looked unmistakably lovely, beautiful in fact. She emerged from sleep just once the previous two days when she opened her eyes just wide enough to acknowledge Miki and Jack by her bedside. "I love you," she uttered before closing her eyes and fading back toward oblivion. Most of her family was in the room then, and there wasn't a dry cheek among us.

So, not only was I struggling on the boat with Mike to find fish, but I was also struggling inside. Half-time custody of my kids was not so easy for me, especially now that their grandmother was gone. I learned that when they were with me, and it was just the three of us at home, I was essentially outnumbered, two kids to one adult. I hadn't realized how much work it would be. It made me appreciate all the more my mother having raised my brother and I as a full-time single mom. Even more difficult were the days when the kids were not at my house, because I felt lonely. Worst were the mornings before they left to go their mother's and the nights before they returned. I couldn't get used to the transition between the different lifestyles: single guy vs. busy dad.

Fortunately, I had stopped drinking and overeating. Problem was that even after a year I was still adjusting to the experience of fully feeling my emotions—both the good ones and the bad ones, not just smothering them with junk food or sanitizing them with booze. I was reminded of the classic 1980 movie *Airplane* where the stressed-out air-traffic controller, played by the actor Lloyd Bridges, continuously complains that he picked the wrong week to quit his various vices, including smoking, drinking, and taking amphetamines. When death and destruction seem certain for the airplane, he finally declares, "Looks like I picked the wrong week to quit sniffing glue."

As an angler, I had occasionally used a drop of glue to secure certain knots or a rubbery part of a lure to a metallic head or hook, but I had thankfully never been tempted to inhale the stuff, or for that matter take other drugs. The only vices remaining were caffeine from strong coffee and fishing. I took a long swig from my mug out on the *Scout* and observed to Mike, "Could be our final trip of the year."

"We can still do some shore fishing. Break out the waders."

After yet another fruitless retrieve, seemingly out of nowhere the words "The Bahamas" sprung to mind. I had never been to the Caribbean—in fact I'd only been on a couple of vacations ever—but the words conjured balmy beaches, sparkling waters, and winter fishing.

"You want to go to the Bahamas this winter with me, Mike?"

"Can we fish down there?"

"Do stripers piss in the Canal?"

"They do, and so do I."

Before we knew it, we were descending aircraft stairs on the tarmac in Nassau. The sun felt hot on our heads, necks, and arms. Palms waved, and not a flake of snow fell for a thousand miles. Selfies from the day show us making silly faces like college kids on spring break. Although it was only for a few days, it was the first "resort vacation" of my life, made possible for Mike and me only through the increased success we were both starting to manifest with our books. Truly it was a validation of the paths we were working together.

After passport control, we picked up a rental car. Notably, the female agent was sullenly rude in the disgruntled way I've since learned many locals are in poorer countries with resort areas filled with privileged visitors. Her slow movements, mumbled phrases, and refusal to look at us eloquently communicated, "Don't waste my time with your small talk."

When I grew up on Cape Cod in the seventies and eighties, I too resented tourists invading every summer with what my friends and I considered loud, pushy ways. I now know a big part of it was envy. We all worked at least two jobs every summer, often menial ones, while the visitors seemed to frolic carefree.

Mike and I drove to our mid-tier resort. The staff was accommodating but similarly standoffish as the rental car woman. The rooms were clean, if dated, the grounds stunning, and the sunshine spectacular off the waves in front of the property's wide, sandy beach.

I had decided that if we were going to the Bahamas, I might as well start researching a book about the place. We'd try to visit the most popular sites while there. A guidebook purported that a particular hill in Nassau offered fantastic vistas of the sea. After visiting it, we planned to walk around town, check out the nearby National Art Gallery of the Bahamas, take notes and photos.

We arrived at the parking area for the overlook hill about midafternoon only to find it closed. It seemed to have been closed a long time, evidenced by litter everywhere. Having visited many similar sights throughout the United States to do similar research, I wasn't going to be deterred by one closed parking area. We left the car along the road about a quarter mile down the street from the entrance, in the residential neighborhood that bordered the viewing hill.

Mike and I were still ecstatic to be in an island paradise together. Leaving the car, we strode blissfully up the road toward the parking area. I slid on my new sunglasses, bought specifically for the trip.

"Nice shades." Mike said. "It always surprises me what a difference polarized glasses make when spotting fish. They're like x-ray vision through the water."

"I know, like fishing superpowers. They're Ray-Bans."

As my eyes adjusted, I took in the neighborhood. The run-down houses had bars over their windows. There was a lot of garbage on the ground. I heard distant music and caught the smell of both cigars and pot.

"You don't need designer glasses," Mike declared. "Any polarized ones will do."

But I wasn't listening. I was looking into the open garage door of a nearby house. It was dark but there were at least half a dozen guys inside, a couple sported wife-beater shirts, one guy was bare chested and ripped. They were smoking, drinking, and blaring hip-hop.

Just then a lean guy with dreadlocks started eyeing me from the mouth of the garage.

"Mike . . . " I said, as he started walking ahead of me. But he didn't hear. I saw a second guy come out of the garage with a bottle in one hand, a cigar in his mouth. They were looking us over in a not-very-welcoming way.

"Mike. I think we're going the wrong direction. Come on," I called, raising my voice a little.

"No, the path up to the hilltop is this way."

If I'd learned anything from years of travel, it is to listen to my instincts. The thought hit me that my nearly $200 shades would likely fetch a few bucks at a local pawnshop. What was I going to say if those guys decided to walk across their yard and tell me to fork them over, or my wallet filled with travel cash?

Just then a third guy stepped out. He was even bigger than the other two. They were talking about us. I had the unmistakable feeling I was "not in Kansas anymore," never mind Cape Cod.

"Mike . . ." I said, trying not to sound as concerned as I felt.

I did not want to go through the negotiation process he and I too often underwent when out on the *Scout* trying to decide where to fish next.

I turned abruptly back toward our car, held the keys over my head, "I'm going back Mike. Bye!"

He had no choice but to follow. I opened the door to our subcompact, slid into the already scorching hot front seat, and started it up.

"What's the matter?" he asked when he got to the car.

I told Mike I didn't like the neighborhood. He just rolled his eyes. "I saw them too. Those guys were fine."

Having decided to put the scenic viewing area aside for the time being, we headed for downtown Nassau to park and explore. Along the way, we got a little lost and soon found ourselves in a very run-down neighborhood. House after house was sorely neglected, many also had bars on the windows and the doors. We also saw several barefoot, dirty-faced children, from preschool to preteen. None looked happy in what amounted to a tropical slum. It was hard to imagine that countless seaside resorts were just a short drive away in almost every direction.

Just then a political ad came over the radio. It opened with the rat-tat-tat sound of machinegun fire. It was sponsored by the opposition political party. "The Bahamas leads the Caribbean in gun crime and homicides. It's time for a change this election . . ."

Mike glanced at me, "Are we lost? This is a bad neighborhood, and it's obvious as hell that we're tourists."

We eventually made our way to the main street near the government buildings and cruises ship landing. There we encountered a dozen soldiers in flak jackets and fatigues, toting machine guns. They patrolled the street directly in front of designer clothing and jewelry stores that were obviously there for visiting cruise ship passengers.

"I'm thinking most visitors stay in their resorts here, or they just come into town from cruise ships to party on the main drag and then leave," Mike commented.

Once back at our resort, we went to the concierge desk to look for something to do the next day. Mike and I had sticker-shock at the $600 half-day fees for charter fishing boats. We were used to spending $25 to $50 in gas for days of fishing from the *Scout* with its efficient ninety horsepower outboard. We asked the concierge for other options and were encouraged to sign up for a snorkeling trip that included a "Swim with the Sharks" activity.

"Everybody loves it," he insisted.

It did sound like an adventure, and it was only a fraction the cost of fishing.

Next morning, Mike took full advantage of the breakfast buffet. I don't think I've ever seen anyone eat as much. My theory is that Mike's frenetic creativity burns a lot of calories every day, allowing him to eat whatever he wants and stay lean.

Afterward, we took a resort shuttlebus to a tiny marina where warm water lapped countless mangrove roots. We collected snorkeling gear at the dive shack and boarded a shipshape catamaran operated by a captain and a first mate. Both were local Bahamians with easygoing attitudes and who seemed like competent mariners. Mike tried to talk fishing with them but they too were unreceptive.

The weather was perfection, mid-seventies with gentle breezes and flat waters. As the sun rose higher, the captain motored to three different snorkeling locations. The first two were coral reefs. Sadly, the coral there was mainly brown and remarkably lifeless, with only a few tropical fish here and there.

"I understand coral reefs are dying or dead all over the world," Mike said.

"We're polluting the planet," I returned.

And yet I had to recognize my part. There I was on yet another motorized boat spewing fumes, having just flown 1,250 miles on a jet aircraft that created plenty of pollution itself. Those dead and dying reefs were no more an affront to me than to the barefoot Bahamian kids or gun-toting soldiers. I like to think of myself as a sort of neutral witness of the world about me. But as a tourist staying in a resort there myself, I was actively participating in the system that created those situations.

Our third stop was by a small-engine plane that crashed in shallow waters years before. A few of us were stung by jellyfish near it. The first mate passed around a spray bottle with vinegar solution to counteract the sting.

"Mother nature can bite back," I said to Mike.

Then the captain got everyone's attention with a loudspeaker announcement.

"Now I'll take you to swim with the sharks."

After a short ride, the mate dropped anchor near a small island. He told us to ready our masks and fins. He started stuffing frozen fish heads and tails into metal cans with holes in them and lowered them into the water on ropes. We could see them perfectly through the crystal waters. Brownish-red blood billowed out of the holes as each can warmed.

"This will attract them," he declared, flashing a bright smile.

The twenty-five or so snorkelers on board were all quiet at this point. The mate continued. "I'm going to float this rope off the back. You can snorkel holding onto it and watch the sharks swimming below you. But the rule is you don't let go of the rope. There is one more rule, nobody flushes the toilet while we're here. If it gets in the water, the sharks can get excited. We don't want that."

Some fellow tourists tittered at that comment, not entirely certain if the mate was joking or not. Mike and I exchanged glances. Surely they didn't release the boat's wastewater into shallow waters like these.

"Okay," he continued. "Do I have any volunteers? Who wants to swim with the sharks first?"

I don't know what got into me. Maybe it had something to do with my life changes. Maybe it was the southern sun. I don't know, but my right hand was all of a sudden above my head. "I'll go," I heard myself announce nonchalantly.

I did not imagine any actual danger. No one had spotted any sharks around the boat yet, and whatever did come by would surely be as harmless as the jellyfish. The tour was recommended by a reputable resort, and

I was on a handsome boat that took people out for trips exactly like this one, every day of the week.

Once in the water, I noticed a crowd of fellow snorkelers along the edge of the boat staring at me, mouths agape. They were clearly curious to see if I'd suddenly go under in a boil of red water, eaten alive like the skinny-dipper at the start of *Jaws*. I made my way out to the end of the floating rope, adjusted my mask, and began peering below for sharks. The sound of my breath echoed in my snorkel. Slowly, I became conscious of others joining me in the water.

At first there were only a few small sharks around the periphery. As they materialized, they seemed as wary of us as we of them. Steadily, though, as the long floating rope filled with snorkelers, I started noticing larger sharks lurking. Many looked about five or six feet long. Then there were a couple more like eight feet. The water was shallow, less than twenty-five feet deep, so they were not very far below our fluttering fins. No one identified the various species for us.

The sharks circled lazily, edging slowly in below us and our boat, particularly toward the "fish pots" that continued to emit blood.

The population grew until there were perhaps twenty or more sharks. I also noticed a few even larger, perhaps nine or ten feet. They were starting to swim faster. I could hear the pace of my own breathing picking up in my snorkel. I was getting colder, and I was picking up on the growing energy of the curious sharks, as well as the disquiet of my fellow snorkelers. It was astonishing to see sharks so close, to be with them.

I checked my watch and saw I had been in the water nearly fifteen minutes. Just then the first mate raised his voice bossily: "Put your hand back on the rope. You don't want to lose a finger, do you?"

I didn't realize he was talking to me. I looked up at him through my mask. He looked annoyed. Meanwhile the smaller sharks were starting to almost dart around.

It occurred to me that I was in fact in open waters, connected with the entire Atlantic, and for that matter all the oceans of the world. Any shark of any size and of any disposition was perfectly able to swim here. I hadn't identified any hammerheads or makos or great whites. Were those the primary man-eaters? What did I know about sharks?

Then some sense came into my head: "I'm a tourist. I don't know shit, and I'm clinging to this rope like a sea worm on a tube trolled behind the *Scout*."

I decided to make up for being the first one in the water, by being the first one out. On my way up one of the ladders off the stern, I notice Mike right behind me, following my cue.

By this time all but a few of our snorkel-mates were out on the rope. The catamaran was all but empty. I drank some Gatorade and decided to take a pee in the head. I'd like to emphasize here that there remains some controversy around this next point. I couldn't testify in court that I did not do so, but Mike maintains that he's "fairly sure" he heard the toilet flush before I came out. I'm "fairly sure" I didn't flush.

When I returned to the stern I noticed commotion in the water. The boat was equipped with two sets of very narrow stairs off the stern into the water. There was a family of three on board where the two parents were clearly disappointed because the captain and first mate had told them they could not let their four-year-old son swim with sharks at such a young age. (Yes. I did just write that, "They were disappointed . . .")

To appease the boy, they sat him on one of the two sets of stairs where he could dangle his feet in the water. Their main concern was keeping him from crying. The problem was that more and more snorkelers were realizing what Mike and I had, that our crew had zero influence on what types of sharks were attracted by the blood or what those sharks were going to do. The sharks were now higher up in the water table too, much closer to the swimmers. Suddenly, like birds on a wire all the snorkelers wanted to get back in the boat. Yet there was only one ladder for more than twenty people. It wasn't yet a stampede, but there was a palpable panic in both the air and the water. Everyone was jockeying for position to get back on board. In short, it was a nightmare waiting to happen.

Things got even worse when a couple of heavier, older women struggled to climb the one free set of slippery stairs, compounding the logjam. It was at this point Mike and I started playing heroes by helping swimmers up onto the deck without the ladder, taking them by the hands and hauling them out. Mike says he'll never forget the panic-stricken look on one young woman's face as she stared at him from the sea and mouthed,

"PLEASE." After we grabbed one of her arms each and yanked her up, she slid and fell right on the back of the man who had come out before her. Still, she never stopped repeating gratefully, "Thank you. Thank you."

By this time the captain realized we were close to a riot and came down from bridge. He cleared the boy from the ladder. Then he stated the obvious: "Time to come out, the sharks are coming up!" This only made matters worse. No one was holding the floating rope anymore, and the congregation at the ladders was a confusion of flailing, splashing snorkelers drawing further attention from the sharks.

Mike swore later, "I saw one of those monster bad boy sharks shoot up from the depths like a torpedo, not turning until it came within a foot of a swimmer."

The mate even jumped in the water to help get people out, repeating, "Calm down, mon. Calm down. Go nice and slow."

Just before everyone was out and he reboarded himself, Mike and I saw a terrifying fin surface above the waterline behind him. The sharks could taste the fish blood, but there were no fish to eat, just fleshy snorkelers rapidly disappearing.

By some luck, there was no shark attack that day. But when we got back to the resort, Mike was bubbling over. "Those guys are training sharks to associate people with food! I've got to find out about sharks in the Bahamas. Did we really just do that?"

He broke out his laptop and started Googling.

We soon learned that the most recent death from shark attack in the Bahamas was only a couple of years before, with others in the previous decade. Most disturbing was the report that "a diver almost had his arm bitten off" in a shark attack when a glass-bottomed tour boat dumped chum to attract sharks for viewing. The article castigated the crew of the tour boat for wantonly disregarded the nearby diving flags.

Another article described a group fishing south of Nassau who caught a twelve-foot tiger shark. When they pulled it next to the boat and shot it in the head, the shark promptly regurgitated a human foot, completely intact from the knee down. The men then tied a rope around its tail and towed it in. When they returned to port, the Royal Bahamas Defense Force cut open its belly and found the torso of a headless man, including his undigested driver's license from one of his clothes pockets. He had been a member of a fishing party of five on a small boat (not all that much bigger than the *Scout*) that lost power south of New Providence. He and a friend jumped overboard to swim ashore, which turned out to be a fatal error as they both died, whereas the three who stayed with the vessel were eventually rescued.

That night I gratefully viewed a three-quarter waxing moon above the palm trees outside my resort room balcony and considered that while I may have escaped the winter for a few days, I had not escaped my own craziness. While those dead fishermen had not intended to get anywhere near sharks—they had only wanted to swim to land from their malfunctioned boat—Mike and I had just paid good money to swim with them.

Before we left the island, we did at least manage to squeeze a few hours of fairly mundane fishing in with a flamboyant local guy named Elvis who owned a little skiff with a twenty-horse outboard. He made us laugh a lot. He loved the Bahamas and said he had made a living from the sea there since he was a teen. But he was also either so stoned or so drunk (we never decided which) that he accidently threw his anchor and line in the water without securing the line to the boat.

"Oh shit, mon, I lost another anchor," he announced to no one in particular.

We were in a shallow, protected cove where we didn't think sharks would likely be, so Mike decided to dive back into those Bahamian waters and rescue the anchor and line for our new friend, saving our fishing trip in the process. (Mike does have his priorities in order, after all.)

Before leaving, we also rented a jet ski for a few hours from a teenager who was hawking its use up and down the sands. It led to my favorite moment of the trip. Neither Mike nor I had ever jet skied before. We had always stuck our noses up at them as "noise machines" for people who like zooming in circles. I also fleetingly wondered what its carbon footprint was. But before we knew it, Mike and I were hooting and hawing on it, zipping across a jewel of a bay at forty-five miles an hour, hot sunlight reflecting off everything. We even hit the wake of a massive motor yacht and caught air for a long second before a perfect landing and a synchronized "Yippee kai-yay!"

On the plane back to Boston (and to winter, and to both our recently divorced lives), with more than a little sunburn on our noses and cheeks, I considered that the Bahamas are no more paradise than anywhere else. In direct contrast to the lessons that I and my generation had gleaned from TV when we were kids, there really is no *Fantasy Island* or *Love Boat* or *Gilligan's Island* to run away to. I reclined my seat and closed my eyes. People suffer in the Bahamas aplenty. They, just like me, love nature but live lifestyles that too often pollute it. They resented tourists in the same way Cape Codders often do. They also have their crime problems, just like pretty much every other place on the planet.

Then another idea came to me: Mike and I had a great time together, and we barely fished. Perhaps it was possible to be nurtured by Mother Ocean without fishing rods in our hands. It was just a thought.

CHAPTER 15

Great Whites, Human Sharks, and the Power of Determination

MT

With our trip to the Bahamas behind us we were back on home waters, but the subject of sharks kept coming up. I'd heard reports of great white sharks in Cape Cod waters as early as 2001 when a fishing charter captain angling off Chatham said a fourteen-foot great white snatched a striper he was reeling in. Then the shark passed beneath the vessel and slammed into it, apparently going after a second striper they had been battling. The captain said the jostling was hard enough to knock him off balance and he was worried one of his customers would be knocked overboard. The shark then circled the vessel and the captain had his passengers sit low in the event the shark bumped the boat again, while the captain slowly motored away.

Another early report of a great white occurred in 2004 when one of these massive creatures was spotted in a cove off Falmouth. The frequent sightings of this 1,700-pound fish and the efforts to guide it out of the cove received around-the-clock news coverage. Crowds of people descended on the cove hoping to catch a glimpse of it, and tour boat operators fielded calls from around the world from people who would pay any price to see this fourteen-foot great white. The *Boston Globe* reported that one woman told officials she wanted to swim with it because she could "heal it." Another asked permission to be taken to the shark so they could "talk it out of the lagoon."

The circus-like atmosphere and incredible interest were a reflection of how rare great white shark sightings were at the time. There had only been two fatal shark attacks recorded in Massachusetts since the Pilgrim's landed, one in 1670 and another in 1936. Adam and I never gave sharks a second thought. That started to change, however, as the years went by. In 2007 I remember fishing with my friend, Mark, off Chatham, and we heard a desperate call on the marine radio.

"Coast Guard! Coast Guard!"

The Coast Guard asked the nature of the emergency and location.

The boater answered in a French accent that he was in a small boat off the tip of Monomoy Island, which also happened to be where we were fishing. He then said, "There is a great white shark circling my boat! It is huge!"

The Coast Guard asked him to repeat his message.

"Great white shark! It is now under my boat!

"Did you say you have a great white under your vessel?"

"Yes, yes! It is bigger than my boat!"

"Then we suggest you move."

Mark and I cracked up when we heard this. Up ahead we saw a small boat gun its motor and go screaming away. Since I had never seen a great white, and the only one in the area I'd even heard of was the one in the cove at Falmouth, I didn't believe the Frenchman.

"He probably saw a basking shark," I said to Mark.

"Don't be so sure," replied Mark. "There's a few great whites around. All those seals on Monomoy Island are multiplying and the sharks are coming."

"Have you ever seen one?"

"Yes. I was surfing off Nauset and wiped out. While I was in the water one cruised right by me, looking me over."

"What did you do?"

"I lost control of all bodily functions! It was the scariest thing I've ever seen. When I told people about it, few believed me. But I know what I saw and some charter boat captains who I know said they have seen them as well. Soon there's going to be a lot more with all these seals for their dinners."

Mark's prediction turned out to be quite accurate. While we've always had a few great whites in the Northeast, they tended to stay south of Martha's Vineyard and in deep water. Over the next few years that would change. The sharks hunted the seals and the seals were often near the beach. Maybe the sharks have a way of communicating to one another and if so the word got out: "There's good eating off Cape Cod."

More great whites arrived, and as the seal population grew and expanded their range, the sharks followed. By 2010 there were enough sightings off Chatham that tourists flocked to Lighthouse Beach with binoculars and cameras hoping to get a picture of a big dorsal fin going by. Chatham businesses that catered to tourists saw an increase in foot traffic and sales from people coming to the town in hopes of spotting a great white from the different vantage points overlooking in the shore. This prompted the Chamber of Commerce to tell the *Boston Globe* that "Anything that brings people to town is going to help our economy." Local television reporters breathlessly reported every time a shark was sighted, and they did so with glee. Seems just about everyone was happy to have the toothy visitors getting familiar with the waters off Cape Cod. I certainly wasn't. Boogie boarding off the National Seashore had long been a hobby of mine, but the presence of great whites made me stop. And I wasn't happy about the huge number of seals, figuring the fishing off Monomoy for stripers would probably be going downhill with them hunting stripers. And that is exactly what happened. (Biologists say stripers are not a primary part of a seal's diet, but I'm not buying it. Even if I'm wrong, no striper in its right mind is going to stay in an area where seals are hunting.)

I also wondered if the business people and tourists on the Cape would still be welcoming the great whites when attacks on humans occurred, which I thought was just a matter of time.

One of the earlier indications of trouble occurred in 2012 off Truro's Ballston Beach. A man was body surfing when he said he was attacked by a shark and sustained severe cuts on both legs. A sunbather on the beach saw the attack and told *Cape Cod Today* that, "All of a sudden between the two swimmers we a saw a fin come up and something came through the water. It was a very large fin, easily fifteen inches high and came across and torqued a little towards the second swimmer and within seconds we realized it was a shark, and the swimmer had been attacked."

By 2014 a couple of great whites were being seen on the bay side of Cape Cod, and that's when I stopped plunging off Adam's boat for a swim whenever it was warm. Giving up that swim was a big loss for me. Whenever I fish the experience is usually intertwined with swimming or snorkeling (to try and look for the fish I couldn't catch). I often use fishing as an excuse to swim and float in the river, lake, or ocean I'm fishing in. There is nothing like the refreshing shock of cold water followed by sunbathing where warm rays embrace bare skin. But now, on the ocean of the outer Cape, those days are over, and something is missing. Swimming made bad days of fishing still special, and a way to connect with environment more intimately.

I also feared the increased presence of great whites and seals in Cape Cod Bay would soon impact the fishing in a negative way, and I commented about that to Adam during a day when the stripers were thick in shallow waters. "Enjoy this day to the max," I said, "in a few years a day like this may be unheard of if the seals take up shop."

Also in 2014 one of the scarier attacks occurred, this time to kayakers off Plymouth—in the exact spot where I'd been trolling for stripers from my kayak a couple months earlier. Two women were paddling near shore, enjoying the water and photographing seals when a great white attacked them. It slammed into both of their kayaks so hard that it flipped them over, sending both women into the water. That's when one of the kayakers came face-to-face with the beast, clearly seeing its eyes, grey pointy snout, and its teeth before it submerged. The two women screamed for help and people on shore called 911. Meanwhile the women, who were treading water, had no idea where the shark went. Efforts to get back inside their kayaks were unsuccessful, but they managed to survive the ordeal until the Plymouth Harbormaster rescued them. Later their kayaks were recovered and one of them showed that the great white had actually bitten into the kayak! The Division of Marine Fisheries confirmed that the bite was from a great white based on a tooth fragment and the bite radius. "I don't think I'll ever kayak again," said one of the women. "It was petrifying waiting in that water for the harbormaster, not knowing if anyone was going to come get us."

That incident got me thinking. Did the shark mistake the kayak for a seal? Probably, but that means anyone in a kayak could be at risk for the same fate. And I wondered if it was also possible the shark saw the women in the kayak and intentionally attacked. . . . Either way I began rethinking some of my kayak trips. While I still go fishing for stripers from my kayak, I won't go anywhere near places seals are known to frequent, and I will no longer kayak at night. Adam's forty-four-inch striper that he caught from his kayak off Barnstable Harbor at night is a feat that I'll never equal. Nor will I be like the thrill-seeker featured in the local paper who, from his twelve-foot kayak, went miles offshore and caught a 157-pound bluefin tuna! He explained that "you go for a sleigh ride," and said he once hooked into a tuna that pulled him five miles offshore!

The encounters with great whites increased over the next few years, culminating in two attacks in 2018. The first was a serious assault off Truro that occurred when William Lytton was swimming about thirty yards offshore. He told the *Cape Cod Times* he felt a terrible pain in his leg and when he turned around "there was a giant shark on my leg that was thrashing and writhing. It was to the point where a good part of the shark's head was out of the water." Lytton hit the shark with all his might, breaking a tendon in his forearm. That blow might have been the reason the shark released him. Lytton, who had severe injuries on his leg, made it out of the ocean alive. Just one month later twenty-six-year-old Arthur Medici was attacked and killed while boogie boarding off Newcomb Hollow Beach in Wellfleet. Witnesses said he was only about thirty to forty feet from shore when he was ambushed.

Experts believe that the great whites mistook these men for seals, and that the sharks are cruising the channels of water between sandbars. And instead of attacking from below with a vertical launch, the way great whites usually grab prey, these sharks were engaged in lateral attacks because of the shallow water they were in.

So even if you are wading in waist deep water to cast your plug, you might have company. I know of fisherman wading on the flats who had an eight-foot great white come check him out. Imagine standing still while an apex predator does a lazy loop around you.

I have no desire to see a great white. Charter boat captains have told me how they have seen great whites do a total body breach out of the water as they make a grab for a striper being reeled in. The younger Mike Tougias would have loved to have seen that because I'd take risks in my efforts to be close to nature. Back then I would have probably gone into a shark cage where the operator then puts chum around to attract great whites. But the snorkeling experience with Adam and the sharks in the Bahamas was enough adrenaline for now. I can say I've snorkeled with stingrays, sea turtles, and manatees in the ocean and brackish water. In freshwater I've snorkeled up to beaver, snapping turtles, and once even got close enough to see a loon dive for a fish. I don't need to add a great white to my list.

The fishing friends of mine who have seen a great white up close say that to witness such a spectacle is a sight to behold. And I'm sure it is, but I'd be quite happy if they moved out of the area and I never have the opportunity. Unfortunately, with the seal population protected by law, the seals will keep increasing in numbers around the Cape and so too will the great whites. According to the Massachusetts Department of Marine Fisheries they identified sixty-eight individual great whites in 2014 in the area. In 2016 that number jumped to 147, with the experts estimating approximately 250 separate and distinct individual great whites having cruised the waters off Cape Cod in a three-year period.

When I'm leaning over the boat to bring up a striper or a blue fish it's possible that either a seal or great white will want the same fish, and we might come eye to eye. I'm convinced that both the seals and great whites have learned that the vibrations from boat engines is like a dinner bell—there could be a struggling fish near the boat. An article in *On the Water Magazine* theorized that most of the great whites that take a fish off a line are juveniles, not quite ready to hold onto a five-hundred-pound gray seal. Still, a "young" ten-foot shark breaching behind our boat or suddenly appearing when I'm lifting a fish in would be enough to scare the bejeezus out of me.

If there were fewer seals, there would likely be fewer great whites off Cape Cod. The seals were protected by the 1972 Marine Mammal Protection Act, and their resurgence has led to talk about trying to get an amendment to the law so their population can be culled around the Cape. I would be all for that, but I can also see the other point of view that says let nature take its course, and defining "over-abundance" can be in the eyes of the beholder. Some people simply like having large populations of seals around. While seals are clever, and some people call them cute (their heads look very much like a dog, especially a black lab), they are predators just like the rest of us.

So how have the seals impacted fishing in my home waters on the Bay side of Cape Cod? Anecdotally, I can say that from 2019 to 2022 the shallow water fishing were my worst years in the last twenty. I observed that there were almost no large stripers on the Brewster or Chapin Flats during their usual June forays. And Jon Hyde, who fishes the flats weekly, confirmed that, and we both think it's because of the increasing presence of seals.

***

While I have no desire to see a great white, Adam and I saw something far bigger in our home waters. At first we thought we were seeing a great white shark's dorsal fin, but as we motored closer we realized it was basking shark, bigger than our eighteen-foot boat. This was no seal/man-eater, but a harmless plankton eater. The basking shark uses its enlarged mouth with gill rakers to catch plankton as it filters the water.

The basking shark looked remarkably similar to a great white. Experts say there are different ways to tell them apart: the basking shark has numerous gills and its dorsal fin is more rounded at its apex. But if you are swimming or in a kayak, I don't think you want to take the time to try and examine these two distinguishing features. Which leads me to a kayaking incident that happened off a beach in Sandwich one evening. I was fishing from shore and struck up a conversation with another angler who was paddling by in his kayak just a few feet away from me. While we were talking a dark object caught my eye.

"Holy shit," I said, pointing at the ocean, "there's a giant fin farther out there."

The man in the kayak quickly spotted it, while he sat motionless in his kayak.

"I think it's a basking shark," I said.

"Yes," the angler responded, "I think you're right, looks too big to be a great white. Amazing that something that big is so close to shore. I'm going to take a closer look."

"Whoa! I said *I think* it's a basking shark, but what do I know."

"It is, I'll just go take a quick look." In the dimming light he began paddling toward the fin.

"You might be making a big mistake!"

The last I saw of him, he was paddling toward the area where we saw the fin, moving at a fast clip. I couldn't see the shark's fin any longer. Soon the kayaker was far in the distance, and I characteristically soon got back to fishing. I assume he made it safely to shore, since I never read about a missing kayaker in the paper, but he sure took one hell of risk, especially in the fading light.

***

Although Adam and I have never seen a great white, a shark of a different kind caused us serious pain. This shark was a human, and the pain was financial. Adam mentioned in an earlier chapter how a slick distributer pocketed money from our *Blizzard of '78* book. This human shark took the money from a giant, multi-store retailer who purchased our book but never paid us. Adam would have liked to sue the distributor, but he was protected by declaring bankruptcy. We never did get a cent for the biggest sale either Adam or I had landed up until then.

While the financial loss was bigger for Adam than for me, that incident made me doubt I was on the right path having become a full-time writer. There were other negative experiences as well, such as a problematic agent. Also, my nearly lifelong struggle with insomnia hadn't improved, and I could no longer blame it on the corporate world.

Eventually I learned to live with this issue, and found that a 2 p.m. power nap, between thirty and forty minutes, was the way to go. If I could squeeze one of those into my day I felt reenergized. Sure, it was an inconvenience, but I told myself the whole country of Spain, and many others, is in the napping tradition!

Adam understood my lack of REM sleep, and there were many days I'd take a quick nap at his house and then we'd go fishing. I never felt I needed a therapist's counsel, because I'd bounce any challenge in my life off Adam and consider his advice.

And so Adam's boat became both the brainstorming center and a psychoanalyst's office with handy access to fishing rods. He knew about my battle with insomnia and the challenges of my transition to full-time writer. Adam frequently asked the insightful questions that made me pause or he offered an idea I had not thought of. The fact that Adam was a risk taker was not lost on me either. His publishing business involved equal doses of taking big chances and capitalizing on any rewards, and he would soon try a new endeavor that required real conviction. I had always considered myself a calculated risk taker, and he inspired me to accept even more risk if I could live with the consequences of the inevitable setbacks that come with spreading your wings to their full extension.

Long ago I decided to exclude people from my life who were energy drainers or drama specialists, and only associate with those who challenge and lift me up. Adam fit the bill. And that's how our conversations went on the boat—each of us encouraging the other. We reminded ourselves that our dreams of successful writing and publishing businesses were in the works, that our determination would make it happen.

CHAPTER 16

Other Species

AG

Mike's encounter with an ocean sunfish in the Cape Cod Canal is one of my favorites of his fishing anecdotes. I had never seen an ocean sunfish myself until the first autumn we had the *Scout*. Mike and I spotted a fin waving above the waterline from a distance and sped over to investigate.

"What's that?" I asked.

"It's an ocean sunfish," replied my knowledgeable pal. "Its scientific name is *Mola mola*."

"I better cut the engine."

We floated a short distance away from this blob-like being which was apparently lying on its side at depths that varied from right on the surface to three or four feet underwater. I couldn't make its shape out entirely, but what I could see was an unattractive, mottled, blotchy, pale-white creature, perhaps five feet generally around. It had a small puckery mouth and a drowsy but intelligent-looking eye. It was like someone dumped a giant vat of pizza dough in the bay which coalesced and came alive.

It had no scales and no tail. It bobbed like a gargantuan jellyfish, sluggish, unwieldy, and to put it bluntly, ugly. I perceived it as helpless. I thought of a five-foot-around mushroom top with an eye and mouth. I wondered why predators—sharks or seals, for example—weren't munching it alive.

After a while, this one appeared to start making its way toward us. Mike and I both leaned over the low gunnels of the *Scout*. As it approached, it peered up at us with its skyward facing eye in an unworldly way. It gave the impression it was as curious to know us as we were to know it.

"It's looking at us."

"It is."

"*Mola mola,*" I said, "meet *Homo sapiens.*"

As odd as that sunfish appeared, in the years leading to my divorce, while drinking and overeating, I wasn't all that different from what I perceived it to be. I had maxed out at more than sixty pounds overweight. I was just as bloated, pale, and helpless as the sunfish appeared. Mike has noted that in German the sunfish is called *Schwimmender Kopf,* meaning "swimming head." I've also read that in Polish it is called *samogłów,* meaning "lonely head." That was me to a T during the years leading up to my divorce, and for quite a few afterward, lonely and trapped in my own head.

Fortunately, our fishing friendship helped save me. Being around a fellow man, who spoke with appreciation and positivity, who had noble goals for his life, was nothing short of therapeutic. Humans have been involved in group hunter-gatherer activities since we have been a species. I'm convinced that activities like fishing with a friend tap into very basic aspects of our psyches. They satisfy our primal longings to be close with one another, to be outdoors, to collaborate and problem solve, and to obtain food, activities that are often sorely missing from life nowadays.

I have an uncle named Donny who is in his mid-seventies. Uncle Donny is possibly an even more avid fisherman than Mike and me, except that he doesn't bother with saltwater. He prefers the serenity of lakes and ponds. During fishing season, my uncle goes fishing at least twice a week, weather permitting, and in winter he icefishes whenever he can. He has done this consistently since he was a boy. He and his closest fishing buddy, Bob, have made it a point to explore different lakes and ponds across southeastern Massachusetts for thirty years together, so far. When they fish on weekend mornings, Bob brings coffee and breakfast sandwiches, and when they meet weeknights, my uncle brings deli sandwiches and a six pack. Together they have plummeted the depths of more than two hundred different bodies of water. My Uncle Donny has had a

lot of relationships through working, raising a family, and active partici-
pation in civic life. He told me that the single most important friendship
he has had is that with Bob. His wife, my Aunt Judy, goes even farther
and says they are every bit as close as family. This is perfectly consistent
with my friendship with Mike, even though we have only been fishing
together for a comparatively short twenty-five years, so far.

I'm not going to pretend that having a fishing friend was the key to
surviving my addictions, although it helped. Actually, my overindulgence
in alcohol and food played a very practical role. They helped me live with
the feelings of worthlessness I clung to as a kid. Even while the drink
and junk food steadily hamstringed me and kept me performing below
potential, they allowed me to get by with my deep discomfort, one drink
at a time, one ice cream overindulgence at a time. I told myself that I
was "working hard and playing hard," that I was "taking big bites out of
life." But I was anesthetizing myself to the point that the anesthesia was
poisonous.

Less than a year after my divorce was finalized, my mother died.
Then, within just another twelve months my only brother, Matt, died
unexpectedly. Then, just a few months after that, my Uncle Billy, who was
perhaps my closest family member, had a heart attack and passed away
as well. I went through a divorce and the deaths of three close family
members in just two years.

One friend admitted to me later that during those days he had
sometimes wondered if I was going to make it through without a tragedy
befalling me too. One of my employees later confessed that for a period,
he sometimes worried that he might show up to our office some morning
only to find the doors locked and a sign reading "Closed Permanently."

"It happens all the time," he said. "But you kept showing up, Adam,
so I did too."

The fact was that all that loss around me made me desperate to
change.

My maternal grandfather, who took a fair amount of responsibility
for my brother and me after our father died, had witnessed just such desperation when he himself was a young child. Once, after his parents were
divorced, he and his older brother spent the day at a lake house with their

father and their father's new girlfriend. At some point the couple decided to leave the young boys on the beach while they paddled along the shore in a canoe. Their father, my great grandfather, was a very good swimmer, but his girlfriend did not know how to swim. When their canoe capsized, she panicked and clung her arms about his neck with such fierce desperation that he could not resist. The pair drowned together, flailing, the young boys watching and hearing them helplessly from shore. I believe I have some idea what that desperation feels like. I became life-and-death desperate to change.

Mike and I also shared a belief that helped save me. It is the article of faith that each of us has the capacity to overcome our sufferings, even to transform them into something better. Mike mentions it in the very first sentence of this book: "I have this crazy belief that I can turn any—well almost any—bad event or disappointment into something better."

I had absorbed this belief while attempting to practice Buddhism for many years. I don't know where Michael adopted it from, perhaps from his father, perhaps from his life in nature and literature. Ultimately, I think we both have to credit this belief as the lynchpin, or the cotter pin (which is the name of the pin that keeps a boat's propeller on) that allowed us to motor toward our personal challenges, to face them directly.

There was a Fourth of July weekend some years after my divorce that helped me see how it had been working. I was out on the boat late in the morning with Miki and Jack, just the three of us. A perfect summer day on Cape Cod Bay, we were wearing our bathing suits under azure skies decorated with pristine, puffy clouds. We were just beginning to grumble at how slow the fishing was when Jack pointed in a direction and asked, "What's that over there, Dad?"

About a mile away, there seemed to be a disturbance on the water of a type I didn't recognize.

"Let's check it out," I said. "Lines in, you guys. Let me know when you're ready."

"All set," they announced once their rods were back in their holders. We shot off toward the spot which was not far from the shoreline.

When we got there, both kids exclaimed, "Dolphins, dolphins!"

It was the first time I had encountered them in those nearshore waters. There were at least sixty following some kind of bait. I cut the engine.

"They are beautiful," Miki declared.

Sleek, muscular, curvaceous, and glistening, they were all speed. Surfacing and submerging, arching just above the surface, they were waves themselves.

After a few delightful minutes of admiring them from a distance, just floating with our engine off, the pod unexpectedly moved in our direction. Soon, we were surrounded by the speedy mammals. For a long couple of minutes, they frolicked all around us. We were each leaning over the gunnels—as Mike and I had years before with the sunfish—when three different dolphins came right up adjacent to the boat, one after another, twisting in the water in such a way that, as they whisked past, we could see they were clearly looking at us.

"They are checking us out," Miki yelled.

It was the first time since the encounter with the sunfish that marine life had intentionally approached the boat.

"You can tell they are smart," my daughter beamed.

"They're playing with us!" Jack exclaimed.

As the dolphins started edging away toward deeper waters, I took notice of a recreational fishing boat, a center-console very similar to ours, a hundred or so yards away. I looked at the two guys fishing off it and realized they hadn't even noticed the dolphins, or if they had noticed them, they decidedly didn't care. They were completely focused on fishing and reminded me of Mike and me.

It was about then that I spotted a near-shore lobster boat on the other side of them, motoring steadily our way. I estimated it was on a heading that would bring it uncomfortably close to our boat. I considered that I better move us out of its way when I realized it was on a collision course with the recreational fishermen between us.

"Watch out, watch out!" I hollered at both vessels. I hit the boat horn button on the dash. "Heads up!"

The recreational fisherman near the helm heard me and rapidly assessed the impending danger. He dropped his rod, ignited his engine, and tried to accelerate out of the way of the oncoming lobster boat. His boat lurched forward awkwardly, but it wasn't enough to avoid being struck by the larger craft. Fortunately, he moved just enough to evade a square ramming on his starboard, a hit that would have surely resulted in an ugly mess. The near-shore lobster boat had a lot of mass to it. Who knows how many gallons of gas were in their tanks? Fortunately, the smaller craft only suffered what amounted to a sidelong glancing strike from the lobster fisherman. It was the first and only time I've seen a collision at sea.

Immediately after the bang, a man's head popped up on the lobster boat. The guy running it had been completely distracted by something he was focused on below his steering wheel in his small cabin. The bump he felt had all of his attention now. He and the recreational guys started exchanging heated words. My kids and I had a drama in front of us. For a second it looked like a fistfight was in the making. It also became clear from the lobsterman's face and voice that he had been drinking and was drunk, apparently having started his Independence Day weekend celebration too early.

Fortunately, it didn't come to anything serious, and the two parties went their separate ways. Before they were out of sight, I found myself quietly overwhelmed with gratitude that I wasn't that drunken man on his lobster boat that day. I had been without alcohol for perhaps four years by then, so not only was I no longer a menace myself, but I was also alert enough to help prevent a potentially bad accident.

I was even glad not to be one of the recreational fishermen who were too preoccupied to enjoy the dolphins.

Just then I also notice a bucket floating in the water at the site of the accident. It had apparently been knocked off the stern of the lobster boat. We motored over, and the kids worked together to scoop it out with our dock pole. Today, I still have that perfectly serviceable ten-gallon bucket in our garage, a souvenir of sorts.

Another experience with other species came later that year. It was September, sunny, bright, and warm with light, pleasant breezes. The sun reflected everywhere.

I was fishing on my own, trolling a swimming plug that was supposedly designed to mimic the motions of a real fish. The boat puttered slowly. I looked at my line off the stern and was surprised to spot two eyes peering back at me from out of the water, a long fifty yards or more behind the boat. I gave them a double take. I couldn't make out a head or body, so I had no idea what creature they belonged to. They just bobbed out there and peered at me, then disappeared.

About five minutes later, just as I had forgotten them, I suddenly spotted them again. They stared directly at me. It was unnerving. Then they were gone again. It was the third time they appeared that I realized they belonged to a large seal that was keeping its head low to the water.

I now suspect it had either spotted my swimming plug and was curiously following it, or perhaps there were fish following my lure, and the seal was in pursuit of them. One thing I don't doubt is that the seal saw me looking back at him or her. Maybe the seal was wary of me, or maybe playing with me a bit. I could not tell.

Yet that encounter was not the high point of the trip, not by a nautical mile. A little while after the seal's eyes vanished for the final time, another creature shot up out of the water, perhaps a quarter mile to the north. It came down hard with a walloping splash.

"Whale," was my immediate thought.

Then, just seconds later, another exploded out of the bay in a different direction, maybe half a mile to my west. It was just as big as the first, bursting above the waves before crashing down and sending sprays into the air and sun.

As he has pointed out, Mike and I have seen several such breeches together. They always come unexpectedly. There is an upward explosion of whitewater followed by a creature in the air whose shape never quite seems clear. We eventually figured out that they were sunfish breeching, a phenomena that still seems incredible based what they look like when basking on the surface.

Prior to that day, it had been rare for Mike and me to spot one or two sunfish breach an entire season. Now I witnessed two in a matter of seconds. I was in for a real gift. At least forty sunfish breached in sight of the *Scout* that afternoon. There was even one particularly intense half-hour wherein I witnessed more than a dozen hurl themselves high into the air, sometimes as much five or six feet above the surface. It was such a calm, bright day, each caught the sunshine in increasingly novel ways, often tumbling end over end. It was like Cape Cod Bay celebrated itself with all that bursting and splashing. They proved to me in no uncertain terms that sunfish are no helpless blob-beings, victims to the whims of waves and currents.

CHAPTER 17

Bad Luck, Good Friends

MT

Dolphins racing by the boat, ocean sunfish breaching, bluefish rocketing, and stripers making runs where we worried about being spooled. So many great trips. But not all. We had our share of bad trips. Everybody does.

I'm not a superstitious person, except when it comes to the ocean. I saw a direct corollary between one of our crap days on the water and the food Adam packed for a snack. A banana. You simply do not ever, and I mean ever, bring a banana on a boat. There are different theories about why bananas bring bad luck, and I believe them all. One premise is that crates of bananas sometimes house poisonous snakes and spiders that can run amuck on a vessel. Another is that boats with bananas from Central America often come around the tip of Florida and then up the Gulf Stream, which can be a deadly place in a storm. (The Gulf Stream flows northeast and if winds are out of the northeast that combination, or should I say collision, produces some of the biggest waves on the planet. I'm convinced it's that current of water and not the so-called mysterious Bermuda Triangle that caused boats to disappear.) Yes, it's possible that the banana gets a bad rap simply because they float; and so if a boat sinks and all that is found are bananas, they get the blame. But I think it is something more. People who ignore ocean superstitions do so at their peril. In my cowritten book *So Close to Home*, guess what the vessel we focused on was carrying? Bananas. Guess where the vessel is now? The bottom of the sea. Guess what floated by the people struggling for their lives in shark-infested waters? Bananas.

Guess what happened when Adam brought a peanut butter and banana sandwich on the boat? A piece of the propeller fell off. That's right, my captain who had reliably guided me to some of the best fishing days of my life broke the cardinal rule of the sea. He brought a banana on the boat, and our trip was over within fifteen minutes of leaving the dock. He even admits he was well aware of the superstition but thought he could trick the gods of the sea by sneaking pieces of a banana inside a sandwich. You simply do not bring a banana—or parts of said fruit—on a boat. It's taboo, it's inviting trouble, and it's not some silly myth.

Just three months ago I was fishing on my friend Opie's boat with another buddy, Dale. I took them to all the spots Adam and Jon Hyde have shown me. Those locations and the techniques that work there come from their combined fifty years of fishing almost exclusively in these home waters. And those sites always yield fish—maybe not a keeper striper but at least you can enjoy knowing you are going to catch a schoolie or a small blue. Yet on the outing with Dale and Opie we caught zilch, nada, a big goose egg. I felt like I had let my buddies down, and as we motored back to the harbor, I happened to glance behind me. There was Dale, sitting in the seat at the stern, happily eating . . . a BANANA!

Other superstitions? There are plenty:

- Never change the name of a boat. Legend has it that renaming implies you were trying to trick the gods. But if you do decide to change the name you must first have a virgin pee on the vessel. (Certainly an odd myth, but, yes, one of my books features a vessel that had its name changed, and it sank.)

- You don't whistle on a boat. Why? Because you are "whistling up the wind." You're challenging the wind, trying to declare your dominance. (You might be able to get away with this, but only if you are whistling John Lennon's "Jealous Guy." It's so beautiful I can't help whistling it—even on a boat.)

- Try not to clap on a vessel—it conjures up a storm with thunder and lightning. (Jon Hyde says of all his bad trips, nothing compares to the fright of being at sea in a small boat during a lightning storm. "There is nowhere to hide and it's terrifying." I believe him, and you won't find me clapping when I catch a keeper.)

- Never leave port for an overnight voyage on a Friday. The origin of this one may be tied into the fact that Christ was killed on Friday. (Yes, once again I have proof that you should take this superstition seriously. Just read *Fatal Forecast*.)

- Never kill an albatross. Read *Rime of the Ancient Mariner*. Seabirds, particularly albatross, are said to carry the souls of sailors lost at sea.

- Don't go to sea with a redhead. (Sounds like a stretch, but the fear has been around for centuries.)

- A woman on a boat brings bad luck. The superstition probably was propagated by some captain, knowing a woman on a vessel would distract the men from their duties. (This one is total bullshit. I've researched almost a hundred vessel disasters and almost all them had an all-male crew. If the women myth were true boats wouldn't be referred to as "she" nor would the figureheads on the bow be of a woman. And besides, I caught my biggest striper with Jon Hyde and two women. Case closed.)

- And finally, one of the stranger superstitions I've heard. It goes something like this—if someone falls overboard you may not want to save them—the vengeful ocean will sink your boat. Obviously we can't let this silly myth rule us . . . but there was a time . . .

The time in question occurred when Adam guided the *Scout* near shore where mud banks, covered with marsh grass, met the tidal flat we were in. The depth of the water next to those mud banks was about a foot, and somehow Adam, in just two feet of water, had maneuvered us to within casting distance of the shore.

It sure didn't look like fishy water.

"Cast right up near the grass," Adam instructed me. "You stand up in the bow. Keep the floating soft plastic on. If you don't get a hit there, slowly cover as much water as you can until you are casting at that weed bed out where the water's a little deeper."

I cast, and muttered under my breath, *No fish in its right mind is going to be in crystal-clear water one foot deep under a full sun. This is really . . .* Then bam! The water exploded and I was into a nice striper that was off to the races seeking deeper water. After that day, on future trips, I always said, "Why don't we try the marsh grass."

Now jump ahead a few years to the bad luck trip that happened in the fall when the marsh grass was the color of straw under a cloudless sky. Adam, being a kind soul, let me stand in the bow as he positioned the boat just off the grass in about three feet of water. He killed the motor and we drifted.

Adam positioned himself at the stern to fish behind the *Scout*. On my third or fourth cast a bass crashed the lure, and I whooped and hollered. Normally, bass don't jump, but in a foot of water I guess it had no choice, and it catapulted out of the water.

From the peanut gallery at the back of the boat, Adam said, "Why do you grunt when the fish first strikes?"

"Do I?"

"Yes, you do. It sounds like a third-rate porno movie up there."

I thought about that for a moment, wondering if it was an insult. But not wanting to be sophomoric, I moved the conversation to more serious topics that men often discuss while fishing. "Adam," I said, "is it considered cheating on your mate if a man gets a rub and tug?"

"I'm not touching that one," said Adam. Then he was silent as he too started casting.

I went back to playing my fish. I guessed it was just short of keeper size. Had I thought it was a big one I never would have spoken while battling the fish.

Behind me, I assumed Adam had also hooked into a nice striper because I heard a big splash. My fish was running and I kept my rod tip up to let it take some of the shock when the fish changed direction or pulled harder. This fish was a fighter and I was locked in, determined not to lose it. I turned around to tell Adam that I thought I had a nice fish on.

Where's Adam? I thought. Not being the brightest bulb, it didn't immediately occur to me that if I didn't see Adam he wasn't in the boat. After all the *Scout* is only eighteen feet. Sherlock Holmes I'm not.

I didn't want to lose the fish, so I calmly said, "Adam?"

I waited a second, and not hearing an answer, repeated, "Adam?"

His voice answered from somewhere unusually far away, behind the boat. "I was wondering when you might notice."

He had fallen from the vessel and into the water—that was the splash I heard.

I glanced behind the *Scout* but couldn't see him. Rather than run to the back, I said, "Do you need help? I've got a nice fish on but I could slowly walk back to you."

"Oh, I wouldn't want to interrupt your fishing. You just go ahead and play the fish, and don't worry about your friend in the water."

"It's not over your head is it?"

Using the back of the motor, he climbed into the boat, and started shedding his wet clothes. Then he asked a rhetorical question, a tad on the melodramatic side, "What if I had fallen overboard way out in the ocean? How long do you think it would have taken you to notice?"

"That depends if I'm playing a fish or not. I've got a good one on right now, so I was kind of focused on the fish."

"You know what I think," said Adam, "I think you'd say to yourself, *Well, if Adam doesn't show up in the next hour or so then I'll stop fishing and look for him.*"

I didn't take the bait, and Adam didn't say anything more. He must have been freezing after his little swim. I was about to tell him that it can be bad luck to retrieve a man overboard, but this didn't feel like the right time.

Adam explained how he fell in. "I had raised the engine because we were in such shallow water. One of my back casts got caught on it. In leaning over to free the lure, I lost my grip and fell in. I could have drifted to Nantucket by the time you noticed I was missing."

The fishing was really good that day. And that turned out to be a problem. When there are big bass around I'm so in the moment, I'm childlike, and forget everything else. More than once I've rushed to cast so quick to a rising fish I've forgotten to open my bail, and instead watched the lure snap off and sail away. In fact one time a fish hit the sailing lure as soon as the lure met the water. Too bad my line snapped off from the lure.

And so on that magical day of big fish in shallow water, I forgot about the time. Adam did too, but he had the excuse of being kerfuf-fled from falling out the boat. (It's okay to use the word kerfuffle when describing Adam). Anyway, when we realized we better get out of the shallows as the tide was dropping we found ourselves stuck on a sand bar. I took a cast, said, "Shit, I'll get out and push," and promptly hooked into a schoolie. While I played the fish, Adam went back in the water, and started pushing from the stern.

I did my part by keeping my weight in the bow, but figured I might as well keep fishing.

After five minutes of heaving the *Scout*—like Sisyphus pushing the rock up the hill—Adam had the boat in a little channel which he felt was deep enough, so he climbed back onboard. He knew the waters so well he drove the boat parallel to the shore, understanding this little dip in the sand would soon lead to another channel that would take us to deep water.

The sun was going down on what was a perfect day for me. I put my hand on Adam's shoulder and said, "What a great trip. But you really should have taken me up on my offer to push us off the sand. You had already been in that freezing water and you're the captain."

"Yeah," Adam sighed, "I heard your offer. But you made no move to take your sneakers off."

Jeez, he had me there. I thought about mentioning that at the time I did have a fish on the line, but again thought better of it. Instead I said, "Next time I won't get so locked in to the fishing. It will be my job to monitor the time we are in the shallows."

He laughed so hard I thought he'd fall out of the boat again.

***

While that "bad" trip I just discussed (for Adam, not me) was more of nuisance, a sudden change in the weather can be deadly serious. In our early days of boating, we responded too slow to changing conditions. We were lucky the worst that happened was cold, pounding rides back to port, getting drenched by spray the entire time. On one trip we made far offshore the outcome could have been nasty. It was late in the day and the wind was picking up as we turned toward our home port. We bumped into a pod of feeding bass and of course we stopped, killed the engine, and silently drifted up to the fish. We did our usual top-water casting, and we each caught and released a couple of big fish. We did a high five, noted the sinking sun, and knew we best get moving.

When Adam went to start the motor, it would not turn over after a number of tries. Let me tell you, that is one sickening feeling when you are a long way from port. I kept my mouth shut, and Adam waited a moment or two—we probably both said a silent prayer—and he turned the key again and the engine coughed to life. Relief flowed through me and I said, "Let's not stop again for any fish."

"That'll be a first for you," Adam responded. "But yes, we're going straight back. This chop is nasty and it's getting late."

It was dusk, and I was a relatively new boater at the time, and it was little disconcerting that we couldn't see shore. This was before we had GPS or cell phones. A half hour later—it was now dark—after pounding into the wind, the channel marker for our harbor came into sight through the gloom. I let out another sigh of relief. I started to tell Adam how we learned another lesson, and how it flashed through my mind that there was one weak link in our plan to get home safely.

"What's that?" asked Adam.

"If our onboard radio conked out we'd have been screwed."

"A lot more than that could have gone wrong."

"Like what?" I asked.

"Well, I didn't want to mention this to you but since we are entering the harbor, I will. Take a look at the fuel gauge."

I did and my stomach did a little flip. The red arrow was on empty. There was no banana to blame, just our own stupidity, and we vowed right then and there to make changes in the way we boated. We would have check lists for long trips. And I added another rule of my own—to not trust the weather forecast the night before a fishing trip. Too much can change. From now on I vowed, I'd check the marine forecast before I left my house in the morning.

***

In this book we've shared a few fishing tips, but now I want to share what I've learned from survivors of boating accidents whom I've interviewed. I've described lighthearted moments so far in this chapter. I don't want any reader to mistake my humor for an indifference to safety or disrespect of the sea. Nothing could be further from the truth. Adam and I always took the ocean seriously, but we probably should have taken a boater safety course. In one respect, however, I was learning from some of the most knowledgeable people on the planet about safety and mistakes—survivors of deadly or near-deadly accidents who I had interviewed for my books.

A few takeaways have stayed with me. Wear a life jacket (rather than, "Where's my life jacket?"). The most functional jackets are the ones that auto-inflate upon contact with the water and also have an activation cord. They are not bulky and easy to fish with. And if you're boating alone use the kill switch cord. (One end of the quick release cord is attached to you and the other to the vessel, if you are thrown from the helm position the connection to the vessel detaches and the engine stops.) Have an EPIRB onboard if you're going far offshore. Bring your cell phone and make sure it's charged. Have a strobe light attached to your life jacket—it might be your only hope at night. Be sure to have a marine radio onboard. At the first sign of trouble on a boat, err on the side of caution and call the Coast Guard. You are not giving them a Mayday but simply alerting them to the fact you have an issue at sea. That issue can turn into a full-blown emergency, and you may not have a chance to make that call. Stay hydrated while you're out on the boat—dehydration could cause you to pass out.

And perhaps the most important step to take before a trip: tell some-one where you plan to be fishing and what time you expect to be home. There's nothing worse than finding yourself treading water, knowing no one is searching for you. On the other hand, knowing that a concerned friend or loved one is onshore and will alert the Coast Guard can give you the hope and strength to hang on until help comes.

I'm just scratching the surface with these tips, but the message is simply to put safety first. Adam and I made our share of mistakes, but we learned from them. We know accidents can happen just a stone's throw from shore, and we didn't want to test blue water until we were more experienced and in a bigger boat. Our goal was to keep our bad trips as either annoyances or fishless days, not life-threatening.

Even if you don't follow all these safety tips, do yourself one simple favor, if only out of your most basic sense of self-preservation—whatever you do, do not bring a banana on the boat.

CHAPTER 18

Sleeping with the Fishes

AG

This chapter is about the opposite of fishing. Rather than hauling something up out of the ocean—a fish—it's about leaving something in the ocean, in this case the remains of a dear friend.

George was a soon-to-be retired shipping consultant when we met a couple years after my divorce. He not only helped me with the shipping needs of my publishing business, but he also quickly became a friend and even a mentor. Ironically, George was also the name of my actual father. By that time, I had grown more or less accustomed to my new divorced life, but I still had not yet completely moved on from the recent deaths of my mother, my brother, and my uncle Billy.

George was in his early seventies. He wasn't a fisherman, but he loved being on the water as much as anyone, and he owned a sailboat for many years. He and his wife, Chris, lived in a small house called Swan Cottage along the banks of a tidal creek that flowed out of Cape Cod Bay. It was an antique that had originally served as a one-room schoolhouse. George had known the woman who resided in it prior him and was so charmed by it that he came right out and asked her, "If you ever sell Swan Cottage, would you give me a chance to buy it? I love it!"

According to George, he had forgotten all about his request when many years later he received a call from her. She was moving into a nursing home.

"I said I'd give you first refusal, George. Do you still want the house?"

Swan Cottage does not have a modern foundation but is set on top of large granite blocks that form a half basement. About a month after George and Chris moved in, there was a very high tide in the creek that brought water in through joints around the foundation blocks, fully flooding the half-basement. George immediately called his friend at her nursing home.

"I hate to bother you," he told her. "But I'm worried. The creek flooded the basement with seawater. Do you know anything about this? What do you think I should I do?"

"Oh yes, George. I know about it. Swan Cottage has been on that site for the better part of two hundred years now. What happens is that the tide comes in, and the water comes in. Then, after a while, the tide goes out, and the water goes out. That's how it works."

"I guess if it's been going on for nearly two hundred years, I won't worry about it," he responded.

"Don't," she told him.

It's a classic Cape Cod story if there ever was one.

My relationship with George was very different from that with Mike. Mike lived more than an hour's drive away, and we mainly met on our fishing trips or for publishing related business. The friendship with Mike went further back, but George lived close by, so we saw one another a lot. We boated together a little and had some good times on the water, but for the most part we mainly met for breakfast and lunch meetings, that kind of thing.

One summer's day, we were scheduled to grab lunch, but I got a message from him that he wasn't up for it. He had a bad headache and couldn't make it. Not twenty-four hours later, Chris called and explained that his headache turned out to be the result of a brain aneurism and that George died in the night.

It was completely unexpected.

It was the same thing my brother died suddenly from just a few years before.

When I went by to visit Chris the next day, she was on her way to meet with George's siblings to discuss an unusual request he had left. George wanted to be buried at sea, and not just his ashes, his entire body.

George was apparently adamant about this. He had never mentioned it to me, but apparently he had an intense discussion on the topic with his brother Tom. Tom is another ocean person, so much so that when he retired from full-time work, he took a summer job as a ferryboat captain.

Tom explained to George he didn't think they still performed burials at sea in this day and age, to which George responded, "Well that's what I want. Bury me at sea. If you must, just take my body out on your boat and dump me in the ocean, please."

Tom said, "First of all, if you die, I'm not going to be in any kind of emotional state to do anything like that. Second, we are not in the mafia, so we don't go dumping dead bodies in the ocean."

Apparently, George wasn't satisfied. But as is often the case with such things, he and everyone else simply assumed there would be years before he would die, and no plans were put in place. Now his family had to figure out what to do.

To everyone's surprise and relief, it wasn't such a problem after all. Tom found a company called New England Burials at Sea that specializes in it. As many people commented afterward, "Who knew?"

Soon the burial was scheduled, and I was honored to be one of only a couple non-family members invited. In fact, Chris allowed me to drive her to the boat that morning, as well as to the funeral home later where a second ceremony took place that was open to the public. This later event was fairly traditional, except perhaps that most of the speakers told stories about George that were hilariously funny. From his childhood friends to his coworkers, it was plain that he had spread a lot of joy. I had never heard such laughter at a memorial.

The burial at sea, on the other hand, was something else.

About forty of us gathered early at a dock in Plymouth. The boat we were to board would be familiar to anyone who has ever been on a small whale-watch or ferry boat. It featured two main seating areas. The one on the lower level was fully enclosed with windows on three sides. It included a small galley with snacks and refreshments. There was an open deck upstairs. A walkway encircled the craft on the lower level, with standing room at the stern lower level as well. This was where a dark body bag (referred to by the company as "a natural burial shroud") was laid out.

New England Burials at Sea provided a licensed captain who served as the master of ceremonies. He was not a licensed funeral director, so one was also provided, as required by law. The cost of the event—including the ship, shroud, and personnel—was in line with that of a cemetery burial. Of course, there was no cremation or embalmment fees, no plot, no casket, and no headstone.

The proceedings began with a bugle player sounding taps and a flag ceremony led by the US Army at the dock. George had been entitled to this due to having served. Chris was handed an American flag just like the one that had been handed to me a few years previously for my brother, the same that countless family members of US military personal have received.

Soon after, the captain gave us an obligatory boat safety speech, and we left the dock.

By law, a burial at sea needs to be in at least one hundred fathoms, which equates to six hundred feet of water. In order to reach these depths, our boat took us more than thirty miles east-northeast across Cape Cod Bay beyond the end of the peninsula. The forecast called for winds and choppy seas in the afternoon but calm in the morning, so the captain aimed to get us out and back promptly.

Plymouth Harbor was in full summer splendor. It is well protected with north and south barrier islands. Stately Plymouth Lighthouse stands watch on a bluff above its mouth. Unlike many indoor funeral ceremonies, where somber parlor rooms and sacred church spaces typically either include heavily draped windows or stained glass, sunshine danced freely in the fresh air around us glittering off an infinitude of waves. Even the loveliest cemeteries and churchyards I've visited paled in comparison with Plymouth Harbor and Cape Cod Bay that day. The 360-degrees of views from the top deck evolved around us as we motored out. Instead of grey headstones, terns and gulls squawked, waves lapped and splashed, wind whistled.

Over the next hour or so, many stories were shared featuring the words "Uncle George" and "my brother George" and "dear George."

Meanwhile, his shrouded corpse lay silently at the stern. Individuals occasionally visited it to pay respects. Eventually, I too sat with his remains for a while. I offered a prayer and soon found myself transfixed by the mesmerizing geometries of the ship's wake behind us.

Just before leaving the stern a vertical shaft of spray on the northern horizon line caught my eye. I recognized it as a whale's spout, leviathan breath shooting into the air. We had cruised about forty minutes across the bay by then. As time passed, one fellow passenger after another began calling out sightings.

In no time, we were virtually surrounded by whales, most some distance away, but in all directions and a few close by. Their exhalations misted the air over and again. Eventually, many breached, sometimes coming full out of the water. We saw tails, backs, fins, belies, even some of their eyes, mouths, and faces. It was like a ballet but on a stage grander and more majestic than any human performance. Probably everyone on board had been on a whale watch trip at some point or another. But this was different. Whale watches trips usually entail seeking and find-ing them, prior to hanging around them. In this case, the magnificent mammals simply appeared, while we just motored by them with our own business to attend to. There were so many at so many different dis-tances, I couldn't believe it. I was reminded a little of the sunfish show I had seen the previous season, but the whales dwarfed them. The sunfish simply shot up from nowhere, spun in the air a second, and were gone. The whales on the other hand tended to lumber and loll on the surface, inhaling and exhaling, turning their bodies and churning the waters. Yet simultaneously the whales, like our boat, were but tiny dots in the expanse of sea and sky.

Elephants, the largest terrestrial mammals, are well known for their sympathetic responses to the deaths of members of their herds. They are known to mourn their dead. But what about whales? Are leviathans less complex than pachyderms? What, if anything, did these giants conceive of death and dying?

According to New England Burials at Sea, human remains require somewhere between three and six months to decompose in the ocean.

We eventually reached deeper waters that were nevertheless within distant sight of Provincetown, at the tip of Cape Cod. There, the captain

announced we were in more than a hundred fathoms and invited us to
gather in the stern.

A selection of music was played. Two of George's brothers shared
readings. There was one from George's favorite book, *The Prophet* by
Kahlil Gibran, titled *On Giving*.

It made me realize that even on his passing, my friend had given us
the gift of this trip.

The captain fired a small cannon as a salute. No balls were shot, only
blanks, but real cannon balls were included in the ceremony. Three fif-
ty-five-pounders were placed in a special pouch at the bottom of the bio-
degradable shroud to ensure that it went directly down to the ocean floor.

Finally, some of George's nephews served as pallbearers. They moved
the board that his body lay on to the rail at the stern of the ship. They
then raised the shipboard end of it until George's shrouded corpse slid off
it and plunged into the dark blue waves. Gone in a moment.

Our boat then circled the GPS-marked location three times, while
mourners tossed flowers into the water.

The return journey to Plymouth was neither quiet, nor solemn. A
pleasant comradery had grown up among everyone by then. More stories were shared. There was a sense of completion. I especially enjoyed
talking to one of George's nephews who was a little younger than me.
He was a passionate recreational tuna fisherman who loved nothing more
than bringing his young kids out for long days fishing, until they would
eventually fall sound asleep on the boat's seat cushions heading home. I
told him I focused on inshore striper and blues fishing, but I understood
exactly what he meant.

When I told another fishing friend of mine named Greenleaf about
George's event, he responded, "That's why we fish, so we can have amazing trips like that while we are still here."

I eventually found myself sitting alone staring up at the sky, every
bit as unfathomable as the ocean we floated on, in which George's body
now rested. Images emerged of spreading my Uncle Billy's ashes with
family at the beach where he had once worked harvesting quahogs; of
my brother's boyhood friends at his army funeral; and of the disabled
individuals my mother had worked with as a teacher who had attended

her memorial; even of my grandparent's church in Buffalo where there was standing-room-only for my father's service.

Somehow the bittersweet serenity of saying goodbye to George out on the water—where I have spent so much time fishing—extended to these other deceased loved ones. The ocean has the power to destroy. George's remains would be consumed by it. But the ocean is the original source of life too. Mike and I have fished the waters near that ceremony since then many times, during which trips thoughts of George always drift into my mind, as does a certain sense of peace.

CHAPTER 19

Plenty of Fish

MT

Back on terra firma, my freelance full-time writing and speaking career surprisingly kept me afloat through the Great Recession. By putting my head down, working my ass off, and casting a wide net I weathered the storm. Now I decided to take that same approach to the dating scene. Having been married twenty-five years, I was ill-suited for this new challenge and had my share of "bad dates" just as I had a few bad fishing trips. The only difference was I couldn't blame the bad dates on superstitions.

Since Adam became single within a year of my divorce and he too was navigating his way through the dating experience, we could compare notes, analyze successes and failures, and more importantly have someone who understood dating is no walk in the park. In many ways it was a lot like fishing: there were plenty of sharks out there, presentation of your offering was crucial, and success was often dependent on the little things, the subtleties often overlooked. Except I never looked at dating like a sport, but more of a part-time job, a quest, like trying to write a bestseller, only this was to find the right partner. It would involve work, and any guy who thinks otherwise either is deluding themselves or is Tom Brady. And I'm sure it's just as difficult for women, if not more so.

The fact that Adam and I were experienced fisherman helped us. We both borrowed the fishing expression from Jon Hyde "on any given cast" and applied it to dating. And as anglers we were quite familiar with having our offerings rejected. To help us through the rebuffs, the near-misses, and the flat-out disasters we added a second term to our dating jargon, and that was, "Next." We told each other just move on, and keep hunting, the way we did for stripers.

Employing fishing tactics helped us keep our eyes on the prize. For example, many times on the *Scout* we found blitzing fish, but they were all small schoolies. One of us would invariably say, it was time to move on and find bigger fish, even though some anglers say never leave fish to find fish. But we did. And so it was with dating, we had to leave some nice schoolies and gamble that we could find a keeper, but it would involve considerable time, effort, and energy.

On the boat we'd compare dating notes, and realized that we made a few of the same mental mistakes when we first started fishing. Sometimes we tried to set the hook too early and other times we scared off a potential keeper by roaring in too fast. Some keepers can be skittish, and I remember saying to Adam, that on my next date I'll slow my motor down and drift a little more to let the fish come to me. That approach, however, was easier said than done for an impatient guy like me. I was all for finding out quickly if the potential keeper was really worth the effort. And so my method—a bit different than Adam's—was to cut out as much wasted time as possible. Online dating can facilitate that approach through the screening method. I followed what I thought was a logical procedure.

1. Look at the woman's photos (yes, I know that seems shallow, but I'm just being honest).

2. See if we had common interests. For me, being fit and loving the outdoors were essential, and I searched for those key words.

3. Exchange a message. Notice I say "a" message. Here is where I differed from most people. I was not looking for a pen pal. Back in 2010 I didn't even text, and if I did I would have skipped that dance. Instead, if the woman responded to my message positively, I'd say let's talk by phone and maybe we can set up a time to meet. Talking by phone can yield some good intelligence, and I often found it a

useful tool for screening out someone who . . . how do I say it? . . . was crazy!

4. Be efficient. Here again I took a different approach than many men. I learned not to invite the woman on a traditional date, because if you are a polite person, as I think I strive to be, you can be trapped with someone for a couple hours knowing the whole time it could never work. My first couple dates I took to dinner, and I had the same feeling I had the day Adam and I got the *Scout* stuck on the sandbar and had to wait two hours for high tide. So, learning from these experiences, all future first meetings (I'd call them interviews, not dates) would occur at a coffee shop. That way she or I could politely leave any time after the coffee was finished—about a half hour. This method not only avoided the sand bar hazard, but it was also a heck of a lot more cost effective than buying dinner and drinks.

5. If the coffee went well we would plan a date. Often it involved a bike ride or a walk and then out to dinner. During that time I'd let my date know that I was an independent, restless soul who was often away on fishing trips or at my cabin in Vermont. I knew that would be an issue for some women seeking steady companionship, so I figured it best to be up front about it. (In the spirit of full disclosure, I did shave a couple years off my age on my profile. I wasn't fooling anyone however, because they could easily find out my true age by Googling and finding me as a published author.)

Adam and I had certain advantages and disadvantages in the online dating world. A real strength is that we could not only spell, but we could also actually write. Our profiles looked good, and we made suggestions on each other's. I still have my write-up, and I think it was straight and to the point of who I was and what I was looking for. Near the end of the profile I wrote, "I'm looking for someone who is active, in good shape, has an adventurous spirit, and enjoys laughing at the silly things. Chemistry can't be explained, but it's either there or it's not, and you usually know it pretty quick."

Chemistry is something scrolling through online dating profiles will never uncover. Reading about someone or viewing pictures is never enough. You have to be with the person and then see how you *feel.* In my dating experience I *liked* almost every woman I met, but the mysterious chemistry only surfaced a couple times. What is chemistry? I don't really know except it includes both a physical and mental attraction resulting in both people feeling happy when together. It sounds like such a match would be easy to discover, but it's not.

Even when I did find someone with whom I thought the chemistry might work, I quickly learned many dates were like walking through a minefield; one misstep and I could blow the blossoming relationship to smithereens. One woman told me I was too forward—after she started talking about sex in the middle of dinner! Stupid me, I thought that was a hint. Another woman whom I dated several times got angry when I sent an old-fashioned card sealed in an envelope to her home address. She said it upset her pre-teen daughter. Stupid me, I should have been clairvoyant.

I always recovered quickly from these failures, however, because I tried to think of myself as a manuscript that I was shopping to publishers. I could send my manuscript (similar to a dating profile) to forty publishers, and get rejection after rejection, because personal taste is so subjective. But how many publishers does a writer need for his book? That's right, just one.

Ironically enough, the online dating website I used was Plenty of Fish. I chose this on the recommendation of my dental hygienist who said she met her husband there. But I viewed Plenty of Fish as a place to get started, to practice, figuring later I'd move on to Match or EHarmony, the two bigger sites people over forty used the most. On some of my dates, however, I learned that many of the women kept a profile on both Plenty of Fish and one of the other sites too. I also understood that certain pictures of women were red flags. I share these thoughts with prospective daters:

1. Don't date a woman whose main profile picture is of her and her horse. You will hear about that horse nonstop until the only way you want to see the beast is in a can of dog food.

2. Don't date a woman whose main profile picture is of her and her motorcycle. Same reason as the horse (minus the can of dog food).

3. Don't date a woman whose pictures show her scantily clad or posing too provocatively. Something is usually wrong.

And in the interest of helping men who find themselves suddenly thrust into the dating scene here are two "don'ts" for fellow anglers:

1. Don't use a profile picture of you holding up a big fish. No matter how proud you are, most women do not find it appealing. I know, I asked. I also asked women what about a man showing a picture of himself bare-chested. The overwhelming answer was "Don't post it . . .

2. Don't set up a date right after you go fishing. I tried that in Vermont after fishing a river in spring. I was a sweaty, smelly mess but the river was too cold to jump in. I did have a change of clothes, but it was me who smelled. I went to a gas station, bought a couple gallons of water and poured them over my head out in the parking lot. What do you think the odds are that the woman I was going to meet drove by at that very moment? Not long enough. "No that, wasn't me at the gas station . . ."

Adam was the smoother dater between us. I can illustrate by describing our separate dates. One evening, when Adam had custody of his kids, I was at his house when he realized he had mistakenly set up a date on the same night. I loved his kids Miki and Jack, and had spent countless hours with them on the *Scout*, so it was easy for me to offer to hang out with them and make sure they went to bed on time. Adam took me up on his offer. He quickly showered and put on some freshly dry-cleaned clothes and a sport coat. Then he said, "I've got to leave soon because I'm stopping at a friend's house to use his Corvette, and then I need to get flowers for my new girlfriend."

That night got me thinking: sport coat, flowers, Corvette. I was going on my dates in my usual blue khakis, sans flowers, and in a Honda CRV. On one of my dates, I was in my car and the woman surprised me by kissing me. Then she looked in the back of the car where I had all manner of gear—from fishing equipment, to food, to a new comforter. She said, "How are you going to get me in the back seat when it's covered with all that crap?" That line didn't bother me, but the next one did: "Don't tell me you're sleeping in your car after you do those book talks . . . And it looks like you're subsisting on nothing but Snickers and peanuts. You poor thing, I'll take care of you."

I did clean up my car after that. On another date with someone I really liked, the incident in question was not entirely my fault. We were biking on the Cape Cod Canal when blood started dripping from my neck. I kid you not. I had nicked myself shaving in the morning and there was lots of blood but it soon stopped and I covered it with a small bandage. But now on the bike path, the blood was really flowing and my shirt was a mess. The woman I was with sprang into action and said, "I've got to get you a big bandage." We were biking by one of the campgrounds adjacent to the canal and God bless her, she rode into that campground and found people at an RV who had a big piece of gauze and bandages. She applied them to my cut, but still the blood oozed out. "I'll find some surgical tape," she said, and back she went into the camping ground. She returned in a flash, but instead of surgical tape she had silver duct tape. "It's the best I could do," she said, "and you're bleeding like a stuck pig."

And so I biked the rest of the canal with duct tape wrapped around my neck, unable to turn or twist my head. I'm surprised someone didn't come up to me and say, "There's an easier way, you could have jumped off one of these canal bridges or just taken sleeping pills."

Both the woman who thought I slept in my car and the one who biked on the canal were special people, whom I kept in touch with and if they read this, I know they will laugh. Both had a great sense of humor, but for one reason or another it wasn't meant to be.

I did take a couple dates fishing, but that was a bad idea. I felt the pressure a guide must feel when they really want to put their "client" on some fish. Shore fishing is hit or miss, and without the advantage of a boat those trips were more "the walk along the beach" type than real fishing. The experience was the same as when I'd take my son and his friends fishing—I'd try every trick in the book to get the kids onto fish but time and again we would come up fishless. I'm sure those two women I took fishing couldn't understand why I was an avid angler after those boring, fruitless afternoons of casting into the sea.

When Adam and I compared notes while fishing on the *Scout*, one common theme emerged. We may not be Prince Charmings, but much of our competition was pitiful. Women would tell us stories of ex-husbands who wanted nothing more to do with their own kids, failed to pay child support, or who only worked sporadically and the rest of the time lay on their couches watching sports. One woman told me that before our date she made arrangements to drop her kids off at her ex's. When she arrived, he said with all seriousness, "There's one thing I forgot to tell you. My rate is $15 an hour, and I'm deducting it from your child support."

The stories women told me about some of their earlier dates were even worse. One described how she went out on a date and things went fairly well. She considered seeing the man again—until she turned on her phone the next morning. The guy had sent her a text with a photo of his private parts. What a way to wake up.

Another woman told me that she and her date were at a restaurant, and a friend of the man's came up and said, "Thank you for that great stock tip." The woman thought nothing of it, but through the course of the evening different friends stopped by, saying, "Nice home run at the softball game," and another, "Thanks for taking us on that great vacation to the Bahamas." The woman wasn't stupid and could see the whole thing was a setup designed to make the guy look like he was something special when he probably lived in his mother's basement. And of course there were the all-too-familiar stories of men saying crap like "I bought you dinner, the least you can do . . ." or "Let me show you how happy I am."

Rule number one for men should be very simple. Show respect and courtesy.

Chapter 19

***

So at the end of my first year of dating, I had gone on no fewer than seventy meet-and-greet coffees. I was fifty-five years old and about to close my Plenty of Fish account for a while because the "part-time job" was wearing me down. Then someone reached out to me—which was a pleasant surprise in itself—and we hit it off for awhile. The first person I told was Adam, and the second was my eighty-year-old dad who was hard of hearing. I called my dad on the phone and said, "Well, after seventy dates I finally met someone who I think is special."

His response? "What? She's seventy! Wow isn't that a little old for you. But that's okay, it's all about the personality."

I think it took me three calls before he understood the seventy did not refer to age.

CHAPTER 20

Catch and Release

AG

As noted, fish often arrive boat-side tired from fighting against what is undoubtedly to them an incomprehensible force that pulled them into a hostile, alien environment in which they cannot breathe. As if that were not traumatic enough, fish also have a protective, mucus-like film over them that when rubbed off can make them vulnerable to all sorts of illnesses. Fish also often suffer from different forms of rough handling by anglers, including being dropped against unforgiving decks, bounced off the sides of the boats, being tangled in nets, having hooks removed in sometimes brutal fashions, and the list goes on.

In catch and releasing a fish as humanely as possible, it is critical to limit its time out of the water. The state of Massachusetts recommends using a dehooker tool that essentially twists the hook upside-down, so the fish's own body weight dislodges the hook, ideally resulting in the fish falling gently back into the water from a low height, perhaps even while still partially in the water. Mike and I have only tried dehookers with stripers a few times and didn't particularly favor them. Neither of us know other striper anglers who use them. I prefer to land stripers by hand, usually by sticking my thumb in their mouths and then lifting them out of the water by their bottom lip. I then quickly remove the hook with my free hand and—unless keeping the fish—put it gently back in. Except for situations where the fish is seriously injured by an unfortunate hook placement, the vast majority of stripers Mike and I have caught swam off energetically. This situation changed for me somewhat in 2016, when I finally sold the *Scout* and joined the Freedom Boat Club. Although it's not for every fisherman, this boat-sharing organization works great for me. I do recommend it, depending on one's circumstances and needs. Boats in the club are typically larger than the *Scout* (often twenty-one feet or twenty-three feet long, rather than the eighteen-foot *Scout*) with gunnels that are considerably higher above the water. Subsequently, both Mike and I have been using a long-handled net to help us boat fish. We specifically use nets with rubber-coated mesh, because they are less abrasive to the fish's skin than nets without it.

Mike did a lot of catching and releasing one unforgettable trip the spring after our Bahamas vacation. It was at a time that I was still struggling to adjust to divorced life, but at a point that he had become somewhat seasoned in the dating game, as his divorce had taken place nearly a year before mine. The *Scout* was at full capacity that day with Mike and me, my two kids, ages ten and seven, as well as Mike's newest girlfriend. I certainly would not have admitted it to him, or probably even to myself, but I was envious for at least a couple of reasons. First, although he is twelve years older than me, his date was my age. I was still brand new to divorced life and confused as to why Mike was having such success meeting prospective partners, while I was still "striking out" regularly. The bigger reason I was jealous would be immediately apparent to anyone who has ever brought elementary-school-aged children fishing. By definition, I was not actually going fishing. I was "spending quality time" with my kids. In short, while Mike was on a bona-fide flats fishing trip with an attractive date, I was parenting.

After some scouting, we arrived at one of our favorite spots just after high tide.

"There are fish here," I said, noticing a very large shadow move along the edge of a nearby weed bed in about eight feet of water.

"Oh my," Mike stage whispered to the boat. "I just saw a whopper!"

I soon set the *Scout* up on a drift that would bring us slowly across the area, port first, allowing us to cast off that side in the direction of the fish. This allowed three or even four of us to throw simultaneously. Mike and his girlfriend began taking casts with topwater lures from the bow area. Meanwhile, my daughter Miki cast off the stern, while my son Jack sat next to me.

I saw a swirl behind Mike's very first retrieve. He instantly stopped his return and dropped the tip of his rod, allowing the lure to float in place a couple of long seconds. We both had learned to do this with stripers, as they often swipe at lures first with the sides of their bodies, probably to stun what they perceive as prey, before returning to consume it open-mouthed. Mike's lure was a good twenty yards from us when it vanished below a tiny splash. He instantly raised his tip to set his hook, and his reel started singing happily.

"Yes!"

The boat went silent. The four of us watched Mike fight what was obviously a big keeper for the better part of ten minutes. When he finally hauled it onboard, it was nearly as long and as heavy as Jack. It was the largest either of us had seen since the previous fishing season—not counting the sharks we swam with in the Bahamas.

Mike hefted it high for his girlfriend to inspect.

"Wow!" She declared and smiled admiringly at him.

"Okay, put it in the cooler," I said flatly.

For the next couple of hours I grew increasingly jealous, as Mike established himself as the undisputed hero of the *Scout*, landing monster striper after monster striper, catching and releasing many, while keeping a couple of beauties. It was one of the best days of fishing of Mike's life.

In the meantime, try as I might, I couldn't coach my kids into hooking a schoolie. Between my untangling their lines, refastening their lures, offering instructions, doling out snacks and drinks and lunch, and captaining the *Scout*, I barely squeezed in a handful of casts of my own, all returned without a bite. Lady luck was all Mike's that day, and she didn't give me the slightest glance.

There was one moment when I felt the urge to renounce my parental duties, ignore Miki and Jack, and get in on Mike's epic day. I wanted nothing more than to throw a temper tantrum and insist that Mike and his now most unagreeable (to my mind) girlfriend help my kids with their fishing, so I could fish too. Thankfully for my kids, for me, for Mike, and for the blossoming romance in the boat, I thought better of it. I couldn't articulate my feelings, but by the end of the trip a certain alteration had begun to creep in over me, like a steadily rising tide over a parched sandbar. Despite my frustrations, it was the first time I had gone fishing in my life with a greater emphasis on getting my passengers into fish than catching them myself. I was growing up a little.

Now, I don't want to make too close a comparison between fishing and romance (women are not fish!), but as was the case with Mike, fishing unquestionably helped me learn how to date.

My first breakthrough came the day after the above-mentioned trip. I was standing in line at the local post office when an attractive woman in the line to my right turned her head and looked at me and smiled at me, or at least I thought she did. I was still so emotionally needy back then that my heart nearly took wing and soared out of my mouth.

"This could be the one," I thought dreamily.

My mind raced for something to say to her. "What can I say? What can I say?" But I couldn't answer myself. Several frustrating minutes crept by. Then I watched her pay for her postage, turn around, and—without giving me a second glance—walk out the door and, as I thought melodramatically "out of my life forever."

I had been married since college, so I had no actual experience dating actual adult women. To make matters worse, the circles of my life were small and did not put me in touch with many single females. My intense frustration reminded me of the first season Mike and I fished from the *Scout*, not knowing what we were doing and regularly getting skunked. In a flash I recalled that the key to improving our fishing had been our hiring Jon Hyde the fishing guide.

It may sound outrageous, but I decided to look for a "dating guide." I figured if it worked for fishing, why not for romance?

Sure enough, a few Googles later, and right there on my computer screen was the number of a handsome guy who billed himself as a professional dating coach. I gave him a call, and to my surprise he answered on the second ring. What convinced me to hire him was that rather than telling me about pickup lines or other techniques, he emphasized that he had a principle-based approach where I just had to learn to be my best self.

We soon met in a hotel lobby in New York City, where I travelled regularly for publishing. There he explained something extremely rudimentary that simply had never occurred to inexperienced me. When out at a club or at a bar or other known singles place, the vast majority of women were there for the very same reason I was: because they want to meet someone.

"If it were just to hang out with their friends, there are more entertaining activities than a loud, expensive nightclub," he said. "Let's face it, most aren't here to drink either. It's way cheaper to drink at home. If they weren't at least casually interested in meeting someone, few would go to all the trouble of dressing up, going out, and paying cover fees."

Again, this was not a profound observation. It had simply never occurred to long-time-married me. In my mind things were far more convoluted. On some level I imagined men had to somehow manipulate circumstances to get women interested in them.

I had a similar realization in the early years of my striped bass and blues fishing, which also had been a mystery to me. I thought anglers had to possess some kind of mysterious skills to hook a very big fish. The fact is that most striped bass and bluefish spend the majority of their time hunting for food. Even when they aren't hunting, if a good opportunity is presented, they will often eat anyway. An angler's task is simply to find fish and then offer them a presentable target. Now, in seeking a relationship, it was my challenge to get in harmony with a new environment and make myself as presentable as possible.

Actually, Mike had dramatized this for me with his own quest for a partner after his divorce. I had noticed that Mike never pretended to be someone he was not. For example, he usually suggested they do things he naturally enjoyed, such as going for walks or bike rides.

Of course, this novel new idea, that single women are often seeking partners themselves, also implies a very simple rule that for some reason had never been obvious to me either. I had to go where single women were. I had never enjoyed clubs or dancing or bars. Now that I wasn't drinking alcohol, they were even less appealing. But my guide pointed out that those are the places where single women congregate. If I wanted to become comfortable talking and interacting with women, I had to go where they were. "Duh," I thought. Waiting to bump into someone at the post office wasn't exactly playing the odds. We soon identified other places such as art openings, coffee houses, parties, and—of course—online dating websites.

Mike and I had learned the same fishing: go where the fish are. We even coined a phrase to counteract our tendency to fish unproductively in the same places for far too long, "We have the boat for a reason." That of course, is to get us where the fish are likely to be, not to stay where they aren't.

My great friend Alan Brown put it a little differently: "You can't catch what's not in the water."

A corollary lesson, which Mike has noted, is that even when catching a lot of small fish, you still sometimes need to leave them in order to catch a keeper.

When I told my guide the story of my having been completely tongue-tied at the post office, he offered another lesson that coincided with fishing. "Seize the moment." It's very common to motor up to fish that are feeding on the surface. At such times, it's often critical to *immediately* cast into them, because they frequently disperse quickly. Either they realize there is a boat nearby and feel uncomfortable, or the conditions just shift and they move on. I've often seen inexperienced anglers fritter such opportunities away. When the boat stops, they take their time assessing the situation. They look around for their rod, get hold of it, prepare it, adjust their stance, and only then cast. In the same time period, I've witnessed efficient anglers—my cousin Donny, a truly gifted fisherman, comes to mind—cast and retrieve not just once but sometimes even twice or three times. Such anglers often land fish before slower ones get their lines wet. There is a direct correlation between the number of casts made and the number of fish caught.

My coach explained further, "Look, most women don't just go around looking unknown men in their eyes and smiling at them. If they did, they'd probably be bothered by all sorts of guys they don't want around. So, if a woman in a club or similar environment makes direct eye contact and smiles, she's probably intentionally sending the signal that she is interested. If she does this, you've probably got a 90-percent chance of being able to strike up a conversation with her. Every minute you let pass after she smiles at you, your chances are halved. Think about it, if she went to the effort and took the risk to send the signal, and you ignore it, or if you take a long time, you are sending back a negative signal. Seize the moment."

I have also seen many anglers (especially new ones) panic in the presence of feeding fish. We've all done it. We fail to open our bailers, we throw our lure ineffectively to the wrong spot, or we hook something on the boat with our back cast (such as the time I hooked the raised engine behind me on my back-cast and then fell in the water trying to get it unhooked). Panic creates all sorts of trouble. Probably one of the primary skills of good fishing is the ability to remain composed.

Through steady practice, I was soon able to confidently approach women and strike up casual conversations. For example, I remember being in a music venue in New York's East Village. Against all my natural instincts, I walked over to a table of six attractive women and successfully started a conversation that lasted a while and even included a couple laughs. I didn't ever see any of them again, but I enjoyed talking with them. Interestingly, not fifteen minutes later a different woman in the place approached me.

Another important detail is that presentation is everything. For an outdoor and formerly longtime married man like me, who has never been focused on my looks, this was something to consider. The fact is most women are turned off by unkempt, sloppy guys. This means taking care of one's fingernails, hair, dental hygiene, going to the doctor regularly, and staying in reasonably good shape. In fishing terms, few anglers are going to land trophy fish with rusted hooks or ratty fishing lines, never mind a faulty reel or rod, or old smelly bait.

This brings me to what I knew was my Achilles heel: smiling, or in my case, lack of smiling. Having gone through the challenging times already mentioned, I had become way too serious.

"Smile. Smile. Smile," my coach insisted.

My smile was so rare that he eventually put it this way, "I want you to smile so often and so hard, that you feel like a complete fool. Then, Adam, you'll probably be smiling as much as an average person."

In the years that followed, the power (and pleasure) of smiling has amazed me. The way smiling affects my children and their friends, business colleagues, even strangers, continues to impress. A simple smile has the power to set everyone at ease. I feel a little embarrassed to admit this, but I spent a number of sessions back then practicing smiling. Readers should give it a try. Plaster a big fat smile on your face, no matter how inauthentic it might feel. Now hold it for two minutes, and while doing so try to feel depressed. It's almost impossible.

This brings me to my favorite lesson from my guide: "Wherever you are, you need to be your own good time." The concept of going out in the world to seek a new partner who would help me have a good time, or who might make me happy, had to be smashed. I needed to learn to enjoy being me, even if I didn't meet anyone special on a given day, month, or year.

Without my knowing it, fishing had been imparting the same lesson.

"I have to catch a fish. I have to catch a fish," had been an inner mantra. But that meant I had to catch a fish in order to be happy—obviously not a great way to fish, or live. Put another way, you cannot control what you catch. You can only control how you fish. Today, I have a blast when fishing, whether catching them or not. I'm almost always grateful to be on the water, regardless of the outcome. Oddly enough, I'm sure that has increased my productivity as well. I'm more relaxed and thus more likely to be in the right place at the right time, doing the right things.

Another fishing friend of mine named Larry (more about him later) passed on some wise words to me from Oscar Wilde, "To love yourself is the beginning of a lifelong romance."

This brings up yet another similarity between fishing and seeking romance. It happens far too often while fishing that out of nowhere a big fish hits an angler's line, gets the angler excited but then spits out the hook and disappears. Nowadays, in dating, they call this being ghosted. An attractive woman seems interested and genuine, but then without any explanation, she just stops returning calls, texts, and emails. When this first happened to Mike and me, we would ask each other, "What do you think? She suddenly stopped returning my calls. Should I try again?"

We'd then encourage one another, "Keep calling her," or "Text her again. Maybe she just didn't get your message."

Eventually we learned better. One of us asked the other, "If you were Brad Pitt what would the chances be of her missing your message?" The answer was obvious: "Zero."

Mike and I learned that when we were ghosted, it was simply because the woman decided she wasn't interested. In other words, we had been "caught and released" ourselves.

And this is an area where fishing and dating are also similar. Both activities are about interacting in meaningful ways with other living beings. (I know, "women are not fish," but just bear with me here.) The best anglers I've been with always treat their catch respectfully. There's something about the way they get a fish back into the water that communicates profound respect.

Of course, my dating coach emphasized the critical importance of interacting with everyone with kindness and consideration, including people I was not interested in romantically. I'm not saying that every woman I met during the seven years after my divorce and prior to my meeting my current wife would say I treated them perfectly. Dating is not an easy activity. But I do know that I tried my best to lead with respect and kindness.

And how did I finally meet my new wife? It wasn't at a bar or restaurant or even through a website. I met her through a chance encounter, through friends of friends. By then it had been many years since I had seen my coach. Yet I had learned to feel relaxed and be to my own good time, to look presentable and to seize the moment . . . even to smile as much as an average person.

CHAPTER 21

Sharing the Water

MT

I've described some bad trips where we were at fault, but there were some when another boater soured our outing. Some boaters simply have no etiquette when it comes to fishing. Imagine you have spent the day searching for fish on the surface, scanning the horizon for birds or "nervous" water, and after hours you finally come upon bass slashing the surface to a froth with a handful of terns hovering above them. You slow down, determine which way the breeze is blowing, and carefully position your vessel up wind of the pod of fish, making sure to stay a good seventy-five yards away so as not to spook them. You shut the motor off, and let the breeze carry you toward the feeding fish—a sight you dream about. Just as you are about to cast you hear the rumble of an approaching boat, going full throttle. Those boaters have seen the same commotion. But instead of slowing down and circling the school of fish, they blast right up to the mix, with anglers casting while the boat is still moving.

The fish are gone in an instant, put down by the roar of the motor and then by the vessel itself. That happens all too often. In some instances I'll throw my hands up to let the other boater know they just scattered the fish, other times Adam and I just sit down, wait for the other boat to leave and hope that by us being still the fish will regroup and pop back up somewhere within sight.

A blitz on the surface can happen frequently some days, or not at all, depending on the bait in the area. Knowledgeable anglers know that when this occurs, sometimes the really big bass are below the fish on the surface, lazily picking off bait that is wounded and fluttering downward. So fisherman going after size will bypass the top-water lures that the smaller bass or bluefish will hit, and send their offering down deep, perhaps along the edge of the frenzy. I've done that with mixed results, but over the years I've come to realize that sometimes I'd rather catch a smaller fish on the surface where you can often see the strike or swirl, than get a bigger fish on the bottom with a slow retrieve. It's the same thinking when I use a fly-rod. Every angler has their own preference. But the key for all anglers is DON'T DRIVE THE FEEDING FISH AWAY.

On the flip side of the coin, I've seen some boaters act like they own a mass of feeding fish, and no other boaters are allowed in on the action. I've seen the commercial fishermen in Florida, targeting Spanish mackerel, think they can intimidate all other boaters from feeding fish. I understand these commercial guys are chumming and that keeps the fish near their boat, and they don't want an interloper catching fish that have come to their chum. But sometimes they go too far and act like they own an area as big as the state of Rhode Island.

There's a happy medium and it's called respect. Keep your distance from other boats, don't go racing into feeding fish, but don't act like feeding fish are yours and yours alone. I'm happy to say the vast majority of fisherman are not only courteous, but also helpful.

I still remember the day I was fishing a stream in Montana and covered a good portion of it with a small wet fly without a single strike. The setting was spectacular, so different than the way a western writer—whose name escapes me—described the New England woods as feeling he was in a salad bowl. Here was a crystal clear, deep flowing stream, with a mix of meadow, some arid rocky patches and timber nearby, while framing the scene were jagged mountains rising in the distance. I remember thinking this really is big sky country, incredibly majestic, even if I couldn't catch a single trout. Then I saw two anglers coming toward me from the opposite direction and they literally caught a fish on every cast. They used a leapfrog approach each giving the other one little section of pocket water. When they came to the spot I had just worked I figured any trout would have been spooked by me, but I still wanted to watch their technique so I sat on a rock and observed. They immediately caught two fat trout in the very pool I thought was either devoid of fish or spooked.

The two anglers asked how I had done, and I said not even a strike. They were from France, and one of them, with a thick accent, said, "Come on over." I crossed the stream, said hello, and he showed me the fly at the end of his line. It was a microscopic nymph. He then said, "Hold out your hand" and he gave me two of the nymphs. It was a wonderful gesture.

Now to make this story complete, I'd like to say I then caught trout after trout, but I continued to be skunked. They were simply the better anglers. Maybe I was rushing. The light was fading and I only fished for a few minutes, knowing I had a long walk back to the car. And because I was in grizzly bear country, my car held more appeal than trout.

But every now and then you get anglers who are the exact opposite of the Frenchmen. I don't flyfish on the ocean very much, and I recall walking to where a creek met the sea and asked two fly-fishermen if the fish were biting. They looked at me a half second, glanced at my spinning rod, and didn't even bother to answer. Just to make sure they heard me, I walked up to one of the men and said, "Any luck?" This time he didn't even bother to look at me but continued his casts.

I'd like to say I walked down a few yards and made a long cast with my spinning rod and hooked into a monster fish. And . . . that is exactly what happened! The two rude fisherman paused their casting to watch. This fish was a brute, and it must have taken me a good ten minutes to get it into the surf. For a moment I couldn't feel his weight anymore and feared the bass used its tail on the sand to shake the hook as has happened to me before. But the fishing gods were good to me, and the bass finally got close enough for me to grab. He was all of forty-two inches. The two anglers left without a word. Man, did I feel great.

The Frenchmen, friendly and helpful, or the saltwater fishermen rude and cold—which do you want to be? I know I want to be helpful. The older I get the more I realize that is part of the beauty of the sport; anglers wanting other anglers to enjoy the day, the setting, and the peace that comes from being on or near the water.

Chapter 21

***

Thinking about the Frenchmen on that Montana stream makes me pause and consider some similarities and differences between my fifty-five-year quest for trout and my shorter twenty-year passion for stripers. Some anglers only do one or the other, but they are not so very different.

Hunting for stripers on the shallows of the flats has some similarities with stalking brook trout on streams in Vermont. Stealth and proper casting skills are necessary—you can't just race up to a pod of stripers in your boat and start flailing away, nor can you clomp down the middle of a trout stream and expect any fish with half a brain to not be hiding. When Adam and I are on the *Scout* in fishy water, a slow advance, or better yet a drift, will get us in position, then we'll cast to the outside edge of the striper pods so as not to spook them. The same is true with the trout on a narrow stream running through forest. You want to approach the potential trout holding spots slowly, wading one careful foot at a time heading upstream. When you see riffles moving into deeper water or into a tangle of roots, you should freeze and think about the cast you want to make. Where should your fly or lure land? How can you get a bit closer without alerting the fish to your presence? All these thoughts go through your mind in a flash whether stalking trout or stripers in shallow water.

There may, however, be more differences than similarities in transitioning from stripers to trout. On a morning in early June, I recently fished a stream in Vermont four feet wide with a couple pools about two feet deep. Trees formed a canopy overhead. Wading the stream was like moving through a tunnel of green, crowding the slate-gray ribbon of water. This was a quieter kind of hunting, quite different than standing on the cooler of Adam's boat scouting for stripers with the low drone of the motor humming. Fallen trees crossed the stream and branches made casting difficult. Rather than seeing a school of stripers and casting toward them, this stream required pinpoint casting, which in turn caused more than a few casts to get hung up in a branch.

Some people might wonder how I could get excited over trout that rarely reach more than ten inches long when Adam and I had been catching bass up to four times that length just a week earlier. It's the setting. The size of the fish is in proportion to the body of water, and instead of an endless ocean, the stream in the forest was intimate. Any trout above six inches would be a victory. At sixty-five years old, I still get a kick out of locating and stalking native brook trout of any size.

Few people fish streams this size anymore. Kids are too busy on their phones and involved in organized activities, and fly-fishermen have no room to cast. In forty years of fishing this stream I've yet to see another angler, footprint, or any evidence that it was of interest to fishermen. That was fine with me, and good news for the native brook trout that lay unseen under roots or log jams.

When I work this stream I always move against the current because resting trout have their heads pointed upstream and I'd be approaching from their one blind spot, the rear. And by wading upstream any debris I accidently kick up would be carried downstream away from the fish I was hopefully sneaking up on. If I do catch a fish, it is less likely to spook fish upstream in the direction I'm moving. I've experimented with every lure on the planet and my lure of choice is the Panther Martin. The little concave blade puts out a vibration and keeps a tight spin that trout can't resist.

Alone in such a quiet setting, I lost myself in the hunt, becoming one more predator on the stream, no different than the otter, raccoon, or mink, whose footprints I saw in a muddy bank. I lacked their dexterity however, and at one point, when I was up on the bank scouting a pool, I forgot to look where I was going and felt myself falling. This has happened to me so many times, I have a routine that usually saves me and my equipment from harm. I automatically throw my rod to the side as I feel myself going down, and then try to twist my body so that I fall backward onto my ass. On this fall I landed in a three-foot ravine, and luckily my butt hit dirt rather than rock.

After the tumble, the morning continued to be frustrating. My little ultralight rod and two pound test line was giving me a headache, with the bail sometimes closing on its own during the casting. A smattering of black flies also harassed me, but at least did not bite thanks to the bug dope I'd smeared on.

The stream was clear from lack of rain the week before, but that made the trout skittish. Little ones of four and five inches would hit the lure, but the bigger fish would dart out for a look and either not strike, or strike and get off with a quick shake of their head. I caught one fish of seven inches, but the bigger ones came out from their lair, swiped at the lure, then retreated, not to be fooled again. After walking over a mile, sweat dripping from my forehead, I bushwhacked back to my car, with little to show for two hours of hunting.

As I was driving back to my cabin I passed a lake and then a bridge over the stream, remembering how years ago I once caught a brown trout here during the height of summer. The trout likely came out of the lake to seek the cooler water of the stream or maybe to be first in line for the insects the stream carried toward the lake.

Maybe, now in June, another brown might be feeding here, or perhaps a rainbow had entered little stream ready to spawn. I hit the brakes and pulled over.

The only way to get to the spot where I caught the trout—without going through an alder thicket that looked impenetrable—was to follow the stream through the culvert that carried it under the road. This metal cylinder was about five feet high, and I had to walk hunched over. I'd be moving with the current and any trout at the end of the culvert might see me coming, so I had to be extra careful. When I could see the little pool outside the other end of the culvert, I crouched down into a squatting position and made my cast. Nothing hit my lure. I'd learned that usually the first cast is your best shot at catching a trout in a confined space so my second cast was a half-hearted one that barely cleared the end of the culvert.

The trout grabbed the lure as soon as it hit the water. It felt heavy and I worried my two pound test might break as it first ran downstream a few feet and then back upstream and dogged down in the deepest section of the pool. I talk to myself while trout fishing and whispered, *Don't force it*. I moved to the end of the culvert, careful to keep tension on my line. That's when I realized the predicament I was in. The pool was a deep one, probably four feet deep and water from the culvert cascaded into it, dropping down about a foot. A log lay across the waterfall. There was no way I could horse the trout over the log and waterfall without breaking my line, and it was impossible to enter the pool without either falling or having water up to my chest which would have filled my hip waders.

You're going to have to try and fling it onto the side of the stream. I figured that was my only option and once the trout was on land I'd go back through the culvert, lay my rod down and then cross the road and force my way through the alders to either get the fish or release it.

It was a good plan, but it didn't work. When I tried to fling the trout onto the shore my yank put the fish in a branch directly above the pool, where it squirmed wildly. The trout was a big one and I was amazed my line didn't snap.

I had a net with me and tried to reach the struggling fish but came up short. The trout was wiggling every which way and any second would free itself or snap the line. I had to act fast. I put my left hand on the top of the culvert and then leaned over the pool with my right arm extending the net. It was a recipe for falling headfirst into the pool, but I was able to scoop the trout into the net, pull it toward me, and break off the branch. The trout was mine. It was a brown trout, all of thirteen inches in length, but for that little stream it was one of the biggest I'd ever caught.

This tale of the stream illustrates the similarities and differences between fishing for trout on a stream and stripers on the ocean. My big takeaway is to approach fish slowly—you have better luck, you don't upset other anglers who might be working the same area, and you appreciate your surroundings, whether on a tiny brook in the hills or on the seemingly endless sea.

But no matter how many years I fish with Adam, I doubt we'll ever catch a striper inside a culvert.

CHAPTER 22

The Finest Hours

AG

My first season of striped bass fishing came in my mid-twenties, years before meeting Mike. At the time I worked as a full-time freelance shell-fisher in Nauset Marsh in Eastham, digging soft-shell steamer clams out of the mud with a short-handled, long-tined rake. It was hard work, the word backbreaking comes to mind, because it meant being bent over from the waist down for hours. It seemed well worth it at the time though to make a living in a place that was only exposed at low tide and that was submerged the other half of the time.

My hands and feet sunk into the saltwater mud where they rubbed up against seaweed and seaworms, and where the infinite sky expanded over my head, the fresh salt air abounding. The pungent smells of low tide. Snowy egrets. Great blue herons. Herring and blackback seagulls. Terns. Sandpipers. Plovers. Healthy human bodies, especially those in their twenties, require exercise. They long for intense exertion. Mine did.

As I mentioned briefly, my Uncle Billy had also worked as a shell fisherman on the Cape. That was two decades before me, when he too was in his twenties. Unlike me, he harvested quahogs, which required the use of a long-handled, short-tined rake. Quahog clamming had him standing upright in the water. He tossed his rake out directly in front and then pulled it back along the ocean floor, gathering them toward him. Uncle Billy often talked of an old-timer he clammed with named Walter.

Walter gave him all sorts of advice but especially cheered him on with the words, "Pick up the clams, boy. Pick up the clams."

"You know the legends of various cities where the streets are paved with gold?" Uncle Billy asked me when he rode in my car, teaching me how to sell books to retailers. "It's like that with the waters around Cape Cod, only they aren't paved with gold, they are seeded with clams. All you have to do is pick 'em up. There's money lying all around us. Pick up the clams, boy."

Uncle Billy smiled as he encourage me to "go on into that bookstore there and introduce yourself. You are in the business of making friends. They probably want nothing more than to make a new friend today." I can hear him now, "There is wealth all over these streets, Adam. It's everywhere. Pick up the clams."

Of course it wasn't half as easy as my uncle made it out. There were many long days of difficult sales where finding the owner or manager of a store was next to impossible, or if I did track them down, they simply weren't interested. What he was trying to teach me was an attitude not only of gratitude, but of plentitude. He was asserting that the universe teems with resources, and that each one of us is an integral aspect of that universe with access to it all.

During my first full season of clamming, I started meeting enthusiastic guys at the boat landing heading out and returning from striper and blues fishing. Neither my Old Town canoe, nor the motorized skiff I eventually upgraded to, were substantial enough for boat fishing off the backside of the Cape. But they were more than enough get me from the landing to the clam flats of Nauset Marsh and from there to the outer beach. There I started surfcasting from shore. I typically went once or twice a week that first summer. Not having any idea what I was doing, I didn't catch my first keeper until the evening of my birthday at the very end of August. I landed two thirty-inchers, one after another, using a sand eel rig.

The rig consisted of a three-ounce, upside-down pyramid lead weight that drives its way into the soft sandy ocean bottom where it serves as an anchor of sorts. There are then two hooks, one about a foot above the weight, the other another foot higher, on which sand eels are impaled.

The best way to hook them is to thread the hook through a sand eel's eye and then push the barb down the length of its three- or four-inch body until it exits near the anus. A good cast with a ten-foot surf rod usually puts the rig toward the outside of the breakers along the beach. Once the line is set tight to the top of the surf rod, the eels are set dangling in the surf in wait for stripers who often prowl the shoreline for just such tasty morsels. I will never forget the glorious heft and fight of each of my birthday stripers that August in the outer-beach surf of Eastham. Even though I was in some of the best shape of my life from clamming, each fish strained my arms, lower back, and thighs. They had the powerful ocean surf adding to their roughly twelve-pound masses. Each would have been about eight years old. That night I filleted one of the striped bass I had caught and then fried it up for a birthday supper.

I'll hopefully never forget that I had nearly an entire first season of fruitless striper fishing. Of course, there have been a number of days with Michael where we have barely seen a fish. The absolute worst days, however, have occurred while sight-fishing the flats and finding not just a few fish here and there, but hundreds of fish, and then not being able to get any of them to strike. It may sound like a fish tale, but we have been on the flats on numerous occasions when the water is clear and shallow enough, less than four feet deep, where we have seen fish schooled together for a hundred yards. More often than not on such occasions we have found them very finnicky. The frustration of encountering such motherloads only to have them uninterested in our offerings cannot be overstated. Usually, Mike and I have been able to work these indifferent fish until the point that eventually something in the environment changes and at least some of them "turn on" and start striking. Perhaps a cloudbank shadows our corner of the bay, cooling the waters just enough. Perhaps the tide turns or the sun finally drops low enough. Perhaps two fish who consider one another rivals both spot a lure simultaneously and a strike is motivated. It's difficult to say what eventually changes, but there is usually a point when Mike and I wind up with fish in the boat.

It has happened though, when the fish have moved on away from us, countless numbers of them, without our enjoying a single tug on a line. These instances have left us exhausted.

I was convinced we were having just such a trip one early August on the flats. We had seen hundreds of fish, perhaps not thousands but definitely hundreds, yet they had all been in fast-moving schools and not one had done more than glance at our lures.

After about three hours we found ourselves drifting on the *Scout* away from shore, the sun dropping in the west to our left. I threw what was perhaps my four-hundredth cast of the day. I expected more of the nothing I had all afternoon and nonchalantly started my retrieve when a fish burst the surface behind it. Before its splash settled, line started tearing off my reel, a big keeper running with my lure.

"Damn!" I yelled. "Fish on."

"I got one, too. Yeah!"

Mike and I were forced to switch spots on the *Scout*, ducking under one another's lines not once but three times, as we worked our fish. I was convinced we'd get tangled and lose them, but in the end we landed them both, laughing like little kids all along.

On the way back to the landing that day, Mike told me a story that convinced me we were both well on our way to success in the book business too. One of his brothers had been shopping in a Barnes & Noble bookstore, paying with his credit card, when the clerk noticed his last name.

"Tougias?" she asked. "Are you related to Michael Tougias, the author? I've read a bunch of his books. I love them." Just then Mike's brother noticed that the lady at the next register was buying a handful of my children's books.

"You and Adam are everywhere," he told Mike.

I learned a lot watching my fishing pal grow from a part-time writer who held down a full-time day job, into a full-time author and in-demand public speaker. Actually, I knew he'd make it as a writer when I read his book *Fatal Forecast*. I was on a plane trip from LA to Boston and had the bad luck of getting a middle seat way in the very last row between two broad-shouldered body-builder types, two real macho guys. Back then I never cried, especially not while reading or watching a movie. But when I got to the emotional high point of Mike's book I found myself with tears streaming down my face. Honestly, I felt embarrassed crying in public and didn't want the men to each side of me to see me in such an emotional state. I quickly tucked Mike's book in the seat pocket in front of me. I signaled to the big guy on the aisle that I needed to get up, and went to the bathroom to compose myself. I washed my face and took some deep breaths and pulled myself together, relieved that I hadn't made myself or anyone else too uncomfortable. After returning to my seat, I decided to pick the book back up, and resolved not to get emotional. But Mike's writing was such that—try as I might—not two pages later, I literally burst out in tears including a few badly muffled sobs!

There were also several years when Mike regularly commented to me, "Now I'm focused on manifesting a movie from one of my books."

"*Fatal Forecast* should be the one," I told him without hesitation.

Mike's desire to have one of his books become a movie had caught my attention. The quality of one's writing, I knew, was something an author could control. But having a book selected to be made into a film depended on a lot of outside factors, especially luck. In the years that followed, Mike did at least get a handful of different people, agents and the like, to promise to try and get his books made into movies. Still, his progress seemed slow and unfruitful for years.

Then seemingly out of nowhere he was telling me about some interest in *The Finest Hours*, a book he coauthored about a famous sea rescue off Chatham. First came word that a new agent had inquired about it, then he heard Disney was reviewing it, then that there was a contract to sign. Next thing I knew the local Cape Cod media was abuzz about a movie to be made about local heroes Bernie Webber and crew and their 1952 rescue as described in Mike's book.

Soon Disney built a studio in Quincy, Massachusetts, and there were sightings of Hollywood stars around the region. Next, Mike told me he and his kids were invited to be extras.

"All us extras were told in no uncertain terms that we were not to speak with the stars at all, because they were working, and they shouldn't be distracted," Mike explained with a smile. "But I didn't care. I went straight up to the female lead, Holiday Granger, and introduced myself. 'Hi, I'm Mike Tougias, coauthor of the book. How are you?' Then Mike did the same the same thing with the lead male, Chris Pine.

Mike said both the star and starlet were completely down-to-earth and fun to talk with.

Before we knew it, it was 2016 and Disney launched the feature movie *The Finest Hours*. It also starred Casey Affleck.

One thing I've always struggled with is accepting and enjoying my own successes. When people compliment me, I often responded with statements that basically convey the idea that I didn't deserve the compliment. I'd say things like, "Oh, it was nothing." Or, "I just got lucky." Mike, however, reveled in the whole thing. He kept working hard, kept his feet on the ground, but he also enjoyed himself. It was a great example. Now, when I receive a compliment, I try to respond with words like, "Thank you. I appreciate your saying that." Why had I expected good things to happen to me when I didn't know how to accept them gratefully or gracefully?

When Mike was eventually invited to the big movie premier in Hollywood, he was given two tickets, one for himself and then the standard "plus one." But my fishing pal wanted to attend with *both* his kids, Kristin *and* Brian, so he asked if he could have a third ticket. Unfortunately, he was turned down, not once but twice.

One day out on the *Scout* he told me that he had informed Disney that if he could not bring both his kids to the premier, that he would not attend.

"I'm not going to be forced into making a Sophie's Choice on this one," he laughed. "I'm manifesting another ticket."

Sure enough, Disney relented and Mike, Kristin, and Brian made a family adventure out of their trip to Hollywood. It was a joy to see photos on social media of them clowning around with ice cream cones in LA. The three of them looked downright glamorous on the red carpet, shoulder to shoulder with all the stars at Grumman's Theater, a far cry from the way they usually look out on the *Scout*.

Needless to say, the book was propelled straight onto the *New York Times* best-seller list, another achievement Mike had been actively manifesting since I met him. I couldn't have been any more flattered when he dedicated the young adult version of the book to me and invited me to the Boston premier of the movie. (Tickets were apparently much easier to get to that one.)

My Good Night Books series also took off around that time. From conception, I thought of the series not simply as a collection of different books but as essentially one book, or rather one book project. I told myself that once I had created one hundred individual titles, it would be the equivalent of my writing one adult book. Today there are more than three hundred titles in the series. None of the individual books is yet to have been a national bestseller (we are still in the process of manifesting that), but they have been included on countless category and regional bestseller lists. Moreover, the series itself has sold many millions of copies including in countries around the world.

The most rewarding success has come when parents kindly complain to me that without meaning to they have memorized all the words in certain books in the series, because their child insisted on having it read to them night after night. A boy named Gabe could not fall asleep without his copy of *Good Night Boston* in his crib with him. A girl named Sarah carried her copy of *Good Night Chicago* in her purse for months. When I started the series, I thought that if it could touch just one child's life in a meaningful way, I'd have success. Today, I am overwhelmed with gratitude.

Might the Good Night Books series exist without my friendship with Mike? Probably not. I'll never forget the day I first floated the idea for it past him. A mundane forecast had been called by the weather people, something like, "High sixties with partly sunny skies. Southwest winds ten to twelve knots. Seas one to two feet."

The sky was anything but mundane that afternoon. It was crammed with countless, low-hanging, cotton-ball clouds that meteorologist call *cumulative congestus*. We were working the spot we call the Honey Hole. But despite our usual fishing hyper-focus, the sky actually distracted us from it.

"Wow, look at that," Mike pointed up to the south.

"Yeah. And look at it over there," I responded, jutting my chin to the western sky as I reeled.

Soon we saw what can only be described as heavenly skies, where innumerable golden and silvery sunbeams streamed through the breaks between clouds. Each beam was opaquely radiant yet seemed nearly solid. It was the first and only time I can recall both Mike and I feeling compelled to put our rods down and take photos. I had a small, waterproof digital camera at the time, while Mike was still doggedly using his classic 35mm film camera. Of course, when viewed later, neither of us was able to do the sky justice with our photos. Technology still hasn't developed enough to capture a sky like that.

As we were putting our cameras away, I turned to Mike and told him about my idea for place-based children's books and I said, "So why not *Good Night Cape Cod* and *Good Night Boston*? We can do a whole series."

Mike typically responds to my ideas thoughtfully, with measured words that more often than not temper my enthusiasm. He'll pause, cast his line, start his retrieve, and then tactfully ask a question that suggests he either likes or dislikes it. This time he just blurted, "Can I write *Good Night Vermont*? I'd love to write *Good Night Vermont*. Count me in."

I knew I was onto something.

Today, Mike is the author of *Good Night Vermont*, as well as *Good Night Coast Guard*, and *Good Night Redwoods*.

Yet these specific details about our story together are only minor components of our friendship. They are like our crossing and uncrossing fishing lines. They are significant, but they are like the fish we have caught together, important but no more important than all those fish that we have failed to catch.

Catching fish and not catching fish are not opposites. They are complimentary activities. They are different aspects of the same activity, two sides of the same coin, or two sides of the same fishing lure, if you will. Like all Cape Cod anglers who have come before us, and all who will fish after us, we have had to live through each off-season in order to get to each season. There is no point in getting too worked up over what appears to be the good or what appears to be the bad. They come together as a package. We had to know bad days in order to recognize good nights, and we had to live through the worst hours in order to fully appreciate the finest hours.

CHAPTER 23

New Waters, New Friends

MT

As the number of books I had published grew toward forty, a comment I often heard was "You love to write." And my response was always the same, "No, I don't. I love the research. The writing is hard and lonely work."

What I think I'll add to that comment in the future is that writing *is a passion*, something I'm compelled to do. There are many interpretations of the concept of passion, but for me it simply means a strong feeling. It doesn't necessarily have to make me happy. It could imply hate rather than love. Or put another way, a passion is when you put more energy into an endeavor than is required. Having a passion can mean you are willing to suffer for what you care about. And that's how I feel about a writing project—I give it my all because it's part of my DNA, but I can't say I love the writing. If it was pleasant, it would be a hobby. It would be like fishing. Now that is something I love doing.

There are similarities between the passion of writing and the hobby of fishing, and the most prominent is that there are no guarantees. Writing is not like working for a company, where you do your job and you get paid for your labor. With writing, you put the work in, but have no idea if you will get paid. Maybe a publisher will print your book, maybe a magazine will run your article . . . and then again maybe not. So in that respect you may have zilch to show for all your effort, just as can happen on a fishless day. You have to have faith in your technique and talent, but ultimately somebody (a publisher) or something (a fish) makes the final call if you will be rewarded.

Adam and I both experienced having put in maximum effort and many hours given on a writing project, all for naught. In the two cases I'm thinking of, our projects were halted when Dr. Seuss and Rudolph the Red-Nosed Reindeer presented us with legal troubles. Yes, you read correctly. I had presented a publisher with a humor manuscript that used my own version of *Green Eggs and Ham*. The publisher educated me that while I could write a parody of the Dr. Seuss poem, using mostly original content, I could not use parts of the poem in a satire of another person, and my humor book fell into the second category. A parody can only "bring to mind" the original work, and my manuscript went beyond that and used parts of the original poem. And so the manuscript had to be shelved after the work was done.

In Adam's situation, he wrote and published a Christmas book titled *Good Night North Pole*. The book included various aspects of Santa's village including elves, their workshop, Mrs. Claus, and a stable of reindeer, including "the most famous reindeer of all," Rudolph. Not long after the book hit the shelves, Adam received a strongly worded cease and desist letter from a company he had never heard of before. As it turns out, most of the Santa Claus story is in the public domain and can be written about freely by anyone in an original way, except for Rudolph the Red-Nosed Reindeer, who is trademarked. Fortunately, "Adam's people" were able to work with "Rudolph's people" and a deal was ironed out. Eventually Adam dropped Rudolph from the book altogether, so the issue is resolved. Who knew such beloved icons of children's literature could be so well lawyered up?

Luckily, neither the Easter Bunny nor the Tooth Fairy had any claim on *Fatal Forecast*, *The Finest Hours*, or the other books I was working on. And while a few articles and book projects I put considerable time into never were purchased by publishers, I'd been writing long enough and knew many publishers to get most of my efforts published. My odds improved every year, just as they did as when trying to catch stripers in shallow water.

Adam was a tremendous help in both writing and fishing. With the fishing, it was his boat we were on, his knowledge of the waters, and his introducing me to the joys of striper fishing. For my writing, his help as a publisher was immeasurable. For example, if one of my earlier books went out of print, the rights then reverted back to me, and Adam would take the time to reproduce and reissue the book. He knew these older books were not big money makers, and his focus should have been on his wildly successful Good Night series, but somehow he found the time to take my books on and keep them available to the public.

Having those older books in print was important to my business, because whenever I spoke on a particular subject, say King Philip's Indian War, many members of the audience wanted to purchase the novel I wrote about it, *Until I Have No Country*. Without Adam publishing that formerly out-of-print book, those sales would be lost. Selling the books direct to the public was a significant part of my income, and Adam's efforts made it possible, without me having to go down the rabbit hole of self-publishing.

I could not offer Adam anything as substantial, but I was able to be an unofficial advisor for his growing business. He had asked me to be on the board of directors, but having sworn off attending meetings after the endless "shoot me if I have to go to another" meetings in my former corporate job, I declined. Instead I said he could run any business decision by me, and I'd give an honest opinion. He knew I wouldn't pull any punches. That's what he wanted, and that's what he got. We had started that honest exchange of opinions in our early days of making career transitions, and now we continued it on business and financial decisions. That is the beauty of fishing pals—you can talk while you fish. In other hobbies, that time is limited. Try having a meaningful discussion in the middle of playing tennis or golfing. It's not easy.

With fishing, you and your partner are disagreeing frequently—where to go, what to use, boating speed, and when to call it a day. (I don't think I've ever been the first one to suggest we have fished long enough. It's a problem I'm working on.) These differences of opinions are not taken personally, especially with fishing buddies who have been companions for years such as Opie, Cogs, Jim H., and Dale. Fishermen have thick skins and are used to being second guessed. That's why I'm always on lookout for new people to fish with—I learn something new about fishing, and I seek fresh council on whatever issue I'm grappling with at the time.

Those new friends came by way of Florida. With my newfound freedom of knowing I could write full-time, make a good living at it, and do the work from virtually anywhere in the world, I decided to extend my fishing season and rented a house on Florida's southeast coast for three weeks for several years in row. Once I was comfortable with the area I eventually bought a small villa.

It was there that I met Doug Bernhard while fishing on the beach at dawn. I'm not sure how we struck up a conversation, but I'm sure I noticed Doug out-fished everyone else consistently. I was a newbie to Florida fishing. Doug either took pity on me or saw potential, but he gave advice that immediately helped me catch fish. A friendship was born.

Doug not only helped with tackle selection, casting tips, and best locations, he went one step further and started calling me if the fishing action at the beach was particularly good. He knew about my insomnia troubles, so my dawn visits to the beach were sporadic, but he went every morning and was more than willing to take a moment and call me when the fishing was hot. There was one morning in particular that led to two of the most enjoyable days at the beach in my life. (Notice I didn't say fishing, because it was much more than that.)

Here is how that sequence of events happened. I was asleep, having a nightmare that I was struggling and thrashing in a deep snowbank when I suddenly felt a hand on my chest and tried to scream. Not a sound came out and instead I heard, "Mike, I hate to wake you up."

I roused from my nightmare and sat up in bed, opening my eyes to see my girlfriend at the time. "Doug called," she said.

Boom, I was wide awake. "I'm going," I said, pivoting off the bed.

"I thought you would. But don't you want to hear what's going on?"

Throwing on a bathing suit and shirt, I nodded.

"He says the bluefish are in thick and have the bait trapped against the shore. And I think he said something about the water boiling."

God, I love the sound of boiling. Or frenzied. Or churning. Or any description of water where the fish are on the top and on the attack.

Arriving at the beach I quickly went down to where Doug was casting.

"Put on a cheap plug you don't care about," he said, "they're hitting everything, but there are sharks around too." He explained he had already caught and landed dozens of fish, and lost one blue and his popping plug to a shark.

On my first cast I was into a fish and during the fight I saw a big swirl behind my blue where a shark took a swipe at it. I got lucky and landed the fish without paying the "tax man" (as Doug refers to the sharks).

The water was a clear green-blue and in the gentle waves I could see marauding packs of bluefish. This was different than spotting stripers on the flats, where I'd stand in the *Scout* and look down at the large shadows of bass against the sand. Here on the beach in Florida I could only see the blues when they were in the face of a wave—black streaks all moving in the same direction.

Doug, noticing my wire leader, said, "If a shark takes your next blue, you're either going to have to land the shark or be spooled." What he meant by that comment was that the wire leader would stay intact, and I'd have to fight the shark to shore or risk having it take all my line. Whereas a fluorocarbon leader would be cut by the shark's teeth or its rough skin and I'd at least get my line back minus the lure. We had a running debate about the merits of using wire during our three years of fishing together. Doug was dead set against it. He reasoned many fish can see the wire leader and are scared off. Other fish might be mixed in with the blues and he wants to catch those as well, so he uses a heavy test fluorocarbon leader that will increase his odds of getting hook-ups. I on the other hand always use wire when blues are actively feeding so they can't cut me off. For me, there's nothing worse than tying on a new leader and lure in the middle of a blitz, so I sacrifice the possibility of some hits for convenience.

On this day we didn't engage in our age-old debate, but instead, knowing he was right about the shark taking all my line, I tried casting just a few feet from shore to see if the blues were in close. The sharks seemed to be out in the five-foot-plus depths, so I did a flick-of-the-wrist cast into two feet of water and as soon as my plug hit the surface a blue exploded on it. Pound for pound the bluefish is one of the stronger fish swimming in the ocean and this one was no different, taking line and making me apply more pressure to keep it out of the deeper water and away from waiting sharks.

While I was fighting my fish, Doug pointed out that there were bait-fish, called croakers, about ten inches long, in the foaming wash where the waves met the shore. It took me a minute to pick them out as they darted about, but soon I was able to see them in just three or four inches of water. The bluefish had them penned up against the beach. Croakers, like so many fish in Florida, were still relatively unknown to me. I had just caught my first croaker a week earlier, and after learning they were good table fare, sautéed what little meat I was able to fillet from it.

After landing several blues the bite turned off, so Doug and I took a walk down the beach. We passed the occasional dead croaker which basically committed suicide by swimming out of the surf and up on the sand to escape the blues. I examined one and found that its tail was missing, sheared off by a blue. Predator and prey, the violent side of the natural world.

Further down the beach we came upon a pool of water about six feet wide by twenty feet long. I gasped when I looked more closely at it. Trapped in the slough were over a thousand croakers, swimming frantically in water just six inches deep. The small waves must have formed this depression earlier but now it was separated from the open ocean by a thin strip of dry sand. There was one exit channel but it was only about two feet wide and just a trickle of water flowed through it, no more than two inches deep.

Thinking of how good the croaker tasted a week earlier I decided I'd take a few for a meal. I thought I could reach in and grab them, but they were fast, and even when I had a grip on one it slithered out of my grasp. And so I did what any person would do who doesn't care what he looks like: I got down on all fours and tried pouncing on them like a grizzly bear. It worked and I threw a couple high up on the beach sand. Doug helped by herding croakers toward me as he shuffled down the pool. While doing that, he discovered another method for catching them—he stepped on one then reached down and threw it up with mine.

An elderly couple walked down the beach and stared at us. I can only imagine what they were thinking about two adults acting like five-year-olds. After gathering enough croakers for dinner, we realized the rest of the corralled fish were all going to die if we didn't get them back into the ocean. And so we both began herding them down the pool and toward the narrow channel leading to their freedom. Many of the fish turned around upon reaching the shallow channel and darted through our legs back into the pool, but a few shimmied down the channel and into the ocean. They might have gone straight into the mouths of waiting bluefish, but we did the best we could.

Walking back down the shore toward our cars, Doug's theory about clear leaders paid dividends because he cast and caught a Spanish mackerel. I thought to myself *what a great way to end the morning*. And then it got better.

"Well, look at that," Doug exclaimed. He was pointing at a trough in the sand filled with water, and there, floating in the middle, was the plug that he lost earlier in the morning when the shark took a bluefish he was fighting.

While he picked up his lure I noticed a handful of croakers racing around inside the trough. I couldn't pass them up; grizzly bear fishing for croaker had become as much fun as catching blues with rod and reel. Only now instead of gathering croakers for the frying pan I was throwing them back in the ocean.

"Listen," said Doug, "I gotta go. Don't get too carried away here."

But it was too late. I loved the challenge of trying to catch them with my bare hands and stayed another hour.

Looking back on that day, I think I was simply allowing the hunter-gatherer in me free reign. It's why I'll spend hours picking wild oranges in Florida, wild apples in Vermont, and wild blueberries wherever I can find them. Other people like to search for sea glass along the beach, old coins with detectors, mushrooms in the woods. I'm betting that most of the people reading these words remember childhood days when pleasant, unstructured hours were spent collecting something or other.

Chapter 23

"I was rich in sunny days," wrote Henry Davis Thoreau, "and spent them lavishly."

***

The next day I was back at the same beach, alone this time. The spot where the croakers had been trapped was clean sand. The high tide probably washed them back out to sea. Whether they made it out alive or not is a mystery, but even if they did I doubt it was for very long—the bluefish were still patrolling the shore.

A little while later a family from Canada came by while I was in the midst of fighting a bluefish at the end of my fishing line. The kids were age two, four, and thirteen. The father of the group saw my Coast Guard hat, said that he was in the Canadian Coast Guard and asked where I was stationed. I explained I just wrote about the Coast Guard but never served and that the hat was a gift from one of my speaking engagements.

I asked his thirteen-year-old daughter, Bella, if she wanted to fight the bluefish still racing about with my lure. It was pure joy to watch her eventually land the fish and even pick it up by the tail and put it back into the sea.

The family and I walked down the beach while Bella and I took turns casting for blues. We all came to an abrupt stop when we came upon a bunch of baitfish trapped in a pool. There were a mix of croaker and whiting, both about a foot long and pale colored, darting about in the pool. Bella and I set about trying to catch them. It took a good fifteen minutes for her to get the hang of it, but she managed to get one and shouted in victory. Both fish are good to eat, and we threw a couple up on the sand and the rest back in the ocean (probably into the hungry jaws of the bluefish, but at least they had a fighting chance).

After a few minutes I started cheating a bit. I had taken my shirt off and was now throwing it over fish, pinning them underneath and then tossing them back in the ocean. When I trapped a big whiting I threw it up on the sand, thinking of dinner. That's when the four-year-old boy got into the act. He looked at the whiting flopping on the sand, took off his own shirt, threw it over the fish, then did a belly flop on it, shouting to his mother that he got one!

I spent the next hour with those kids trying to trap and rescue more fish, having just as much fun as they were.

Later, Bella was knee-deep in the surf looking for more croaker while I was standing nearby casting, talking to her mom. A bluefish took my lure when it was about twenty feet from Bella and me. Suddenly a shark exploded onto the surface of the water and grabbed the blue fifteen feet in front of us. It was about four or five feet long and gray. Bella quickly moved backward to shore. Now, some people might freak out having a shark come that close, but Bella and her mom were cool. Instead of screaming, the mom simply said, "Wow, never seen that before!"

I was glad I had company to witness the shark taking my blue, making me think that more kids need to see nature close up, or "contact" with it as Thoreau implores us. He wrote:

> *Talk of mysteries! Think of our life in nature,—daily to be shown matter, to come in contact with it,—rocks, trees, wind on our cheeks! The solid earth! The actual world! The common sense! Contact! Contact!*

***

Catching the croakers was all part of my learning curve in Florida. Friends whom I met on the beach while fishing, like Doug, helped me along. I found that the croaker don't actually croak, but that a fish called jack crevalle grunt like a pig when out of the water. I learned sheepshead look nothing like a sheep, grouper are often solitary, and ladyfish do not act ladylike.

Through trial and error, I discovered snook were adept at avoiding the hook, but I'd increase my odds of catching them at the beach if I casted sideways and jerked my lure through the first trough, close to the beach. Which explained why the few snook I previously caught hit near my feet in the surf—that's where they hunted.

Sometimes I caught species that made me wonder if I was living in prehistoric times. One of them was the ribbon fish or cutlass fish. Narrow as a necktie, and two feet long, it has a head like an eel with rows of sharp teeth. It is by far the shiniest fish I have ever seen.

Even the shark that surprised Bella and me was something new. Doug later deduced it was likely a black-tipped reef shark or maybe a spinner shark. Outdoor writer and friend Ed Killer explained to me that from January to March tens of thousands of blacktips and spinners arrive in waters off southern Florida, particularly off Palm Beach County. Lifeguards I've spoken with say they believe there are almost always sharks near the shore, but they rarely approach people in the water. If they see a large shark they call people out of the water, but they say for every shark they see there must be a dozen more that cruise by unseen. In my three years in Florida I'd seen several sharks from both shore and from boats. Once, in a friend's boat, we observed a large hammerhead shark lazily swimming in circles around our vessel, a bit too close to shore than I'd prefer.

One man from Haiti, who goes by the name America, was a regular at the beach, and I learned a lot from him, just by observing. He used cut-bait to catch bluefish, and he had a knack for finding them, casting just the right distance, and setting the hook at precisely the right time. But what he really taught me was patience and persistence, two things I'm not famous for, as Adam has pointed out. I recall going to the shore two days after the croaker slaughter expecting to find bluefish. I covered a couple miles of surf using a Kastmaster without so much as a hit. Other fisherman I talked to during my walk reported the same results, and agreed that the blues had moved on. Heading back to my car I saw America sitting on a bucket with two bait rods stuck in the sand. I greeted him like always, and we briefly updated each other on our families. Then I commented that the fishing stunk that day. He nodded and in this thick accent and soft-spoken voice said something to the affect that yes, the fishing was slow. Oftentimes he didn't say much more during our visits on the beach but this time he was talkative, and I leaned in close to hear him.

"When the wind is from the south, no good. When flat seas, no good. Better with some wind from the north or east and some chop. But today flat and from south."

"Good advice," I said, "I always wondered if there was a pattern. Maybe next time we will both catch blues."

He shook his head from side to side and stood up from sitting on the bucket. "Still fish are here." He pivoted to his large cooler and opened the lid. Inside were three good-sized bluefish on ice.

It was an important lesson for me. There are *always* a few blues around. In fact, I've never seen America get skunked, ever. I fish with my eyes too much. If I don't see baitfish, or a swirl, or birds hovering, I lose faith that there are any fish nearby. America knows there are unseen stragglers hugging the bottom and understands if he is patient for a couple hours and uses bait that will attract the blues via their sense of smell, he will eventually land a fish. He switches to lures on the days that the wind and surf are favorable. If he doesn't catch a fish in a half hour of casting, he'll switch to bait, and then he will be as still as a great blue heron waiting for a little fish to come within striking distance. Patience and persistence lead him to opportunity. That describes me with my writing, but not with my fishing, although I'm working on it.

Each new friend taught me something new or demonstrated a quality I'd like to emulate. Don, a few years older than me, illustrated that age is just a number, and his enthusiasm for fishing was just as strong as my own. I recall when he hooked into a five-foot king mackerel, he insisted that I take the rod for awhile and fight the fish to appreciate its power. Mike M. demonstrated that a relaxed approach to angling could be as effective as my locked and loaded disposition. One time he joined me and Don on an offshore trip. While Don and I were fiddling with preparing just the right tackle, Mike lowered a hook with a piece of bait and within two seconds was battling a mahi mahi.

Chris showed that a buck-tailed jig retrieved in a slow, varied fashion, was as good as any expensive lure on the market. Mike W. turned me on to the inland waterways via kayak. On one of those trips I saw a couple of boulders and thought I'd wedge my kayak between to the two so that the tide didn't carry me away from the area as I cast. The boulders turned out to be two sleeping manatees that scared the life out of me when they awoke and their tail slaps covered me in spray. Nit taught me how to look into the waves to see bluefish on the prowl, and he and Doug showed me the fine art of adding BBs to my topwater lures to cast beyond the breakers. And Ken explained that sometimes we needed to get our lures on the bottom for Spanish mackerel and bounce them along.

***

New waters like Florida's coast had me back to being a ten-year-old kid again, not knowing what I'd catch but trying anyway. With the help of anglers I met on the beach, and on friend's boats, I eventually caught cobia, Spanish mackerel, king mackerel, sailfish, mahi, and smaller fish too numerous to mention. It was both humbling and interesting to start back on the bottom of the knowledge scale, as happened with Adam twenty years earlier. In Florida I found the kid deep inside me, and tried to be both a teacher and student as the situation called for.

CHAPTER 24

Waves

AG

There is a common metaphor in eastern philosophies comparing human lives with ocean waves. Part of its power comes from the fleeting nature of waves, indicating the same about our own lives. Part of it comes from the infinite variety of them dancing on the ocean's surface at any given moment. Perhaps most important, however, is that living beings are not so much separate entities but rather myriad manifestations of the same great ocean of life.

There is also the idea that when we are born, it is as if our life forces become visible in the material world, like a wave forming on the surface. By extension, when a person dies, it is like a wave losing energy, dissipating, and no longer being visible above the surface or in the world. Yet even though a wave's energies are no longer seen on the surface, they don't cease to exist. Like unseen underwater currents, life energies continue below the surface of things. This part of the metaphor can be comforting for mourners.

The metaphor can be taken even further by considering that waves that are adjacent or near one another often share similar characteristics: wavelengths, speeds, shapes. Likewise, close family members, friends, and loved ones often share similar temperaments, physical characteristics, and personality traits. Not all waves that are near one another are overly similar; many differ markedly. But, again, in its broadest interpretation, the metaphor emphasizes that we are not just related with one another, we are also parts of the same whole, the same ocean.

This metaphor certainly works well enough regarding my friendship with Mike whereby I can imagine that he and I are something like nearby ocean waves rushing along in proximity to one another, each experiencing similar perspectives, weather conditions, tidal forces, and currents, yet different too.

One of the most interesting things about waves for me is the visual illusion that makes them appear as separate bodies or packets of water, whereas they are only the rising and falling of the surface. Stadium waves made by crowds at concerts and ballgames demonstrate the principle clearly, with no one leaving their seat or moving their location, just raising and dropping their hands in synchrony.

Just as there are countless ocean waves, there are plenty fishing trips to go around, as Mike's chapter "New Waters/New Friends" demonstrates.

Among my newer fishing friends is Larry. Larry lives in Cambridge, Massachusetts, and was new to saltwater fishing when I first took him out. Larry is also a writer, so he has that in common with Mike and me. He also served as the officiant at my wife Mildrey's and my wedding. Around the time I started fishing with Larry, the striped bass and bluefish populations were being driven off the flats by the growing seal population. As a result, I started to not only fish farther offshore, I started to look for different fish to target. Hence one of the first spring trips I took with Larry was for black sea bass.

Black bass are quite different from striped bass. They are smaller, maxing out at twenty-six inches. In contrast, stripers have been known to exceed five feet. Compared with stripers, their fins are larger in proportion to their bodies, as are their eyes which bulge more than stripers. Larger black sea bass often take on beautiful reflective sheens that include purples and greens that make them radiant to behold.

We headed out early that morning. It was bright, cool, and breezy. We wore sweatshirts that we shed as the sun rose. The best method for finding black bass is to either go to areas where they have been caught in the past, typically shoals, and then fish and see if they are present, or to simply look for other recreational boats with anglers on them who look in good spirits, or better yet, who are reeling up fish.

We soon found about ten boats that had these auspicious character-istics and set up a drift nearby. We dropped shiny metal jigs, about four inches long, with single hooks hanging from their bottoms. We were in twenty to twenty-five feet. Once we felt our jigs hit bottom, we began lifting them up about a foot or two, letting them fall back down, and then kept repeating the action, varying our rhythms now and then, and occasionally adjusting the amount of line we played out.

"If you feel a hit, yank your rod up to set the hook," I told Larry.

In no time he was yelling, "I got one!"

He reeled like mad, and while laughing loudly soon lifted an eighteen-inch black sea bass out of waves. Larry's enthusiasm is con-tagious. The next few hours we drank hot coffee from a thermos and updated one another on our businesses, kids, and creative endeavors. As time slipped by, it seemed the bay grew incrementally gorgeous. Our talk was punctuated by landing and measuring fish. We also caught sea robins, which are not typically kept for eating due to the relatively small amount of meat on them and the amount of work involved in cleaning them. Those we pulled up were only ten inches or smaller and mud-colored. They are an odd-looking fish with large fins that resemble bird wings when spread open, hence the name. They have spines on their gill plates and dorsal fins that can cause slight pain for a day or two if you get stuck by them. They also croak while being dehooked, making froggish sounds.

We also caught a couple of scup, also known as porgy. These were a foot long each with enough meat on them to bring home. Scup are narrow fish, about an inch or so wide. They are a little longer than they are tall, so these were about nine inches in height. The ones we caught glistened yellowy.

Before going in, we lucked into a tautog of seventeen inches which was legal to keep. "Tog" are a popular groundfish along much of the East Coast. They are ugly compared to striper, and black seabass, though they aren't half as odd-looking as sea robins. Togs have a long, narrow dorsal fin running down their backs and small tails. They also have sizeable lips that seem almost like puckered human lips, with a short row of irregular blunt teeth that they use to crack open shellfish. They can reach a yard in length. Although I had experience with the other species mentioned, this was my first tautog. Without trying, Larry and I had a fishing trifecta, catching three different species on the same trip, though I am told that a "true" Cape Cod trifecta consists of striper, bluefish, and tuna.

Back at the house, we filleted all three species and cooked them simply with olive oil, salt, and pepper. My wife Mildrey, who is from Cuba, prepared rice and beans and fried plantains as side dishes. The black sea bass had a delicate sweetness that was loved by all. The scup had a stronger flavor but very nice and reminiscent of shrimp yet more complex. In contrast, the tautog was disappointing, if only because it was so bland. It seems like a strange criticism of fish, but all three of us agreed.

I had suggested we coat some in breadcrumbs before frying but had been promptly reminded by Larry that he has celiac disease, which means he cannot eat food with gluten in it. That includes breadcrumbs and pretty much anything with wheat.

"This isn't just a preference," Larry emphasized, "It's a medical condition."

The key thing for me that day was exploring a different type of fishing. For years, Mike and I mainly sight fished in the same intense, compulsive way already described. Sight fishing for striper means hyper-focusing for us both. When out on the water, I feel this focus is a wonderful thing, as it allows for what athletes and artists often refer to as "flow," that state where all thought disappears and pure doing takes over. I believe it's the best state from which to manifest happiness and success.

This day with Larry targeting ground fish, it seemed I had reached a new stage where I could fish in a relaxed way, one where meandering chitchat and serene appreciation of the environment were as important as hard hookups and arching rods.

The next week I told Mike about the different fish and how tasty they were. He was impressed and readily agreed to go black sea bass fishing the next workable date. This turned out to be a warm weekend day, so there were many others out on the water. When we came out of the harbor, we approached what amounted to an armada of more than a hundred boats crowded together.

"Before we go join all those people, why don't we scout for stripers?" Mike asked.

"The striper fishing has been slow here lately. I doubt if we'll find much."

"Yeah, but it's worth a try."

"Okay," I relented.

After more than an hour of fruitless searching, Mike agreed that we should join the "parking lot" of black bass fisherman.

During an hour of drifting amid the boats, we reeled in five black bass, three of which were large enough to keep. We also caught and tossed back a handful of sea robins. It was a lethargic form of fishing compared to what we were used to. Even the biggest black bass put up but a fraction of the fight a striper or a blue does. Yet I enjoyed catching up with my old friend and made a point to appreciate the salt air, glittering waters, and broad sky.

"Let's get out of here." Mike finally announced.

"What?"

"We're not catching anything. This is boring."

"Mike, we caught five fish, three that we are keeping, plus sea robins. If we hooked into this many stripers or blues in an hour you'd say the fishing was incredible."

"Yeah but this is boring, and these fish are so small. There's too many boats around here. Let's go hunt for stripers. If we don't find anything, we'll come back."

"Okay."

About an hour and a half later, and after maybe twenty miles of boating, we hadn't found the slightest sign of stripers; and by the time we returned to the shoals, the weather and the tide had changed so the bite was off. We soon called it a day and returned with our three black sea bass, making for a total of six small fillets, three each, which was not quite enough for either of us to have a full meal with our partners.

A little later that spring Mike and I left the dock at about 6 a.m. with a forecast for Cape Cod Bay of gentle winds and cloudy skies. We hunted the flats but were disappointed not to see a single fish after an hour and a half of scouring. Seals yes. Stripers no. Afterward, we headed offshore to Billingsgate Shoals into about twenty-five feet of water where we did encounter quite a few stripers on the surface, some with gulls nearby, others without. We both hooked up multiple times though we didn't land a keeper. We then went to one of our favorite spots where we trolled a tube and worm. Almost immediately—bam—we hooked a twenty-seven-incher, just short of a keeper. We kept at the tube and worm for an additional hour, but not another fish hit. We did, however, eventually catch three more striper casting bottom lures in ten to fifteen feet of water, each just below the legal limit. Then the wind picked up.

"Do you want to call it a day, Mike?"

"I think you have a point the other day. When we're having days like this, where we can't land a keeper, we might as well try to get some meat in the boat. So I brought chopped up clams to try fluke fishing. You want to give it a go?"

I was surprised he had a change of heart about ground-fishing. Fluke, otherwise known as summer flounder, are true bottom fish, very flat, a bit like small throw rugs tossed onto the ocean floor. They have white underbellies with gravely sandy patterns on their upward-facing sides for camouflage. Both of their eyes are on this upward-facing side of their bodies, scrunched together.

"A guy I met at the landing last week told me he nailed them with clams not far from the harbor entrance." Mike said.

We motored over and found a handful of boats scattered about, none of which looked to be into fish. We studied the chart on our GPS for a shoal worth trying, and cut the engine. Mike pulled out a plastic container of clams from his cooler. It took us both about ten minutes to dig our groundfish rigs out of our tackle boxes, string them up, and bait them.

"These clams are disgusting," he said, making a face and handing me some. He was right. My fingers stunk sourly for a long while.

We each dropped our lines and started jigging the clams off the bottom. The sky was grey and mottled, the water dark and choppy. After more than six hours of hard striper fishing, I thought it was nice to just sit and relax and take in the vast spaciousness of it all. Then about six minutes later, my fishing pal exclaimed, "The heck with this. This is so boring. I can't do this. Let's go check the flats again. Maybe some stripers have moved in."

"What? We spent more time setting our rigs up than fluke fishing."

"I know but let's go scout for stripers."

"Okay," I said. "You are one diehard hunter."

"That's me, my friend."

So, Mike and I hunted for another hour but with no luck.

"At least you know who you are, Mike. You are a gamefish man through and through."

Mike and I haven't wasted another minute ground-fishing since, and I don't think we ever will.

In early September that same season, Larry and I decided to try some waters around the Cape I'm less familiar with. The night before I mentioned to him on the phone that I had stopped at the store and picked up a few items to make sandwiches for the trip. I had even picked up some gluten-free bread for him.

"Oh, I love that brand," he told me. "Thanks, Captain."

"No problem."

The next morning, we met at the marina.

"This is wonderful," offered Larry. "Being in the city most of the time, I forget how spectacular it is out here."

"Yippee kai-yay," we both hollered, as we throttle forward through the waves.

After hunting a while, we settled on drifting and casting around a tiny island populated by a colony of terns that squawked incessantly. I admired their angular features and sharp beaks.

The water around the island looked fishy. But by our third drift without a strike or follow, we knew there weren't any fish. Then I noticed a steady stream of terns leaving the island in ones and twos. They were flying off in the same direction. Soon after, I noticed that there was an opposite stream of birds returning, also in ones and twos. The returning terns had small minnows in their beaks. The exiting terns flew about ten to twenty feet higher than the returning ones, but along the same flightpath.

"We ought to see where all those birds are coming from with bait. I'll bet there's fish feeding over there."

"Let's go," Larry said.

We boated the better part of two miles following the flightpath of the terns. Along the way, Larry started munching on the fruit salad I had made: apples, mango, kiwi, grapes, bananas.

"This really hits the spot," he said as I finally found the source of the minnows. There was a big school of feeding fish under a flock of wheeling screaming terns, not another boat around for miles.

Stopping our boat within casting distance, I threw a surface lure into the melee and within two cranks had hooked a substantial fish. It leapt high, displaying its raw power, a big handsome bluefish. It wagged its tail and shook its head fiercely, but the hook held.

Still new to saltwater fishing, Larry didn't cast until after I had my first fish next to the boat. When I got it over the gunnels, it spit up onto the deck a dozen of the minnows we had seen the terns carrying in their beaks. Some were mush, others bitten in two, a few were whole and still wiggling, very much alive.

"I can't believe we found fish by following the birds all the way here."

"Yeah," I replied, thinking I was becoming more present and aware.

As I started filleting my blue, Larry's reel started feeding out line.

"I got one!"

Before long he had it in the boat.

"You keep fishing, and I'll finish dressing off our fish," I told him.

When I got the meat in the cooler, I joined Larry and soon found myself utterly zeroed in. The melee grew even more intense with birds screeching and fish splashing. It was as if all time had stopped for me. I hooked an even bigger bluefish and felt my rod nearly come out of my hand.

"Hey, Adam," Larry called as it ripped line off my reel. "Are these my sandwiches in this cooler?"

"Yeah," I said. But I was way too focused on my fish. Rather than listening attentively to his question, I assumed (and what do they say about the word "assume"?) that gluten-free bread and whole wheat bread look different from each other and that Larry as a gluten-free eater knew the difference between the two by sight.

After I landed my fish, I began filleting it.

"I hate to tell you this," he said to me, "but I think I'm getting seasick."

About a minute later, Larry began projectile vomiting fruit salad everywhere. Big slices of white banana and apple were spewed along the gunnels along with the green kiwi and orange mango. Half a grape bounced toward the bow.

"Oh my, Larry. Try to keep it on the outside of the boat,"

A puddle of puke sloshed along the deck, mixing with the dead minnows and blood from the bluefish. "That's a lot, Larry. Is there anything I can do?"

"No . . ." he said between wet gasps. "I'm just seasick."

I'm not proud to say it, but I decided to keep casting while he finished being sick. Eventually, he plopped down on a seat sick as a dog, or maybe I should say as a boated bluefish.

Fortunately, the boat was equipped with a raw water hose that I was able to use to clean up. We decided to wrap up our trip to get him home.

"Hey, Adam, are you sure those sandwiches were on gluten-free bread?"

"Oh no," I gasped. "Yours were on gluten-free. Mine were on regular bread. Oh my, Larry. Did you eat one of mine?"

"Man, why didn't you tell me there were wheat bread sandwiches in there?"

"I thought you could tell the difference. I was so focused on fishing. I'm sorry."

Now I felt sick. I had imagined I was becoming more enlightened, that I was no longer a hyper-focused fishing maniac. Get me near feeding fish and I failed to even think about the health and safety of my only passenger and dear friend. This was worse than the time Mike had been too busy fishing to notice that I had fallen off the boat.

Thankfully, Larry had immediately vomited up his entire sandwich, thus avoiding digesting much, if any, gluten. Had his body not rejected it so violently, he could have been seriously ill.

He wound up too tired that evening to drive back to Cambridge and spent the night at my place. Fortunately, he woke up the next day good as new. We both reflected on ourselves over a *completely gluten-free breakfast.* Larry realized that he must be even more conscientious in dealing with his food and not trust amateurs like me. I realized I need to pay way more attention.

"I had a great time anyway," he said, "at least up until the end."

If Mike and I are like two waves flowing along the surface of the ocean, I had thought I had veered from our old headings a bit, in a direction a tad less obsessive, but I hardly had. Moreover, a wave named Larry appeared to be on a similar trajectory with us now, like that of many other waves with names like Jon Hyde, Paul, Opie, Cogs, Jack, Miki, Kristin, and Brian, to name a few.

Fortunately, Larry never let my poisoning him slow his fishing down. He doesn't even seem to hold it against me. He was back not a week later with Mike and me, matching our casts from dawn until dusk. (He brought all his own food with him.) Ironically that next trip was the one where Mike got a hook stuck in his hand that I had to help him remove. Mike was not going to let a mere hook in the meat of his palm ruin a good day fishing.

Despite the accidents, and despite the persistent imperfections of our characters, fishing remains both powerful and positive, as the title of this book indicates. Mike has rightly referred to the *Scout* as our floating psychiatrist's couch. I like to think of a day of fishing as a spiritual retreat of sorts. Removed from the regular rhythms of family and work, immersed in the overwhelming beauty of outer nature, connecting with friends or family, and involved in an activity where the regular flow of time often seems to cease, my spirit always feels refreshed and renewed.

CHAPTER 25

Differences and Similarities

MT

One might think that because Adam and I spend so much time fishing together that our approach to the sport would be the same. But we were different in many ways, especially with regard to lures. We had both perfected the action of a lure jerked on the surface to entice fish, and that one technique usually out-fished every other one. Logic would dictate that's the lure we should stay with in shallow water, and that's what Adam did. But there is nothing logical about my accumulation of lures, and I blame it on my insomnia. It's in the middle of the night that infomercials run for suckers like me, and twice they reeled me in like a schoolie striper on his first migration up the coast.

My first purchase was a rubber minnow with life-like action. The infomercial had a video camera at the bottom of a huge aquarium where a couple of freshwater largemouth bass ruled the roost. These bass must have been starved for the past month, because when that lure was cast into the tank the bass attacked it with a savagery that was a sight to behold. *Ah ha*, I thought, *Adam has never seen one of these. If it works in freshwater, the larger size should crush the stripers.* Maybe it was because it was 3 a.m., but I just had to have this minnow. I actually called the number on the TV, and sure enough operators really were standing by. "I'll take the full set," I announced to the tired-sounding lady who took my call. She was probably in Iowa, at home in her pajamas with a headset on, wondering who in the world buys this stuff, especially in the middle of the night. As soon as the deal was completed she probably hollered, "Hal, sold another one to some dumb-ass from Massachusetts. Says he's going to use it on stripers. Far as I know strippers want dollars in their G-string, not minnows."

When the package arrived at my house a week later, I realized that before the minnow could be fished there was quite an assembly required involving rubber bands and weights. It took a while but I put a couple together, licking my chops over how I'd humiliate Adam by out-fishing him with something that could not be bought at tackle shops. He'd beg me to find out how to purchase some, and I'd hold that knowledge tight to my chest until the appropriate time. But first I had to give the secret minnow a test run, just to hone my technique. I think I was with Cogs and Opie when I tried one out. On my very first cast the rubber band went one way, the weight another, and the minnow fluttered to the water's surface where I swear I heard fish laughing.

You would think I'd have learned my lesson, but on another sleepless night I was reading a fishing magazine that mentioned a lure that had a retractable, concealed leader. Why is that important, you ask? Well, let me tell you . . . I'm not sure. But here's the thing: it sounded like it would fool a fish. The words "deploys upon strike" were quite tantalizing. I ordered one on the spot, even though for the price I could have bought a small car. So how did the lure perform? I don't know. It was so expensive I don't dare use it.

That lure sits in my basement waiting for just the right moment. Maybe if I make it to ninety I'll give it a whirl.

But give me credit, I never ordered the Ginsu knife. I'll admit I was tempted; you never know when you might need it to cut a beer can or a sneaker in half, especially right before slicing tomatoes. (I can still hear the infomercial, "But wait! Order now and . . .")

I'd estimate the lures I bought online and in tackle shops are well over eight hundred. (I felt I needed them to go along with the fifty-seven fishing rods I own.) And so I have a garage and basement chock-full of every lure under the sun. But I'm no fool. I have a set answer when people like my daughter say, "You think you got enough fishing equipment?" I respond, "It's cheaper than golf." And along that line of reasoning there is a saying I once heard a fisherman say. "My deepest fear is that when I die my wife will sell my fishing gear for only the amount I told her I spent on it."

Adam is amused by my obsession with trying to find the secret weapon. When on the *Scout*, and fish are in the vicinity, he will often observe me rummaging through my tackle bag to locate a lure I've never used before. Then he says, "I've already caught and released two stripers while you've been hunting in that massive military duffel bag you insist bringing on the boat for some ridiculous new lure. Stay with what works!"

I think he's jealous or trying to throw me off my search because he knows someday one of my late-night purchases will be magic, and he hates the thought of having to beg to find out the lure's proper name and where to purchase it.

***

Most of my differences with Adam are not, however, over equipment, but instead are philosophical in nature. In our early years of fishing together, Adam was just as intense a fisherman as me. But in recent years, he seems to have evolved. A day on the boat where we only catch one or two small fish is not a disaster for him. His brain works something like this: *We were out in the sunshine, we talked, we laughed, and the ocean always has its own beauty. We'll find the fish the next time.* I have slightly different reaction: *What are we doing wrong? Is the fish stock declining? Do I need to buy new lures? I think I'm losing my mojo.*

Adam takes the long view and says we'll find the fish the next time. I do too, but I'm thinking next time should be first thing tomorrow morning.

My friend Opie is even more casual than Adam in that he views a day on his boat as one of fresh air, friendship and conversation, seeing new places, and any fish caught is a bonus. That same day for me is viewed as a hunt, as if our very survival depends on locating the bass. I'm lucky that both Opie and Adam humor my quest by staying out on the water longer than they normally would. And when I'm pushing to go out on a crappy day with strong north winds, they remind me of the unofficial rule for fishing Cape Cod Bay:

Wind from the East, fishing's the least.
Wind from the South, hook in the mouth.
Wind from the West, fishing's the best.
Wind from the North, don't go forth.

I haven't advanced up the enlightenment ladder to simply appreciate a day on the ocean in totality, regardless of whether or not fish are caught.

So yes, I need to grow up. But I'm just being honest—catching fish makes my mood a thousand times brighter. There's a little bit of a gambler in me that loves the somewhat random nature of having that shot of dopamine shoot through me when suddenly a striper crashes my top water lure. Suddenly any fatigue I was experiencing is gone and even the colors surrounding me are brighter. Adam's stories about me getting bored ground-fishing are true. I want to hunt for hard-fighting gamefish on light tackle and not methodically bounce bait off the bottom and then crank up little fish once in a while like a fishing game at an amusement park.

I always knew that was a problem for me, but I figured as I age just the act of being on the water with a friend would be enough. But I'm running out of time for that Zen-like mindset to settle in. I figured by age fifty I'd be Thoreau-like and have his wisdom when he supposedly wrote, "Many go fishing all their lives without knowing that it is not fish they are after." Well let me tell you something, Mr. Smarty Pants of Concord, I'm sixty-five, and it's still fish I'm after.

There is another fishing quote that fits me better, one from John Buchan (1875–1940), which says, "The charm of fishing is that it is the pursuit of what is elusive but attainable, a perpetual series of occasions for hope."

Buchan's right, at least for me anyways—it's the pursuit. That pursuit is even more evident when I'm going after trout in Vermont. Sure, I have my preferred spots on favorite rivers that are productive, but I never stop the quest to find Shangri La: the perfect stretch of water where there are large fish and no other fisherman. That search has taken me to every corner of the state, and I believe that over the last fifty years I've fished every river in Vermont, and more brooks than I can remember. And still the quest (obsession?) goes on.

There is, however, one big difference between my no-fish days on a river compared to on the ocean. Exploring rivers and streams, often hiking for a mile just to get to a secluded area, does leave me in a peaceful state, fish or no fish. I think it's the exercise. On rivers and streams I always take a plunge at the end of the day right up into October. The swimming, the hiking, and the wading, all tend to take the edge off of my maniacal desire to catch a trout. On the boat, my exercise is limited to casting and balancing on the cooler while scouting. So that is my theory of why I can be Thoreau-like on a river and more of a Captain Ahab out with Adam.

Don't get me wrong, fishless days on the ocean do have their benefits for me. I'm so locked into scouting for stripers in the shallows or finding some surface action that the normal dimension of time ceases to exist. After launching at dawn and going into our hunting mode, Adam might say, "It's time for lunch" and I'll be shocked, thinking only an hour has gone by. And that's a good thing—any hobby where you can totally lose yourself, along with the concept of time, is a wonderful change of pace from most people's working days where it's easy to be a slave to the clock.

The only awareness of time for me on the ocean is the angle of the sun. While I hate for the end of the day to come, I know when the sun first sets it's a special period we call "the witching hour." Bass that stayed deep and rejected all offerings seem to turn on at this particular time. Often that single hour accounts for 95 percent of our action, and I love the slow ride back to port, shoulders and arms fatigued from casting and fighting fish, legs shaky from balancing on the cooler. Good aches, a good kind of tired.

One bit of enlightenment I have gained is to appreciate what each fishing friend brings to the table. George M. showed me that rushing from place to place can be folly—he guided me to a keeper bass a stone's throw from the harbor where Adam and I usually launch from. Then we pulled up one of his lobster traps and not only was there a big lobster inside, but also a tautog. Fish can come in surprising places and even unique methods. Jim H. reinforced the conservation streak inside me, going out of his way when on the ocean to pick up trash (particularly balloons that can be ingested by marine life, sea turtles especially can choke on them). He also opted not to chase boats to an area where fish were breaking the surface, saying, "Let's stay right here, they [the stripers] may pop up next to us." And they did. Allen taught me you can catch big stripers by dropping a spoon lure straight down, then bringing it up slowly.

Adam's friend Guong, from Malaysia, demonstrated a childlike delight in fishing, even though he has a PhD. He would ask me question after question, absorbing it all like sponge. And when I asked what it was like for him to instruct medical students at Johns Hopkins University, he said, "I can give my students every tool except one, and that is passion. I can only help them explore subjects and careers in medicine or research until one lights their fire." I knew exactly what he meant—I've explored many jobs, but the passion only surfaced when I discovered writing.

Paul is all about humor: when I brought a keeper home and blood was on both me and the fish, he said, "What'd you do, shoot it?" And I remember him putting a keeper in his backpack with the tail sticking out when suddenly the fish's tail started to whack him in the back of the head. Then there is fishing guide extraordinaire Jennifer C. opening her home to me on Martha's Vineyard so I could prowl the beaches in search of fish. She even directed me to a doctor who outlined the proper steps to wean myself off diazepam for my sleep issue. Only partial success there, but Jennifer's warmth and the doctor's guidance provided much better results than my effort at cold turkey.

My elementary school friends, Opie, Dale, Booge, and Cogs, prove the power of fishing can be the glue that keeps friends connected. They remind me that sometimes the fish that get away are the most memorable—they love to mock my comment during a battle with an especially large striper, "This may take a while." They also frequently quote a line we used as kids, "Get the Gaff!" And after a fish shakes free it's a simple, "Well, you got your lure back," to keep my cursing in check. Cogs also likes to needle me that I'm no different from the fly-fishing purists in that I'm always trying to keep us on the flats even when the fish are most decidedly in deeper water.

***

All of these friends practice patience when fishing, an important trait necessary to be a good angler, but one that is simply not in my DNA. I cannot stay in one spot for long if I think it's devoid of fish. But luckily, I do have another attribute that successful anglers need, and that is persistence. I won't stay in the same spot, but I'll spend from dawn to dusk on the move, hunting for fish and exploring new water. In that respect Adam and I are a lot alike. In fact, Adam's desire to get us in the shallowest of waters to find stripers is an obsession we both share—calculated risk, sight fishing, and being on the move. Sometimes it works out and sometimes not. One of the "nots" occurred when I was in the bow scouting, and we hit a rock and damaged our boat. Simple miscommunication: Adam assumed I'd warn him sooner if I spotted any rocks, and I assumed he'd go slower entering the abrupt shallows.

Our similarities in the way we fish and the appreciation of our quarry outweigh our differences. Adam and I both feel a deep sense of wonder toward the environment. Fishing makes us feel a part of something greater, and every now and then pulls us into a state where we forget we're human, but instead are just one more creature in the ocean—a brief moment of harmony with our surroundings, "contact, contact, simplify, simplify."

Adam's journey to avoid excess puts him in line with my own quest for self-improvement. I remember a comment he made when we were on our Bahamas trip enjoying rich food, a massage, and lazy days in the sun while folks back home froze their butts off in the winter chill. "This is nice, but you and I are worker bees and our work fulfills us."

He was right. While the trip was a nice break, it was all too easy, and we missed the challenge of trying to grow our respective businesses.

***

More than twenty years on the boat together. We coped with the heartache of divorce, loss of our parents and other loved ones, the ups and downs of our careers, and more. Sharing these experiences was only the half of it, more important were the actions we encouraged each other to take:

1. We learned you become how you act, or put another way, consciously engaging in a positive attitude usually leads to positive results. The old "fake it till you make it" is a way to fight through the tough times.

2. We learned manifesting what you want works. Keep a fixed image of your desire in mind, and make a little step in that direction every day. On the boat we verbalized our goals. Through the process I realized the goal is fixed, but the time frame and the plan to get there must be fluid or you set yourself up for disappointment.

3. The fish taught us lessons as well. More than one day started out with a big fish in the first five minutes, where we thought *This is going to be quite a day*, only to be followed by long hours without a single additional hit. Fishing humbles you, and we could all benefit from that message from time to time. I remember saying to Adam, "Man, we're getting really good at this shallow water fishing. I think we got it mastered." And he responded, "Don't you think it has something to do with the fact we have been fishing for eight or nine straight hours and never stopped casting?"

4. Fishing doesn't just recharge my mental batteries, it reinforced my two core beliefs, which Adam shares with me. Belief number one is that we all have the ability to turn almost any "bad" experience into a positive one. You have to work at it, you have to hunt for the positive the way you would hunt for a fish, but what you gain in wisdom and what you discover by being nudged in a new direction can have benefits that outlast the bad experience that started it all. My second belief, really more of a reminder to myself, is "Not so serious is this brief life." I don't think I've been on a single fishing trip where I didn't laugh, often at my own stupidity or something I did, usually involving losing a fish.

5. Adam and I encouraged each other to lead lives of no regrets. We may sometimes do things we wish we hadn't or passed up an opportunity where we should have acted, but we strove to minimize those mistakes. In a book written by Bonnie Ware, *The Top Five Regrets of the Dying*, she interviewed the terminally ill about things they wish they did differently. Those regrets were not about actions they took, but rather what they didn't do. Passivity leads to misgivings and lost opportunities. The five most common regrets were:

   a. I wish I had the courage to express my feelings.

   b. I wish I hadn't worked so hard.

   c. I wish I lived life on my terms and not what others expected.

   d. I wish I stayed close to my friends.

   e. I wish I allowed myself to be happier.

So while Adam and I might have qualms over certain errors, we can honestly say we don't have any of the five regrets listed. Part of that comes from examining our lives while on the boat and being sure to give honest feedback and encouragement.

Finally, during our more than two decades of friendship, we both can be proud to say we did not let our fear of uncertainty stop us from making big changes in our life. The fear was there, and it was palpable at times, but we were not cowards.

And what was Adam's message that has stayed with me over the years? He said it in an email sent after one of our outings: "I was so grateful for your enthusiasm. They say sorrow shared is halved and joy shared is doubled. You tripled it my friend."

Now that's *The Power of Positive Fishing*.

Epilogue
Seeing the Light

AG

Being out on the water is as close as I have come to the infinite: infinite water stretching out in all directions, with unending sky above, a dome of inconceivable space, and with unfathomable depths below. The way that light flows in that environment can be nothing short of magical. When I am aware of it, it is an overwhelm of spaciousness, depth, and profundity. The resultant feelings of awe and wonder surely are related in some way with the idea of spirituality. Perhaps best of all, unlike a view from a window, or from a viewing area, there is no feeling of looking out at something. On the water, we are in it, we are part of the scene, part of the infinite: in the light.

One special play of light first noticed early in our sight fishing days yields what I call the magic carpet effect. The tidal flats along Cape Cod Bay, particularly off the town of Brewster, are in many places so flat that there is no more than a couple of feet between high spots and low spots, literally for miles. These sands are nearly devoid of boulders and other navigational hazards; so that when the tide is in, boaters can confidently cruise at high speeds just a few feet above the sands. The water there can be cloudy, filled with air and particulates stirred up by storms or rains or simply by the tides. In such circumstances, the bottom can barely be seen. But once in a while the water takes on a remarkably crystal-clear aspect where everything becomes visible. Sunlight slices through it, completely illuminating the tiniest patterns of sand, pebbles, seaweed, crabs and their footprints, swimming bait, everything. Looking down from a cruising motorboat like the *Scout*, a mirage occurs where the water seems to disappear, so you feel like you are no longer floating but flying over the flats. Imagine Aladdin riding on a magic carpet just above a vast desert in an Arabian tale.

Yet another favored light occurs on unusually calm days, when it seems the whole ocean is free of waves. There may be a long, lolling roll to the sea but no chop and few ripples. The surface gets glassily flat even miles offshore. On such occasions, it can take on a mesmerizing sheen. The upper edge seemingly captures and contains the light, like a highly polished vase, or marble, or gemstone, only deeper and on an incomprehensibly greater scale. One feels as much afloat on light as on liquid.

Of course, not all light out on the water is smooth or inspiring. On one of our very first trips together, Mike and I encountered an altogether different play of light. Back then, the *Scout* had neither sonar to tell us how deep the water was, nor a GPS to help us navigate. We were still inexperienced and neither of us knew Cape Cod Bay well. I kept a paper chart and a compass on the center console for reference and used them regularly, though not with skill.

We had put in just before sunrise that day, early enough to witness the "rosy fingered dawn" as Homer describes it in *The Odyssey* nearly three millennia ago. We motored around almost randomly looking for fish, yapping away incessantly, forgetting ourselves in it all, when suddenly we noticed we were driving toward an impenetrable wall of fog.

"This doesn't look good," I heard Mike murmur.

Before we knew it, the thick bank shut down all visibility beyond twenty feet. I cut the engine and told Mike we needed to drop anchor to wait it out. I didn't know much about boating, but I was pretty sure that cruising blindly in fog was not recommended.

We both soon learned that waiting out fog can be disconcerting. No matter how thick it gets on land, I've always been able to relate to some firm landmark or another, whether it be a tree or a house of even the edge of a sidewalk or roadway. I've never felt truly disoriented in fog on land. Out to sea, however, floating and with nothing solid nearby, I was lost.

After a while, it became clear that fog can be sublime as well. Everything appears soft. The world turns ephemeral, consisting only of shifting light and moving mists. Even sounds seem both softened and magnified. One becomes unusually conscious of the slaps and drips of waves against the hull, newly alert to the squawks of gulls.

"I guess this is why it's a good idea to have GPS and a depth finder. We better get them," Mike eventually commented.

The *Scout* had a built-in horn, but it wasn't the loudest, so I got out the air horn and suggested that if either of us heard any engine sounds close by we should blast it to warn them away.

Mike took the airhorn in hand and mulled it over.

Not knowing what else to say, and realizing the convenient privacy that the fog created, I announced, "I'm gonna take a leak off the back."

"Do you know how many Coast Guard reports I've read while doing writing research of guys taking a pee off the stern of a boat and dying?" Mike asked me. "They go back there by themselves, lose their footing or whatever, probably while unzipping, and fall overboard. No one hears them screaming above the drone of the engine, so the vessel just keeps chugging away and they are left to drown."

"Well, it's a good thing we're at anchor," I responded.

A short while later, he added: "If we're going to be stuck here waiting for the fog all morning, we might as well fish."

"Good luck," I said, pouring coffee from my thermos.

Then, only a few casts later: "Fish on!"

The next half hour in that fog bank was arguably the best bluefish fishing of our lives. We both used top water plugs which made for endless exciting splashes. Many shot out of the water, some in sight, some hidden by the mists. It was a frenzy.

"I love this fog," Mike declared.

"I guess being lost in a fog isn't always a bad thing."

Akin to fishing in fog is night fishing. Even with modern GPSs, you never know quite where you are or what you might encounter. For example, more than one summertime trip has included the revelation of glowing, green bioluminescent phytoplankton in the water. It is a type of microalgae that sparkles on the surface, like magic green glitter. These nighttime displays are apparently quite common in some warmer water locations. For example, I've seen ads for bioluminescent kayak tours in Puerto Rico. But these strange little creatures primarily only glint noticeably around the Cape on rare summer nights, specifically when the surface is disturbed. Sometimes they sparkle in the boat's wake. Sometimes they are awakened by fishing lures, sometimes they're turned on with kayak paddles. I've even seen the effect while night swimming, every stroke activating their light.

Prior to the moment that these infinitesimal creatures start shining, the water is perceived to be plain old Cape Cod seawater, a substance that I once thought of as being no more than lifeless liquid, except when a fish or other creature was clearly seen in it. But on these unexpected bioluminescent nights, the phenomena forces recognition of just how richly endowed the water actually is.

My favorite nighttime trip occurred one Fourth of July when no bioluminescence was visible in the water. It was about an hour before sunset when Mike and I hit the water with Miki and Jack, then both teenagers, along with two of their friends. It had been one of the first genuinely hot summer days of the year, so it was liberating to be out in the cool air of the bay, especially with four raucous kids. Because of the limited amount of time left before dark, we decided to get right into jigging with wire line. As explained by Mike, using that setup is not our preferred method. Still, it can yield a good catch. It certainly worked a charm that night. We caught four beautiful striped bass by the time darkness fell. They ran from between twenty-eight to thirty-three inches. All of us took turns jigging, catching, landing, and giving and receiving hoots and high fives. One of the kids had never seen a striped bass before.

It being Independence Day, we had heard the sporadic pops and bangs of fireworks across the water from various directions since launching. But as darkness crept in, we started seeing them too. We weren't in sight of any major municipal fireworks. Instead, we were treated to dozens of private displays along the miles of beaches about us, all in the distance.

"It's so cool to see them from way out here," said my daughter. "It's so different that they aren't overhead. They seem tiny from out here but so pretty."

"This is awesome," one of her friends confirmed. "You can see them before you hear them."

After putting up our poles, we decided to stay out a while and drift and enjoy the show.

As the darkness became complete, the water a blackish-blue all about us, Mike pointed straight up overhead and said, "I think I like those fireworks best of all."

"Yeah," the kids agreed.

With no moon, the stars were on full display. We spotted the red of Mars and the bright white of Jupiter. Orion's Belt strung its straight line. The Big Dipper pointed out the North Star. We saw the lights of other boats far off. Airplane lights occasionally blinked overhead. We even spotted a satellite cruising across the firmament.

"I know everyone knows this already," Jack said. "But its so cool that the light hitting our eyes from even the closest stars was created years ago, some of it even centuries ago."

At some point the kids speculated on whether there was life on other planets. The unanimous consensus was that there must be.

"We pulled life up from below us, from inner space," someone commented.

One form of light that seems more common on the water than in any other environment, is the sparkle that appears in our loved ones' eyes when out on the water. Not long before we completed this manuscript, Mike's daughter Kristin married a great guy named George. It was a testament to their relationship with Mike that they chose him to officiate their wedding. But it was just as impressive to me to see that when they chose a location for the ceremony, they selected the waters of Cape Cod Bay, just outside Mike's and my favorite harbor, the main place we had taken Kristin fishing over the years. Our sacred space had clearly become one of the newlywed couple's as well. They hired a commercial boat to take the wedding party out for a cruise and hosted a beautiful ceremony.

Standing with Mike above the sparkling waves, beaming at each other while reciting their vows, their love was readily apparent.

As this manuscript goes into final editing, I'm happy to report that the couple has established themselves as quite a handsome family as well, having just brought their pretty infant daughter, Robin, into the world. And as if that were not news enough to end a book on, I'm delighted to announce that just a few weeks before our last look at this book's page proofs were due, my wife Mildrey gave birth to a healthy baby boy, Nathaniel Gamble. We couldn't be happier. Needless to say, Mike and I have already begun dreaming about fishing trips with Robin and Nate.

About the Authors

Michael J. Tougias is a *New York Times* bestselling author and coauthor of thirty books for adults and nine books for young adults. He is best known for his nonfiction narratives of survival and rescue stories. These include *The Finest Hours, Ten Hours Until Dawn, So Close to Home, A Storm Too Soon, Overboard, Rescue of the Bounty, Fatal Forecast,* and *Extreme Survival: Lessons from Those Who Have Triumphed Against All Odds.*

The Finest Hours has been made into a Disney movie starring Chris Pine and Casey Affleck. *Ten Hours Until Dawn* was selected by the American Library Association as "One of the Best Books of the Year." Tougias also cowrote *King Philip's War* and a novel set during that war titled *Until I Have No Country.* The *Wall Street Journal* and NPR featured Tougias's book about the Cuban Missile Crisis titled *Above & Beyond.*

He has also written several humorous nature books including his memoir *There's a Porcupine in My Outhouse: Misadventures of a Mountain Man Wannabe,* which won the Independent Publishers "Best Nature Book of the Year Award." His latest two books are *Extreme Survival* and *The Waters Between Us: A Boy, A Father, Outdoor Misadventures, and the Healing Power of Nature.*

Tougias's rescue books have been adapted for eight to thirteen-year-olds and are part of his True Rescue Series and True Survival Series. His newest series The True Survival Series features a little-known World War II story, *Abandon Ship!*

Tougias speaks to groups across the country and has a slide lecture for each of his books. He also speaks to business groups on his inspirational lectures sharing what he has learned from survivors and rescuers about overcoming adversity and making decision under pressure. Tougias splits his time between homes in Florida and Massachusetts where he is an avid fisherman, vegetable gardener, swimmer, and bicyclist. www .michaeltougias.com

Adam Gamble conceived, wrote or cowrote, and supervised the production of three hundred titles in the Good Night Books series for preschoolers. The series is distributed by Penguin Random House Publisher Services since 2017 and currently has more than nine million copies sold worldwide, www.goodnightbooks.com. Gamble is also the author of *In the Footsteps of Thoreau* (1997), coauthor of *A Public Betrayed* (2004), and coauthor of a volume of poetry entitled *Under the Table* (1993). He is the founder and publisher of both Good Night Books, LLC (since 2005) and of On Cape Publications, Inc. (since 1996).

Praise for other Books by Michael J. Tougias

Praise for *There's A Porcupine in My Outhouse:
Misadventures of a Mountain Man Wannabe*
"An engaging and insightful book with just the right mix of humor."
—*Metro West News*

"He writes eloquently with vivid descriptions and I looked forward to each new adventure."—*The Boston Herald*

"A good storyteller with a self-deprecating streak that makes for great humor writing."—*Bend Oregon Bulletin*

"A very funny memoir. Tougias learned from his cabin experience and today he is one of New England's leading nature writers."—*Book Views*

"Tougias' book will have readers rolling with laughter." —*Taunton Daily Gazette*

"Porcupine is laugh-out-loud funny." —*Hilltop News*

"There is a great deal of spiritual and reflection in his fine narrative that never gets preachy." —*Telegram and Gazette*

"This is the way natural history should be taught—by a good storyteller with a sense of humor. What fun! And what a great read!" —*Audubon* magazine

"Tougias blends wit and wisdom resulting in a nature book that, fittingly, goes slightly off the beaten path. Lots of laughs." —*Sentinel and Enterprize*

"Tougias describes connections so profound that they speak not just to the mind but to the soul." —*The Union News*

"Tougias recounts his experiences with candor and humor. He blends in the adventures of Lewis and Clark with the vision of John Muir." —*Cape Cod Times*

lamenting only that each page turned brings us closer to his last." —Outdoor Columnist Todd Corayer "Fish Wrap"

"Much of the books emotional power comes from Tougias success evoking his special places." —*The Cape Codder*

"It's a story with plenty of comical moments but *The Waters Between Us* also recounts a tragedy that brought a reckoning for Tougias and his family—and his father's response to that incident gave his son a better appreciation for his dad's values and ultimately brought the two closer." —*Daily Hampshire Gazette*

PRAISE FOR *EXTREME SURVIVAL: LESSONS FROM THOSE WHO HAVE TRIUMPHED AGAINST ALL ODDS*

"Michael Tougias converts the wisdom of survivors into advice we can all use to light up the darkness." —Amanda Ripley, *New York Times* bestselling author

"These really are 'extreme' survivors and they did the seemingly impossible." —WBZ Radio

"In *Extreme Survival*, Mr. Tougias examines survivors of disasters that range from being lost at sea to falls from cliffs, from being trapped in a car for two weeks to experiences in prison camps. The author looks at some well-known disasters such as the *Titanic*, *Apollo 13*, and the World War II sinking of the USS *Indianapolis* as well as many lesser known but equally inspiring stories." —*The Enterprise*